CARE FULLY

CARE FULLY

Critical Care through Making with Food

Kelsey Virginia Dufresne

NC State University Libraries

Copyright © 2024 by Kelsey Virginia Dufresne

This work is licensed under a Creative Commons CC BY-NC-ND license. To view a copy of the license, visit http://creativecommons.org/licenses.

No part of this book may be reproduced without written permission from the author.

Suggested citation: Dufresne, Kelsey Virginia. Care Fully: Critical Care through Making with Food. North Carolina State University Libraries, 2024.
DOI: https//doi.org/10.5149/9781469688824_Dufresne

This material is based upon work supported by the Data Science and AI Academy and The Division of Graduate Education under NSF Award No. 2222148. Any opinions, findings, and conclusions or recommendations expressed in this publication are those of the author(s) and do not necessarily reflect the views of the National Science Foundation.

Aboreto font, Designed by Dominik Jáger. Copyright 2022 The Aboreto Project Authors (https://github.com/domija/Aboreto). This Font Software is licensed under the SIL Open Font License, Version 1.1 . This license is copied below, and is also available with a FAQ at: https://openfontlicense.org

Della Respira font, Designed by Nathan Willis. Copyright (c) 2011-2012, Nathan Willis (nwillis@glyphography.com), with Reserved Font Names "Della Respira." This Font Software is licensed under the SIL Open Font License, Version 1.1.

Epilogue font, Designed by Tyler Finck, ETC. Copyright 2020 The Epilogue Project Authors (https://github.com/Etcetera-Type-Co/Epilogue). This Font Software is licensed under the SIL Open Font License, Version 1.1 . This license is copied below, and is also available with a FAQ at: https://openfontlicense.org

Homemade Apple font, Designed by Font Diner. Apache License, Version 2.0, January 2004.

Cover design: Sophie Dickerson. dellasophiadickerson@mac.com

ISBN 978-1-4696-8880-0 (paperback)
ISBN 978-1-4696-8882-4 (PDF ebook)

Published by the North Carolina State University Libraries

Distributed by the University of North Carolina Press
www.uncpress.org

"To pay attention, this is our endless and proper work."
— Mary Oliver

table of contents

collaborators	iii
preface: I collect cookbooks	iv
Chapter 1. Prep work	**1**
on care + cookbooks	6
the pursuit of knowledge[sharing]	9
what cookbooks know	15
my personal experiences with cookbooks/cooking	22
how to use this book	26
Chapter 2. Tools + frames + theory	**35**
a note on theory	36
intersectional feminism	37
critical pedagogy	46
experiential inquiry	52
critical making	56
critical making + critical pedagogy + experiential inquiry + cooking = this book	61
Chapter 3. Conversion charts: The methods	**66**
interviews	68
images	73
Chapter 4. Care materials	**78**
care as cute	81
care as labor	89
care as radical intersectional feminist action	92
care as survival	96
Chapter 5. Staples	**104**
321 Coffee	105
3 interviews with 321	107
Michael Evans	107
Sophie Pacyna	121
Rene Grunow	128

321's iced honey cinnamon latte	135
Bee Downtown	136
interview with Leigh-Kathryn Bonner	140
Grandma's apple and honey muffins	171
Leigh-Kathryn Bonner's easy honey garlic chicken	172
A Place at the Table	175
a chat with Maggie Kane and Andrew Gravens	176
The Root Cellar Cafe & Catering	180
talking with Chef Sera Cuni	181
Well Fed Community Garden	201
Microbiomes and the science we eat	213
a conversation with Dr. Erin McKenney	215
Dr. McKenney's easy sourdough bread recipe: #TINYLOAVES4TINY HANDS	237
Dr. McKenney's easy sourdough bread recipe	240
Wonderpuff	241
talking with JAC M	244
Videri Chocolate Factory	261
an interview with Sam Ratto	265
Videri's classic dark chocolate pudding	286
Videri's classic dark brownies	287
Two Roosters	289
a chat with Sarah Romeo	292

Chapter 6. Sharing the table — 302

spaces + places for making care	305
the work of care	306
rose-colored care	312
the careful stories	315
the capitalism of care + the care in capitalism	318
equity + justice + making	320
the responsibility + burden of care	323
the capacity of cookbooks for change	330

Chapter 7. A recipe for necessary disaster + disruption: A manifesto — 338

Chapter 8. Cleaning the table — 342

overview + overarching findings	342
contributions	345
limitations	346
opportunities for further consideration	347

references   352

thanks   365

further reading   367

collaborators

321 Coffee	Michael Evans, Sophie Pacyna, and Rene Grunow
Bee Downtown	Leigh-Kathryn Bonner
A Place at the Table	Maggie Kane and Andrew Gravens
The Root Cellar	Chef Sera Cuni
Well Fed Community Garden	Lilias Pettit-Scott
	Dr. Erin McKenney
Wonderpuff	JAC M
Videri Chocolate Factory	Sam Ratto
Two Roosters	Sarah Romeo

preface I collect cookbooks

Every time I get something that comes with a set of instructions, I immediately throw the instructions away. I will not read an instruction manual. I find the black and white linear illustrations that are labeled with A B C D E to be too simplified and the instructions both too direct and too vague. I rather rely on personal instinct to put something together.

But yet how do we really differentiate a cookbook from the instruction manual? It's way better, of course, and there's so many reasons why that we intuitively feel and experience when we hold a cookbook, rather than an instruction manual. Yet, at a rudimentary level, it is also an instruction manual about food.

At the same time, we feel and understand that these are distinctively different forms of instruction. Firstly, we are far more likely to save a cookbook than an instruction manual for a chair, a Lego set, a toy. With this longitudinal utility of cookbooks, I find my favorite aspects of these texts to be that I feel very at liberty to write all over them. I annotate cookbooks just as much as my poetry books. Perhaps more so, since I annotate in ink just as much as accidental smears of flour, oil, chocolate, and butter. I dog-ear and bookmark pages with sticky notes with messages like: "Family favorite" or "Made for Christmas Dinner 2022." In doing so, these cookbooks adopt a more human-feel to them, demonstrating significant evidence of use, experimentation, and consideration — as well as a collaborative nature that does not exist within an instruction manual.

And here is a demonstration of such utility, memoir, and humanness of cookbooks. I[1] made this recipe for panna cotta when we had company over, and it was probably the worst thing I have ever made in my entire life. It tasted like I had made a cup of vinegar for everyone. And you can see, I wrote: *Do not use the vinegar*. I have underlined *not*. I also wrote: *Do not use electric mixer*. I even crossed out apple cider vinegar from the ingredients list. Apparently I was hopeful enough that I would still make it again, because I didn't write: *Do not make this* — and I left the post-it note on top to bookmark the page.

Simultaneously, it is important to consider where we most often find cookbooks: the kitchen. Rather than a library, these works are often housed within the most domesticated and historically feminized space within a home. All the more, many cookbooks came to fruition because it was the only publication and knowledge sharing avenue that a lot of women had. Because of this, I think cookbooks are also exciting because they're subversive knowledge opportunities — subversive avenues through which knowledge, stories, and historically discredited voices are shared.

And while my cooking and collecting of cookbooks is rooted in this exploratory nourishment and fun, not everyone engages with a cookbook or cooking in the same manner — seen in how cooking is, at its basest form, and avenue for sustenance and livelihood, and how food and its

---

[1] Importantly, an identity card for myself might read as follows: late 20s, white, American, cisgender, female, heterosexual, non-practicing and conflicted Catholic, mother, hometown n/a. And with these identifiers, I recognize that I am, and was raised, as a person with extreme privilege — and I recognize that I was raised with a privileged (and extremely limited and problematic) understanding of the United States. I was raised in a military family in a military system. In addition to being born on a military base in Japan, I lived in North Carolina, Texas, Rhode Island, Missouri, New York, and Delaware with my father in the US Marine Corps. For my entire childhood, the US Military dedicated the frequent relocation of my family and the active warfare deployments of my father.

The commissary and stores on base had special parking spots reserved for officers and their dependents, as well as entire swimming facilities. In several instances we would only receive emergency medical attention at the hospital after my dad would call the Officer of the Day at Naval from Iraq. The doctors would then tell my mom: "We didn't know who your husband was." When my dad was promoted to Commanding Officer at Camp Lejeune, my mom went to Commanding Officer Wives training — and we learned that the wives are called COWs. Moving away on my own for the first time, away from the military system in which I was raised, when I went to college resulted in, what I now call, a de-indoctrination from an unrealistic, sacred, utopian understanding of the United States. On my first day of college in my English class I learned the term *ethnocentrism*.

Personal photograph of my cookbook annotations.

preparation have been heavily affected by the social, cultural, and oppressive systems that have existed throughout time. This is seen in how enslaved people were forced to cook for their enslavers and how folks have practiced creative survival cooking during times of hardship and food loss.

But through the use of knowledge and story sharing within cookbooks, in conjunction with a reader's own annotations, cookbooks often have a memoir-like aspect to them that exists between both the author/s and the reader/cook. This once more distinguishes these texts and knowledge sharing objects from an instruction manual because they acknowledge and rely upon that information sharing, eliciting a mode of literacy as well as a mode of survival and enculturation for others.

As such, the cookbook is an interesting object to study, but it's also an interesting avenue through which we can share knowledge and stories. They are colorful, multimodal texts that rely on photos and texts to teach readers and cooks. They also contain homages to families, communities, and homes with a strong focus on hope and positive oriented language. There is a lot of positive, self-efficacy affirming language like: *You can do this!* There isn't a high barrier of entry, because the whole point of a cookbook is to teach you how to do something. In cookbooks we engage with a narrated process model, as well as vignettes and explanations of how recipes came to be in this book. And thus there's a lot of nostalgia and a lot of fun behind these things. Ultimately they're really beautiful and utilitarian objects of design.

To culminate my doctoral studies, I was inspired to construct a text, what I have called an anti-dissertation of sorts, focusing on cookbooks because of my own preference for these books over traditional textbooks and instruction manuals, but also because of my deep admiration for the experience of sitting with a pen, sticky notes, and a cookbook — and how these texts can elicit valuable considerations for how we evaluate and share knowledge, stories, and the process and act of care-giving. This book was born from that work.

Chapter 1.
Prep work

In the United States, there is an increasing discussion of equity (and the banning of these discussions) — of striving for equity in various ways, of prioritizing systemic change, and of devising plans for moving forward. But, this discussion is not enough. We have seen how discourse and conversations surrounding the topics of diversity, equity, and inclusion (DEI) have been appropriated and tokenized, performing pseudo-ethical work that is actually needed. Worse still, these topics then are scrutinized and banned (Doran, 2023), furthering the necessary work to be done.

Because of this pattern of ineffective and/or inept discussion and in a time in which books are being banned alongside Critical Race Theory in classrooms and libraries in the name of indoctrination, the *actionization* of equity is that which is really needed. Many organizations, leaders, and researchers are doing this action work, as seen with Data 4 Black Lives, March for our Lives, And Also Too, and so many more. Interestingly, and perhaps unsurprisingly, many of these action-doers are rooted in community-centeredness for betterment and seemingly display frameworks of intersectional feminist action.

As such, I aim to look to and work with similarly gendered modes of caring, namely that of making with food and its corresponding meaning-making and knowledge-sharing. In food, through its preparation and consumption, we find a form of care that ensures the possibility of surviving and a nourishment that is essential for all living. And while food is essential and vital for all, its care carries a lineage of specific gender associations.

Hill, Janet McKenzie. "The Boston Cooking School magazine of culinary science and domestic economics (1908)." No restrictions, via Wikimedia Commons.

In focusing on the intersection of food and care, I have shaped this text as a public-facing anthology of materials and media objects in the form and performance of a cookbook. In doing so, this anthology features the prioritization of care to do the work of purposeful action for justice. More specifically, this anthology, taking the form of a cookbook for community use and practice, catalogs practices and procedures of making food as experimental and experiential learning rooted in care. This book includes multimodal elements (text, images, art pieces) that provide readers with methods and steps to conceptualize and practice critical care. By promoting a pursuit to experiment and actionize critical care, this work also strives to reinforce knowledge legitimacy through distinctively feminist and feminized modes of production.

Here I look to cookbooks, namely those produced in and through community-based efforts, and explore their capacities as objects and practice of knowledge that are flawed yet hold the capability to facilitate accessible and equitable knowledge sharing due to their participatory, multimodal, subversive, and autobiographical nature. And while not all cookbooks reflect this capacity, we see how many cookbooks follow this tradition and precedent. This is seen in their originating form as collected communal practices of generational, cultural, educational, gendered knowledge-sharing, which I trace and explore throughout this work.

Anne Bower puts it poignantly with: "like many other print and non-print texts, from poems to quilts, from novels to samplers, from letters to gardens, community cookbooks do more than simply 'reflect' the society in which they were published. These books demonstrate the participation of the women who wrote them in the creation of that society" (1997, 138). As such, I aim to rely on cookbooks as archives, autobiographies, and assemblages of stories and materials to investigate a collective participation in knowledge through modes and means that are not regularly viewed, acknowledged, or celebrated accordingly. And this is how I do my research, modeling the objectives and utilities of cookbooks: I want to read, I want to learn, I want to make, and I want to eat and share.

This work takes on an intersectional, material feminism lens to produce a public-facing anthology of food-making practices, materials and media objects rooted in care. This work performs the community-engaged knowledge and production-sharing of a cookbook as it introduces a memoir of methods to conceptualize and practice critical care, reinforces knowledge legitimacy through distinctively feminist and feminized modes of production, and justifies multimodal experimentation for the pursuit and actionization of critical care. Throughout this work, I explore community-engaged practices around food to argue that the forms of knowledge that emerge from these experiences actionize equity and justice, are historically feminized labor and thus rendered invisible, and are rooted in care. As such, I simultaneously investigate the capacity of cookbooks as objects and artifacts focused on such community-engagement and are rooted in community care, feminized labor, and co-creative experiential learning.

Moreover, I explore:

- learning as a vehicle in striving towards equity + justice;
- the actionization of equity and intersectional feminism;
- the (invisible) labor and vital importance of care;
- care's relationship to gender (fatalism) and its role in learning;
- historically gendered + feminized modes of caring, meaning making, and knowledge sharing.

Highsmith, Carol M. [Between 1980 and 2006] "1950s kitchen at Strawbery Banke Colonial Village, a restored city neighborhood in Portsmouth, New Hampshire." No known restrictions on publication. Retrieved from the Library of Congress.

on care + cookbooks

Dwight, Henrietta Latham. "The Golden Age Cook-Book, published in 1898. This is an early American vegetarian cookbook." Public domain, via Wikimedia Commons.

Operating beyond the confines of traditional knowledge production and recognition, as well as the power associated with both, cookbooks have a formula: beautiful, enticing, mouth watering photos alongside direct instructions with a list of materials. They are a perfectly curated catalog of food, yes, but also instructional design — often infused with personal anecdotes, memoir, and reflexivity. In further consideration of the latter, in Donna Haraway's work in situated knowledges (1988) she frames reflexivity as a feminist practice that prioritizes critical reflection and introspection. We see such reflexivity through the inclusion of the anecdotes and memories, but also through the emphasis on *and* opportunity for storytelling found within cookbooks that enables such reflection and personal contemplation. Because of this, we find a more flexible knowledge sharing device.

Speaking from personal experience, my cookbooks have pages that are covered in olive oil, chocolate, batter, and flour. I also notate which recipes I love and how I need to add more salt. I dogear pages and dutifully leave scrap paper bookmarks with notes that say: Make for family dinner. They also sit in my kitchen, in the sun, near plants and my coffee. They are readily available for when I want (need) to make focaccia or chocolate chip cookies. They are the books I touch the most — and use the most, because they are designed to be used. They are not to be pristine objects, but rather reflect our process in creating alongside them. They offer strategies, lessons, and ideas for inspiration, but you are to ultimately take the recipes as a launching point to situate the creations in your own life. As Molly Baz's book expresses titularly: *Cook This Book: Techniques that Teach & Recipes to Repeat* (2021).

They contain careful organization. Some books are organized by meal (breakfast, lunch, dinner, dessert). Some by season (fall, winter, spring, summer). Others by central ingredients (chicken, beef, fish, vegetables). Throughout this, many authors follow this organizational pattern as one display of credibility — for a book of randomness would not be seen as credible, which acts in contradiction to many recipe books and collections that one can find passed down through generations in families. This is also achieved through many introductory statements, where the status as a food preparer (in any form or level) is established and asserted.

In addition to offering strategies for cooking and baking, they also offer advice, informal positionality statements and local contextuality. Small vignettes will often accompany each recipe — notating how the author, baker, developer came to this food and how they found this version that they want to share with you. And if you ask my mom, the best cookbooks have a picture of each recipe made — so you have an idea of what you are aiming for. For some, like Samin Nosrat, this might be illustrations by Wendy MacNaughton accompanied by in-depth discussions of each key ingredient — as seen in *Salt, Fat, Acid, Heat* (2017). For Thalia Ho and *Wild Sweetness: Recipes Inspired by Nature* (2021), this is including photos of food, but also ingredients out in the wild before they find themselves in our kitchen.

Lomen Bros. (1916). "An Eskimo kitchen outdoors." Retrieved from the Library of Congress.

In teaching English classes, we have to teach students how to find credible sources — sources that are from journals or books that contain research that is deemed reputable and solid. Ideas and arguments must be backed up and supported by credible evidence, evidence which is constructed and produced by experts and academics, to verify ideas and explorations. If a student does not follow this precedent, they do knowledge wrong. This is a microcosm of the broader knowledge economy that prioritizes and legitimizes certain forms of knowledge over others. More specifically, the knowledge that adheres to scientific method, has been published, follows prescribed standards and genre/stylistic conventions are valued with more credibility and weight than those that do not comply with this model, including lived experience, family histories, un/published knowledges that do not follow the scientific method, and more. Even more specifically, knowledge produced from a white, heteronormative, and patriarchal, colonialist perspective is awarded more credibility due to its adherence to knowledge systems (which are cyclically designed for and to support such limited and exclusive framings of what gets to count as knowledge).[2]

However, *The End of the Cognitive Empire: The Coming of Age of Epistemologies of the South* (2018) by Boaventura de Sousa Santos critiques the pervasive and oppressive knowledge formations that reinforce systemic inequalities around the globe, writing: "Most of the knowledge that circulates in the world and is relevant for the lives of people is oral and artisanal. However, our universities and research centers value written and scientific knowledge almost exclusively" (p. 297). Through this, Santos argues that "there is no global social justice without global cognitive justice" (p. 296). Santos illustrates the differences in knowledge production and credibility between the Northern and Southern hemispheres, writing: "The epistemologies of the South deal with knowledges present in or emerging from the resistance to and the struggle against oppression, knowledges that are, therefore, embodied in concrete

---

[2] One of the first academic readings I was assigned to read as an English MA student was about how women were statistically more likely to visit writing tutorial centers in college spaces. At the time, and now, I wondered: Isn't this because academic writing is more geared towards "male" voices, devoid of emotion and feeling? Melissa Lozada-Oliva's "Like Totally Whatever" further illustrates this point.

bodies, whether collective or individual. This embodied character of knowledge poses many challenges. The epistemologies of the North are grounded in the idea of the rational subject, a subject that is epistemic rather than concrete or empirical" (p. 87). Moreover, Santos emphasizes the role of the body in knowledge making: "Even though we think and know with the body, even though it is with the body that we have perception, experience, and memory of the world, the body tends to be seen as a mere support for or tabula rasa of all the valuable things produced by human beings" (p. 88). This is seen in how, until recently and only sometimes, writing from first-person perspective was deemed incorrect — and discredited one's writing and arguments.

As such, the objects and forms of knowledge that challenge traditional knowledge systems, arguably, are all those that do not fit (either in resistance or in nature) within the exclusive confines of traditional knowledge.

Like Santos, many scholars, practitioners, thinkers, and writers share their knowledge in forms and manners that deviate from the traditionally accepted/represented forms taught and circulated in the Western Academia. For example, in *Cupboards of Curiosity: Women, Recollection, and Film History* (2007), Amelie Hastie combines an analysis of memory/memoir, self-analysis/preservation/presentation, and reflection by women to investigate the work, lives, and belongings of various women "to show how they appropriate a variety of personal or domestic forms to make their lives public, to reveal their presence in history, and to display their theoretical insights" (p. 5). More specifically, Hastie studies women and their work in the silent film era to explore how these women collected and created their own memory/memoir-making objects with intention for future use by biographers/authors. Hastie claims: "Usually lodged therein, the woman's expertise concerning her own life's story and her place of labor ultimately manifests itself in a kind of knowledge about the production of history, one that inherently intertwines fact and fiction, reminiscence and prophesy, the temporality and structure of film forms" (pp. 2-3). Through this work, Hastie prescribes great value to the knowledge-capacity of personal effects and materials — emphasizing how these items are valuable in relation to their ability to relay history and meaning.

Similarly, Fikile Nxumalo and Marleen Tepeyolotl Villanueva (2020) engage in transdisciplinary feminist theory-practice via "performative assemblages of visual-sensory-auto ethnographic fragments that place into conversation events, memories, poetics, stories, encounters, teachings and relational knowledges and becomings" (p. 61). In doing so, they "want to trouble the marginalization of these knowledges [Black, Indigenous and Black-Indigenous feminist knowledge-theory-practice] while also challenging the assumption that these knowledges are not informed by rigorous theory-practice" (p. 59). They reinforce the importance, rigor, power, and legitimacy of Black, Indigenous and Black-Indigenous feminist knowledge-theory-practices by exploring water precarity in conjunction with early childhood education: "We see water as life and as being a sacred spirit. We speak of water as a living being, a spirit that thinks, hears, has life and gives life. For generations, our elders have told us what many are now beginning to see: water listens to what we say and think. She listens and holds memory. She understands" (p. 70). Like Santos, Nxumalo and Villanueva address the role of knowledge in relation to identifying and fighting against oppression and injustice, recognizing that "racialized and settler colonial hierarchies have (often deadly) implications for those on those always already deemed as less-than within the interconnected effects of environmental racism and settler colonialism" (p. 73).

In *The Mushroom at the End of the World: On the Possibility of Life in Capitalist Ruins* (2021), Anna Lowenhaupt Tsing studies matsutake mushrooms, which thrive in precarity — in environments that are in peril and have faced destruction. Through this focused analysis on mushrooms, Tsing argues that these mushrooms offer a valuable lesson in how humans may survive on a planet that is facing much destruction from our own hands. Tsing writes:

> Matsutake are wild mushrooms that live in human-disturbed forests. Like rats, raccoons, and cockroaches, they are willing to put up with some of the environmental messes humans have made. Yet they are not pests; they are valuable gourmet treats—at least in Japan, where high prices sometimes make matsutake the most valuable mushroom on earth. Through their ability to nurture trees, matsutake help forests grow in daunting places. To follow matsutake

> guides us to possibilities of coexistence within environmental disturbance. This is not an excuse for further damage. Still, matsutake show one kind of collaborative survival. (pp. 3-4)

As seen above, Tsing extensively demonstrates the reliant nature of these organisms, their role in our human-centered cuisine and cultures and that in the broader environmental system/s we are all part of, and how we can look to and learn from them. Moreover, in looking at collaborations across living things, Tsing draws great attention to the role of the assemblage: "As ways of life come together, patch-based assemblages are formed. Assemblages, I show, are scenes for considering livability—the possibility of common life on a human-disturbed earth" (p. 163). Importantly, Tsing's text acts and performs as an assemblage of media — including narrative, photographs, vignettes, ethnographic studies, and illustrations. Through this prioritization of the multimodal, Tsing illuminates the power of stories (especially those that are not limited to exclusively oral or written): "To listen to and tell a rush of stories is a method. And why not make the strong claim and call it a science, an addition to knowledge? Its research object is contaminated diversity; its unit of analysis is the indeterminate encounter. To learn anything we must revitalize arts of noticing and include ethnography and natural history" (p. 37).

Likewise, in *Braiding Sweetgrass: Indigenous Wisdom, Scientific Knowledge, and the Teachings of Plants* (2013), Robin Wall Kimmerer works against colonialist patterns and analyzes sweetgrass through an indigenous perspective. Throughout this work, Kimmerer frames sweetgrass as both "material and spiritual" (p. 5) to ultimately illustrate the power of the world and our relationship with it, especially when humans are not at the top of the hierarchy and instead exist in a communal relationship with all earthlings. While Kimmerer focuses on an analysis of and with sweetgrass, she also studies (and is perhaps studied by) algae, maple sap, tadpoles, her daughters, her neighbors, and more — thus evoking Tsing's assemblage. Kimmerer further illustrates and relies upon the power of stories, memories, and that of non-human living things (including plants, seeds, animals, trees). Through this work of exploring and demonstrating how we can learn from and with plants and the broader world around us,

Kimmerer showcases, and critiques, what gets to be counted as knowledge and as science (specifically botany) in academic spaces — demonstrating that this identification and classification is a continuation of colonialism. Kimmerer writes:

> As an enthusiastic young PhD, colonized by the arrogance of science, I had been fooling myself that I was the only teacher. The land is the real teacher. All we need as students is mindfulness. Paying attention is a form of reciprocity with the living world, receiving the gifts with open eyes and open heart. My job was just to lead [my students] into the presence and ready them to hear. On that smoky afternoon, the mountains taught the students and the students taught the teacher. (p. 222)

Here, Kimmerer demonstrates how learning and knowledge are not contained and confined to the academic classroom nor the academic. By the same token, Kimmerer places great emphasis on the capacity of the world around us to teach us, if we only give it an opportunity to do so.

Both Kimmerer and Tsing created texts that I unexpectedly loved (I don't think we often love academic books — but these texts are distinctively anti-academic in the sense that they pointedly and purposefully prioritize knowledge formations, objects, and sharing that act in direct opposition to what academia produces). By including personal memoir, illustrations, pictures, and blatantly more human-feeling writing, these texts were accessible and full of love and care. I learned so much from these works due to the methodology of care-full writing that was utilized. Likewise, in *The Cooking Gene: A Journey Through African American Culinary History in the Old South* (2018), Michael Twitty relies on metaphor, imagery, quotes, memories, recipes, song lyrics, history, and more to demonstrate a sustained practice in reflexivity and positionality.

As such, these works importantly align with Arturo Escobar's call for recognition of interconnectedness in knowledge production and sharing (2018): "what is thus needed is a politics for an other civilization that respects, and builds on, the interconnectedness of all life, based on a spirituality of the Earth, and that nourishes community because it acknowledges that love and emotion are important elements of knowledge and of all of life" (2018, p. 12) and

"Patriarchal modern societies fail to understand that it is emotioning that constitutes human history, not reason or the economy, because it is our desires that determine the kinds of worlds we create" (2018, p. 13). As Tsing's mushrooms and Kimmerer's lesson on the mountain illustrate, we can, and should learn in communion — with a variety of teachers, feelings, modalities, mediums, and more.

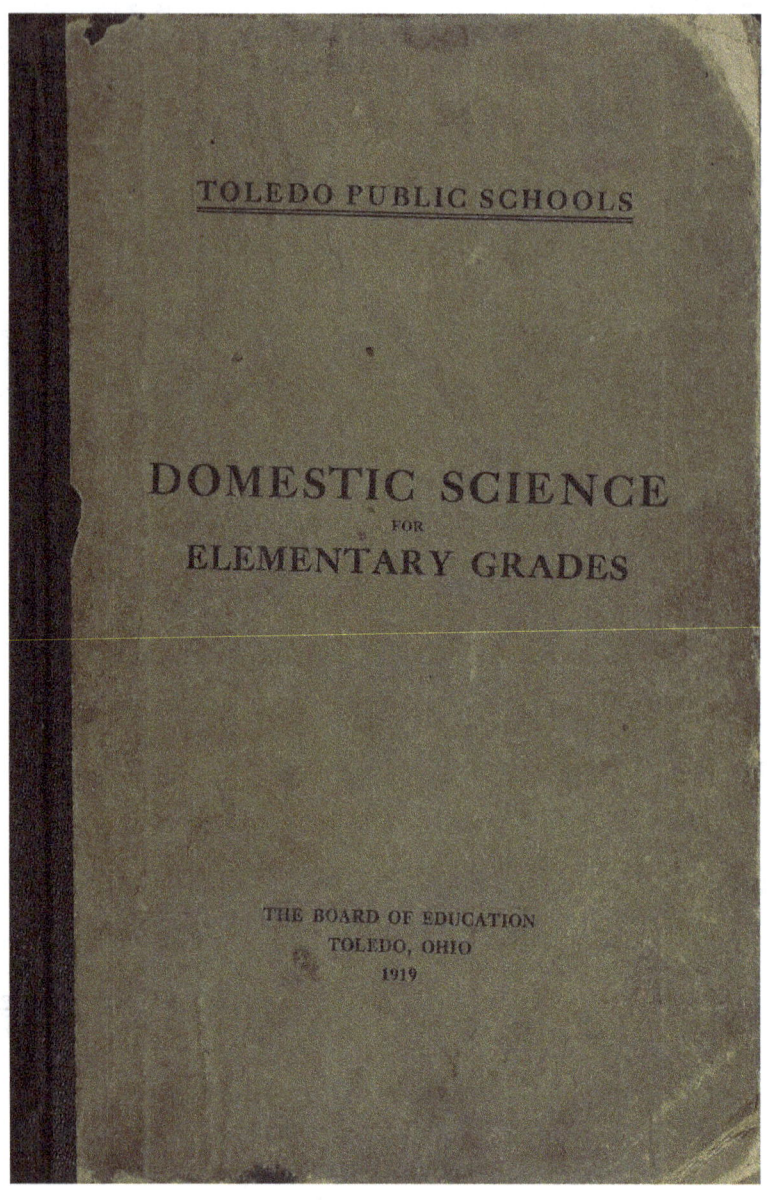

Toledo (Ohio). Board of Education. "Lessons in domestic science for seventh and eighth grade students. Includes lessons in preparing food, baking, and clean up. Created by the Toledo Public Schools Board of Education 1919." Public domain, via Wikimedia Commons.

In consideration of interconnectedness, I look to cookbooks, which are networks of interconnected ingredients, experiences, stories, meals, and more. Sharon Jansen argues that recipes are far "much more than lists of ingredients and instructions" (1993, p. 73). I would agree — and further argue that cookbooks are far much more than a compilation of recipes. In *Cookbook Politics* (2020), Kennan Ferguson writes:

> Their very form, the way in which they are put together and used, breaks up the presumptions of what instructions do and what books are. In politics, we too often conflate instructions with obligatory demands. But recipes and cookbooks are not laws or jurisprudential codes. They suggest and direct without demanding or policing. They entice rather than enforce. They thus allow us to rethink how authority, commands, and directions operate. (2020, p. 6)

Here, I situate academic/traditional knowledge sharing is to instructions (instruction manuals and other forms of technical communication) as feminist/interdisciplinary/non-academic knowledge sharing is to cookbooks.

Of this, I see that Jenna Ashton's feminist manifesto, "The Feminists are Cackling in the Archive," offers alignment to cookbooks through its "performative feminist methodologies, and strategies for disrupting both the archive and modes of knowledge production" (2017, p. 155) that are rooted in both content and processes. Ashton's interventions follow along five points for archives:

1. Selection (what is selected thus has communicated value) → find value everywhere
2. Type (aka: form/genre of object) → look for experience/feeling
3. Facilitation (categorized) → lean into the random
4. Storage & Time (to keep objects pristine and protected) → interact/touch/collaborate with objects
5. Access

These interventions, while intended for archives, are applicable to cookbooks in that they are assemblages of feelings, experiences, materials, mediums — all compiled to provide access and utility for others: "[recipes] contextualize and communalize the land, resources, experience, technology, and care" (Ferguson, 2012, p. 712). Cookbooks serve as tangible archives of images, recipes, stories, ingredients, flavors, textures, temperatures, instructions, tools, and more. Of this, Ferguson writes: "Thus they archive not only physical tastes but also social placements, trajectories of food availability, cultural complexities, nationalities, and even models of authority. They are personal *and* political, local *and* international, historical *and* contemporary, textual *and* embodied. More than any other texts, they connect feelings, flavors, and peoples. Cookbooks archive our bodies, our societies, our values, and our politics" (p. 121). By enabling us to engage and learn about/with other cultures, countries, and communities, cookbooks serve as educational texts that are perhaps more authentic and capable.

Historically, cookbooks were avenues through which women could share their knowledge with interested parties (other women). Janet Theophano writes: "For hundreds of years, women of diverse backgrounds have found the homely cookbook a suitable place to record their stories and thoughts as well as their recipes" (2002, p. 1) and "Despite or perhaps because of their ordinariness, because cooking is so basic to and so entangled in daily life, cookbooks have thus served women as meditations, memoirs, diaries, journals, scrapbooks, and guides" (2002, p. 6). Consequently, cookbooks align with Hastie's analysis and prioritization on the material as a form of feminized knowledge production.

Moreover, Theophano addresses how the form, audience, and very nature of cookbooks provided an opportunity for such authorship, namely because women's lives were "absorbed by the welfare of others" and they did not have the time or capacity to write about themselves (via memoir or journal), the cookbook was an opportunity that aligned with domestic duties and enabled them to "write themselves into being. Women who thought their lives too everyday, too ordinary to be of interest to others often used their cooking skills and prized recipes as a vehicle for making themselves visible" (p. 9). Because of this visibility of their experiences as shared through cookbooks, these texts innately lend themselves to the autobiographical.

Lynne Ireland (1981) explores the autobiographical capacity found in compiled, collaborative cookbooks — addressing how these texts reflected what was prepared, served, and eaten within homes. Like Ireland, Anne L. Bower's *Recipes for Reading: Community Cookbooks, Stories, Histories* (1997) analyzes how "cookbooks tell stories—autobiographical in most cases, historical sometimes, and perhaps fictitious or idealized in other instances. The discourse of the discrete textual elements and their juxtapositions contribute to the creation of these stories, which quietly or boldly tell of women's lives and beliefs" (p. 2). Alongside their autobiographical capacities, Bower identifies that these cookbooks are *texts*: "whether the recipe appears in a commercial cookbook or in a community cookbook, for the most part we read each recipe as a discrete unit of instruction in food preparation, seldom considering the overall story told by the recipes when taken together" (p. 8) and "We consider the community cookbook as a text that enacts within it a group of women's mental, theoretical, thoughtful positions or statements. Indeed, fund raising cookbooks are ideologically motivated, in their form as well as their content" (p. 7). Bower argues that the "stories in community cookbooks might best be described as communal partial autobiographies" (p. 30) that contain and relay setting, character/s, and subtle plots (across individual recipes and the book as a whole). Simultaneously, Bower recognizes that these texts can "also be read as fictions (idealizations or romances of home, of middle class life, of plenty, of the domestic role, of one's subculture or local community)" (p. 32). Through all of these storytelling and story sharing elements, women were able to use and share their voice/opinions, illustrate the importance and power of their domestic role, and express their culture.

Likewise, Colleen Cotter in *Recipes For Reading* observes the role of language in cookbooks and in supporting a story to foster community: "we begin to see how a recipe can be viewed as a story, a cultural narrative that can be shared and has been constructed by members of a community" (1997, pp. 52-53) and "besides the dictionary definition of 'recipe' with which we are all familiar, we will see that the humble recipe can be dressed up for scholarly purposes: it can also be viewed as a text form that is 'locally situated' as a community practice, and as a text that embodies linguistic relationships and implies within these relationships a number of cultural assumptions and practices" (1997, p. 53). As Ferguson explains, these cookbooks and their recipes provide opportunities to "engage a process of community building" (2012, p. 698) through their use of language, storytelling, and textual elements.

Through this, stories, autobiographies, and identities are infused into texts that were compiled by women, often collaborative and by some women that were "only partly literate" — thus providing literacy and educational opportunities for those who participated in their development (Theophano, 2002, p. 5). As such, cookbooks become participatory texts, inviting collaboration and making, rather than relying on comprehension alone. In doing so, cookbooks invoke more complex learning, reaching higher on Bloom's Taxonomy than texts that are dependent on one form of readership consumption, such as textbooks or essays (Shabatura, 2022). As Ferguson claims: "The recipe invites, even demands, a participatory engagement with its own information, inspiration, and pedagogy" (2020, p. 35) and "Their narrative indeterminancy, their infinite replicability, their partiality and specificity: all allow for, even demand, a participatory and experimental engagement. Even if one comes to a cookbook looking for clarity and guidance, one cannot help but participate in its making and remaking" (2020, p. 24).

Cookbooks are vividly and beautifully experiential and participatory. Much like a textbook, we annotate cookbooks — leaving evidence of comprehension, confusion, and/or consumption. The best cookbooks are those that are lived in. As Whitney Sperrazza (2019) emphasizes: "the embodied materiality of recipe books keeps the body at the center... Recipe books record the daily activities of women's bodies." Similarly, Ferguson writes:

> Marginalia becomes part of such recipes, too. The cook remembers remembering: add more baking powder; leave out garlic; add paprika here. The notes taken down, sometimes by the current cook and sometimes by previous generations, become part of the recipe itself. There no longer is an 'official' or originary version; like a folk song or an ancient Icelandic saga, each recipe

> becomes both a template for the current performer as well as a text passed down from an undetermined historical past. (2020, p. 34)

All the more, Ann Romines in *Recipes For Reading* addresses how cookbooks reveal much about the communities that produce them, but also about those who use them — seen in how her own mother made her personal Methodist cookbook into "more completely her own by cutting out the pages, punching holes in them, and transferring them to a black loose leaf binder, into which she also inserted more handwritten recipes and pages from magazines" (1997, p. 79). Romines argues that her mother, and many other women engaging in similar practices, were performing and practicing intertextuality by "transforming the Methodist cookbook into a testament of her own life as a working American woman" (1997, p. 79).

And, of course, cookbooks have and continue to reveal much about gender norms and expectations. Jessamyn Neuhaus identifies how cookbooks in the 1950s "powerfully maintained 'traditional' gender norms" (p. 543) by emphasizing that a woman's primary duty was in the kitchen. Of this, Sherrie Inness illustrates how, throughout the first half of the twentieth century, women were positioned as preppers in the kitchen, and men as consumers — which translates far beyond the home and into our world today: "This division continues to hold sway in the United States: women are still associated with the 'unimportant' domestic sphere, including cooking, while men are associated with the 'important' world of the public workplace" (2001, p. 4). This is further illustrated in which knowledge/s, past and present, are esteemed with credibility.

By analyzing a group called "Lutheran Church Women'' who published aggregated recipes from their congregation into a cookbook that was meant to propagandize their anti-feminist/female subservience stance, Ferguson identifies how community cookbooks are innately feminist due to their focus on women and women's labor, but also complicated in that they often reinforce positionings of women contained to the domestic role/sphere (2012). Ferguson writes: "Even though a woman's place is clearly in the kitchen for the vast majority of these cookbooks, the material, sensory conditions of cookery serve as a form of reclaiming the women's lives" (2012, p. 697).

Yet cookbooks provided and still provide an opportunity to display and enact subversiveness. Joan Newlon Radner and Susan S. Lanser (1987), explores subversive strategies (including appropriation, juxtaposition, distraction, indirection, trivialization, and feigning incompetence) that women adopted "to communicate feminist messages to other women; to refuse, subvert, or transform conventional expectations; and to criticize male dominance in the face of male power" (p. 423). Susan Lanser (1993) investigates women's subversiveness, resistance, and subtle rebellion to domesticity as coded in their daily lives (p. 41). Similarly, Fkeitz argues: "Dissatisfied with their low status in society, women have used language in creative ways in order to have control over their reality and free themselves from oppression. Women have succeeded at this resistance through coding" (2010, p. 3). With this said, perhaps the greatest affordance of cookbooks, in relation to their capacity to preserve and disseminate knowledge, is that they themselves do not perform as knowledge is traditionally expected to.

Furthermore, cookbooks are inherently multimodal, containing images, narratives, essays, instructions, measurements, photographs, while traditional academic scholarship is biased toward textual information. In doing so, cookbooks are able to not only better illustrate the recipes that they contain through a variety of modes (namely written and visual), but they are also better able to share those recipes with a variety of readers and learners — a broader public made up of a diverse body of consumers. As Elizabeth Fleitz (2009) states: "As women have been alienated, oppressed, and ignored by the dominant discourse, it is not surprising that women find it easy to ignore convention, as the convention marks a style they never had access to. Multimodality, then, is women's alternative" (p. 20). Fleitz addresses and argues that women's literacy practices are multimodal out of necessity and patriarchal oppression (2010). Yet, as Twitty's work demonstrates, this is not exclusive to women's literacy — and rather can be identified as a means of subversiveness adopted by many.

Simultaneously, it is important to acknowledge that cookbooks are not utopian modes of knowledge production. Rather they are complicit in upholding and reinforcing systemic barriers, classism, and racism. For example, Ferguson addresses how white women would add recipes developed by cultures and communities that are not their own to cookbooks — claiming authorship and ownership and participating in a cookery colonialism (2012). Ferguson also addresses issues of classism with cookbooks, writing: "The sale of such [community/charitable] cookbooks often served to raise funds for the impoverished and destitute, but the cookbooks themselves were aimed at those with the resources to make new, even unusual, foods... They thus create and reinforce various class boundaries, both in their purpose and in their instruction" (2012, p. 706).

Likewise, Sherrie Inness writes of the classist and racist tensions infused into these texts: "Cooking literature provided a fantasy about how women should live, but it was not always an obtainable one, especially for women of different races or ethnic backgrounds, who were given very different roles to play than Anglo women" (2001, p. 14) and "Popular cooking literature helped promulgate the notion that the 'correct' American housewife was white and middle class; thus, cooking literature not only encouraged women to stay in the kitchen, but also suggested the desirable race, ethnicity, and class for these idealized American housewives" (2001, p. 14). Similarly, Twitty identifies cookbooks as historical white texts that would have been used and associated with "white plantation owner's wife reading the recipes aloud after her reverse journey down the whistling walk. I am the enslaved hearing the recipe, or already knowing it and just humoring Big Missy. There are many things in those books that are not African in conception, spirit, delivery, or form" (2018, p. 15).

Zane Cerpina and Stahl Stenslie also offer a critical reading of all cookbooks in a capitalistic world and dying planet: "any cookbook indulges us into resource depletion, willingly and happily eating our earth empty and way beyond the planetary boundaries. Thus, every cookbook hastens the end of the world that it is written in" (2022, p. 2).

Following an imperative for sustainability and a criticism of capitalism/consumerism, *Cooking with Action Research: Stories and Resources for Self and Community Transformation* (2017) "suggests that, as in good cooking, the requirements of research reach beyond the mechanical application of techniques. Art and science, intuition and hard work, freedom to invent and methodical rigor mix, and from this mix creative transformative action and knowledge emerge" (Hilary Bradbury and Associates, p. 12). Perhaps cookbooks are the template and genre through which we can better reach this action research that relies upon a conglomeration of strategies, frameworks, mediums, and more to produce better, more caring knowledge?

my personal experiences with cookbooks/cooking

My parents both come from farmstock. My mom's family has long owned and operated a dairy and produce farm — and my dad started working on the farm when he was 13.

Unlike my parents' families growing up, mine moved every .5-5 years with military stationing and relocations. Our food reflected that. My mom learned how to cook with spice and pepper seasonings while we lived in Japan. We ate a lot of avocados in Texas when my mom could buy them for six for a dollar on the side of the road. We ate a lot of pork each time we lived in North Carolina — and that people take the vinegar versus tomato sauce debate very seriously. We found out my mom is severely allergic to clams while trying all the seafood in Rhode Island at a restaurant she wanted to try because Rachel Ray recommended it (and I learned I will never be able to prepare lobster myself after watching my parents learn how to make it with our neighbors). We always have the good and the real maple syrup while visiting family in New York.

But while we moved regularly and our lives were often in flux, my mom was an ever-constant (that is the military's "managing and running the homefront"). While my mom was an excellent cook and caregiver, I was fiercely opposed to anything pertaining to the kitchen due to my self-taught feminism.

As I got older, my parents were so dismayed that not only was I not interested in cooking, but I also really did not know how. As my dad reminded me, making Instant Ramen (which was his meal of choice whenever my mom was not home) was an ordeal, whereas my mom began cooking family dinners as a child. And while I understood this as coded sexism of girlhood that my parents wanted me to grow up and learn how to make things in the kitchen (an early example of identifiable gender fatalism), it was also that they wanted me to know how to boil water. In actuality, they were engaging in some slight sexism through these expectations that my brothers didn't have to engage with, but, for my mom especially, this was rooted in a need for her daughter to nourish herself, feed herself, and care for herself without needing to depend on anyone/anything else to do those things for her.

And food became more complicated away from home. At 20, my relationship to making, and making with food specifically, was straining. I enjoyed performing adulthood at times, like trying to make chicken parmigiana like my mom made when I was growing up. In college with limited money and access to food, I turned to Instagram for dinner ideas — and algorithmic bias encouraged me to eat smoothies and fruit bowls with some oatmeal for all my meals. Through social media, I learned about, what I recognize only now, as restrictive eating and harmful diets. I began a dangerous spiral of body dysmorphia that was rooted in a compounded combination of counting calories, eating too many carrots and nothing else, and working out incessantly. Like the Instagram accounts were advertising, I thought this was healthy. And I thought this was caring for myself.

Making with food became unhealthy. I lost weight, too much weight. Friends noticed and family asked if I had always been this tiny. But I was fixated on the (very sexist) pressures to be tiny, to be small. Body dysmorphia came to me through making with food: sexist and infantilizing pressures to not gain a "freshman 15," to look and weigh how I did as a child.

Even now, when I see a calorie counting diet plan suggested on media — I worry for young people that might see this as the only means of being healthy. Severe data collection of the self through caloric intake that ignores and erases other data, such as the joy, nourishment, and care that food brings to us.

Throughout college, my mom would text me and tell me: You need to take care of yourself. At the time, I was frustrated by the insinuation that I wasn't taking care of myself (which I wasn't). But over the years, I realized that my mom, who was largely parenting alone for my entire upbringing, knew that we need to rely on ourselves for care before we can look to rely on any other person or system to do so. Is this what she meant? Maybe not. But I have overtime understood my mom's pressure to learn how to cook and to take care of myself as a call to prioritize the self and one's care in a world that will not do so. Her reminder is to remember that care is independence, of perspective, and to remember what matters.

And so I think cooking and sharing enable the joy of care alongside food. Not only is it really gendered because my family really wanted me to learn how to boil water, but also they really wanted me to be okay for myself.

Now, cooking is a communal activity between my husband and myself. Listening to music, tripping over our dog lying between our feet while waiting for cheese, being each others' sous chef as we fight over who gets to do the next step. Me sprinkling in much more salt when he is distracted. Him refusing to follow any kind of recipe, but instead using them (just the pictures) as inspiration. Usually most dinner making ends with me getting frustrated that he takes over my preparations, but that's because while I like to cook, and enjoy baking even more, he really loves cooking — and, as such, he does 90% of the family cooking.

Also now I see care and cooking, both things my mom excelled at and called for, as feminist practices dressed up in a maternal command. While my dad was often deployed with the military (which operates as extremely hyper heteromasculine as it can possibly be), my mom ran the home front — caring for us. I am not sure my mom would identify herself as a radical feminist, but I think her messages and demandings of care, often through the process of cooking, illustrate that we live in a world and society that do not prioritize care. As such, that burden falls on ourselves.

Gilbert, Lynn. (1978). "Julia Child in her kitchen as photographed ©Lynn Gilbert." Cambridge, Massachusetts. CC BY-SA 4.0, via Wikimedia Commons.

how to use this book

This work emerged from a doctoral dissertation. Importantly: a dissertation is the culminating project, work, and research to be accomplished and performed by a doctoral candidate in their PhD program. The dissertation documents, showcases, and analyzes original research conducted by the student (a PhD candidate) and is intended to provide the opportunity to *perform* as an academic, as a scholar, researcher. Meaning: the dissertation is where students emulate the practices, processes, and traditions of what is expected in scholarly knowledge sharing. And as such, it follows academic modes of knowledge production. This work traditionally takes the form of an extended manuscript, often composed into five lengthy chapters (roughly 30 pages apiece).

This contrasts strongly with other forms of knowledge sharing — like that we can find in nonfiction children's books, museums, scrapbooks, journals and diaries, magazines, and cookbooks. And while these avenues are still informative, educational, and convey knowledge, academic knowledge is often held to a higher esteem due to an awarded prestige. And this is not to discredit the labor and expertise infused into these academic-based works, but that there is a form of knowledge accreditation and elitism that results in these works being siloed within academic communities and institutions and often inaccessible and less readable for anyone beyond these. More specifically, I think of how my mom cannot read something I published in a peer-reviewed academic journal unless I download it through my institution's subscription to the journal and send it to her. She could pay for it, but I have immediate access (to my article and thousands and thousands of others) through my academic position. By publishing within journals such as these, I am contributing to a body of knowledge, I am participating in the academic community, I am performing academic scholarship. However, in *sharing* knowledge in this way, I am participating in a form of knowledge dissemination that is inherently rooted in exclusivity and elitism.

Conversely, as I hope to argue here, cookbooks offer an opportunity to share knowledge that works in opposition to many of the issues presented within academic knowledge production, including that of the dissertation, the traditional textbook, and the broader academic work.

Colford, Anna L. "Front title page of *A Friend in the Kitchen: Or, What to Cook and How to Cook It*, published in 1899." Public domain, via Wikimedia Commons.

While the appearance and contexts of cookbooks vary, a cookbook, as a textual genre, is rather undeniable — most apparently seen in the inclusion of many (many many) recipes. And as Marshall McLuhan famously expressed: the medium is the message (1964). As such, the form and performance of this book and its corresponding research, much like cookbooks themselves, greatly matters. In constructing a cookbook, I simultaneously strive to recognize and emphasize that cooking, baking, and recipe sharing are historically a domestic practice that is largely rooted in the labor and practice of women (Fleitz, 2009; Bower, 1997; Merkner, 1996; Zafar, 1998) — I lean into this to bring this genre to the forefront to emphasize intersectional feminism in knowledge sharing and work against issues present with academic and "prestigious" forms of knowledge.

Through this, I wonder:

1. What role do critical making, critical pedagogy and experiential inquiry play in supporting equity and justice?
2. In considering the role of care in reimaging power, who is responsible for the care, labor, and power of ancestral and community stories, histories, and affect? Moreover, how does gender intersect with care?
3. As seen with the capacities of cookbooks, how can systems and manners of knowing more equitably and critically enable exploration, learning, and care to reimagine power (of care, literacy, and justice) and knowledge (production, recognition, and legitimacy)?

To explore and interrogate these questions, this book is broken into a format that strives to mirror and emulate that of a cookbook, while performing the knowledge-work of an academic text in disguise. As such, this book is organized as follows:

Chapter 1. Prep Work

Cookbooks often begin with the context, history, story of the book and its compilation. Because of this, this work began with the foundations of exploring the advantageous formatting of cookbooks— especially when compared to traditional academic modes of knowledge production, sharing, and dissemination. As such, this session includes the Prep Work, or the introductory materials.

Chapter 2. Tools + frames + theory

Such as cookbooks often include a list and explanation of the kitchen, cooking, and baking tools, supplies, and ingredients that will be needed, this book relies upon this framing to share the frameworks of analysis and theory utilized. The following chapter provides relevant and necessary literature overviews of intersection feminism, critical pedagogy, experiential inquiry, and critical making as they relate to, contextualize, and expand this investigation. My review of intersectional feminism outlines historical and key understandings of this framework, but it also identifies significant faults and limitations — and how this connects to broader faults of academic knowledge production and dissemination. Moreover, I also include an analysis of how critical making, critical pedagogy, and experiential inquiry necessarily ebb and flow into each other as interconnected frameworks of critical production and exploration, especially in relation to a topic such as making with food. Through this, I illustrate how these theories are rooted in knowledge making that are founded upon principles of learning through making, reflexivity, and equitable action.

Chapter 3. Conversion charts

Inspired by the helpful conversion charts that are sometimes found within cookbooks, the Conversion charts offer the methods of this book. In this chapter I outline the methodological processes that guided this investigation, as well as the two knowledge sharing forms that this investigation looks to and relies upon, namely interviews and images. In doing so, I address methodological advantages and connections to the cookbook genre while tracing the justification of their utility.

Chapter 4. Care materials

Drawing from the intentional inclusion of grocery lists found within cookbooks, Care materials offers a framework of analysis as focused upon care. Through this chapter I explore and outline the various different perspectives, understandings, and problems associated with care. In doing so, I illustrate the complex landscape of care and how this investigation exists within these understandings of care.

Chapter 5. Staples

Mirroring the meat of cookbooks (the recipes focusing on breakfasts, grains, baked goods, poultry, etc.), the heart of this work is found within Staples. This chapter includes the conversations, media, and recipes from various folks. Notably, these are included here in the center of the book rather than in the appendix (as may be customary with an academic work), to reinforce their importance, legitimacy, and knowledge value. These conversations include those with the various collaborators and participants:

>321 Coffee
>
>Bee Downtown
>
>A Place at the Table
>
>The Root Cellar Cafe & Catering
>
>Well Fed Community Garden
>
>Microbiomes and the Science we eat
>
>Wonderpuff
>
>Videri Chocolate Factory
>
>Two Roosters

Chapter 6. Sharing the table

Drawing from the knowledge shared and exchanged, as encapsulated in the prior chapter, Sharing the Table offers an analysis of the conversations to explore key themes surrounding the roles of care, community, and making. These findings are derived as a result of the methods shared in Chapter 3. "Conversion charts," and the intersectional feminist principles derived from Catherine D'Ignazio and Lauren Klein's *Data Feminism* (2020) and design justice[3] (Costanza-Chock, 2020) that drove and regulated this investigative effort.

Chapter 7. A recipe for necessary disaster and disruption: A manifesto

Inspired by Haraway's reflexivity (1988), this section performs as a manifesto — outlining processes and opportunities to work towards equity through the ideas and themes presented throughout this work.

Chapter 8. Cleaning the table

Such as we finish a meal by cleaning the table, this book concludes by revisiting the key findings and addressing the contributions and limitations of this investigation, as well as potential avenues for further investigation and research. As cultural artifacts and affective objects of utility, cookbooks speak of and mirror the social values that they mediate. Therefore, working through and with this genre and modality of knowledge, this work will investigate material forms of culture, communication, community, and expression (Latour, 2007; Lievrouw, 2014) — as well as how each of these intersect with care. Thus, this work will draw up cultural studies and materialism as they intersect with feminism and learning.

Ultimately, through the methods of critical making (Hertz, 2016), this work takes the form of a cookbook that shares and contextualizes a compilation of resources, showcases, feminist reflexivity passages, essays, recipes, and public-facing research on care and how we can learn in a more equitable and loving manner to produce a better world. In doing so, this work ultimately aims to actionize care.

---

[3] 1) Heal, 2) Center, 3) Impact, 4) Process of change, 5) Facilitator, 6) Expert on self, 7) Share, 8) Community, 9) Non-exploitative, and 10) Existing.

Read, skim, and flip through this cookbook as you choose. There's no right or wrong way to read this. But do add to it. Add notes, ideas, questions, annotations. Make this yours.

Cramp, Helen. (1913). "The Institute Cook Book." Public domain, via Wikimedia Commons.

Porter, Milton E. (1907). "Baking bread." Public domain, via Wikimedia Commons.

Chapter 2.
Tools + frames + theory

[Photographer unknown]. "*Washington Women's Cookbook* by Linda Deziah Jennings, 1909"
Public domain, via Wikimedia Commons.

a note on theory

When my mom and I talk on the phone, we more often than not find ourselves talking about teaching. We critique her school and county's mandated scripted curriculum and my institution's lack of infrastructural support and care. We talk about what it means to work in a profession that is consistently devalued by those in power. We talk about how her students learn best when she is able to focus on their socio-emotional wellness. We talk about how Common Core State Standards do make room for socio-emotional wellness or how my institution performs care through wellness days. We talk about grading, observing, co-teaching, playing at recess, learning through experiments (and experimenting with our teaching), curriculum development, professionalization, but we never name critical pedagogy, experiential inquiry, or critical making. Yet, these are the things we are talking about.

I begin with this story because my own pedagogy practice and my understanding of all pedagogy is rooted in my experience of learning and teaching, which has been shaped by these informal, frequent calls with my mom as we critique our educational system, envision how it could be better, and ruminate on the joyful teachable moments with our students.

Paralleling these conversations that I am most familiar with, Maxine Greene explores the labor of teaching and the capacity for learning as rooted in imagination for happiness, rather than training. In doing so, Greene positions imagination as a liberatory mechanism. Greene argues: "Teachers may well be among the few in a position to kindle the light that might illuminate the spaces of discourse and events in which young newcomers have someday to find their ways" (2009, pp. 89-90) and "It is a matter of awakening and empowering today's young people to name, to reflect, to imagine, and to act with more and more concrete responsibility in an increasingly multifarious world" (2009, p. 92).

In considering the lessons I have learned with and alongside my mom and Greene's emphasis on the power of hopeful imagination in learning for critical awareness, I lean into hope and classify critical pedagogy, experiential inquiry, and critical making as invaluable strategies for better, more just and equitable learning.

As this note hopes to convey, take from the theory sections what is needed, but remember that, within this context, theory is a name to that which we do or can do. Other names, scholars, and concepts may also apply.

intersectional feminism

I, for better or worse, learned about feminism from a James Patterson novel in El Paso, Texas during my middle school years (despite being taught Janice Woods Windle's *True Women* at the same time).[4] Modeling myself after the young girl protagonists I read about, I was a baby feminist (who did not know what this meant at all — just that I thought it was sexist when I had to set the table for dinner and my brothers did not). I was then taught about feminism for the first time while reading *Gone with the Wind* as part of the Texas school curriculum; however, it was not until years later that I realized I was taught an exclusively narrow and highly problematic form of feminism — one that only focused on white women in the United States.

Because of my own deficits in feminist thought, derived from a lack of understanding and education, below I offer a considerable framing of intersectional feminism as it is used and been helpful for me in conversation with that which this work is concerned with, namely: care, equity, justice, and learning. Through this, I aim to situate my work within these greater conversations of intersectionality and feminism.

I begin with Sara Ahmed, who evokes bell hooks's own conceptualizations and framings of intersectional feminism, who pointedly writes: "Feminism is necessary because of what has not ended: sexism, sexual exploitation, and sexual oppression" (2017, p. 5; hooks, 2000/2015, p. 1). While I was first exposed to feminism through young-adult fiction and then racist historical literature, Ahmed and many feminist scholars emphasize that the fight of feminism is far from over. Ahmed further writes:

---

[4] I never took/had the opportunity to take a class on academic feminism. Rather, the knowledge that comes from experience *is* knowledge and does not need certification from an academy or scholarship to be knowledge. As feminism calls for, my learning of and understanding of feminism ruptures hegemonic structures.

> Feminism is homework... By homework, I am not suggesting we all feel at home in feminism in the sense of feeling safe or secure. Some of us might find a home here; some of us might not. Rather, I am suggesting feminism is homework because we have much to work out from not being at home in a world. In other words, homework is work on as well as at our homes. We do housework. Feminist housework does not simply clean and maintain a house. Feminist housework aims to transform the house, to rebuild the master's residence. (2017, p. 7)

Like many scholars and academics argue, intersectional feminism is key in doing the transformative, radical, and revolutionary housework of feminism as Ahmed illustrates above — and to producing a better, more inclusive and more just feminism that is not looking to a flavor of feminism that suits a powerful few (such as white feminism, which was the historically pervasive form of feminism — and the form of feminism I was taught when reading *Gone with the Wind* at 12 years old).

As intersectional feminism fights against this harshly limiting framing of feminism, Kimberlé Crenshaw, a lawyer and Civil Rights advocate, developed "intersectionality" as a term in the late 1980s to address the overlapping and compounding discrimination from racism and sexism that Black women specifically face (1989). More specifically, the term "intersectionality" was used to explain how people can experience multiple avenues of discrimination that are layered, or intersect, with each other.[5] With this understanding of intersectionality, feminism becomes more critically attuned to the layering discriminations that individuals experience around the world including race, gender, sexuality, dis/ability, religion, class, and more. What this means is that sexism does not exist in isolation, rather some individuals might experience sexism, but other individuals can experience racism, sexism, and ableism all at one time with compounding effects.

---

[5] Simultaneously, other scholars have identified how the term "intersectional" has become too oversaturated and overutilized. I hear this argument, yet lean into the overarching capacity of this term and framework as a form of feminist that is rooted in equity and justice, while recognizing and fighting against uneven power and privilege distributions.

Moreover, Patricia Hill Collins further explores the necessities and capacities of intersectional feminism by situating Black feminist thought as a critical social theory that aims for justice and prioritizes the knowledge developed and work accomplished by Black and African American women, which have been undervalued, underrecognized due to the systemic oppression of white heteronormativity and supremacy: "Because elite White men control Western structures of knowledge validation, their interests pervade the themes, paradigms, and epistemologies of traditional scholarship. As a result, U.S. Black women's experiences as well as those of women of African descent transnationally have been routinely distorted within or excluded from what counts as knowledge" (2000, p. 251) and "This dialectic of oppression and activism, the tension between the suppression of African-American women's ideas and our intellectual activism in the face of that suppression, constitutes the politics of U.S. Black feminist thought" (2000, p. 3). Moreover, Collins's work draws together Crenshaw's understanding of intersectionality and the conceptualization of the matrix of domination to illustrate how systems of oppression work like lattice — reinforcing each other to purport injustice and domineering subordination and instances of power (p. 18).

This necessary focus on injustice is exemplified through sharing personal experiences and stories of sexual assault and authoring of #MosqueMeToo and #IBeatMyAssaulter, Mona Eltahawy (2020) argues for a "feminism that is robust, aggressive, and unapologetic" (p. 6) in the #MeToo movement and a world/history of sexual violence inflicted by the patriarchy across the globe. In her book, *The Seven Necessary Sins for Women and Girls*, Eltahawy introduces the "seven necessary sins women and girls need to employ to defy, disobey, and disrupt the patriarchy: anger, attention, profanity, ambition, power, violence, and lust" (p. 10). In following and enacting these "sins," Eltahawy wants to enable and teach women and girls to fight, not just survive, the patriarchy (p. 14). Importantly, Eltahawy illustrates the universality of patriarchy:

> Patriarchy is so universal and normalized that it is like asking a fish *What is water?* It enables and protects men who sexually assault women, and it demands that only other men "protect" us. As long as we obey and behave in ways it

> approves, it will "protect" us. And if we disobey, you can be sure that that protection will be revoked quicker than you can say "patriarchy." But I don't want to be protected. I just want patriarchy to stop protecting and enabling men. I don't want to be protected. I want to be free. (2020, p. 5)

Due to this, Eltahawy calls for a universal feminism — and a feminism that is not led by white women: "I also want feminism to be led by the nonwhite and the queer, who don't have the luxury of fighting *only* misogyny. We must fight the multiple systems of oppressions that patriarchy often intertwines itself with: racism, bigotry, homophobia, transphobia, classism, ableism, and ageism" (p. 6). Eltahawy's call for intersectionality in feminism aligns with Collins's framing of the matrix of domination — as well as hooks's critique of feminism (what we might call white feminism), claiming: "Most American women, particularly white women, have not decolonized their thinking either in relation to the racism, sexism, and class elitism they hold towards less powerful groups of women in this society or the masses of women globally" (2015; 2000, p. 45-46).

Here, Eltaway's critique of feminism reminds me of the first wave of feminism in the United States with the Suffrage Movement, which focused on achieving the right to vote for white women — not all women. As such, the voices of white women have long been dominant in the feminist movement/s; however, there has been a pronounced pattern of exclusion and racism within this dominance.

This is exemplified further by Mikki Kendall's *Hood Feminism: Notes From the Women That a Movement Forgot* (2021), which demonstrates how mainstream feminism currently focuses and centers the most privileged, while consistently ignoring and not-serving those who need it most and who should be centered. In doing so, Kendall also interrogates why feminism is not doing more regarding issues that greatly impact women, namely women of color — such as hunger, poverty, sexual violence, abuse, gun violence, and more. Through this, Kendall defines hood feminism as a means in which we recognize that the solution to a problem, and challenging that problem, may be messy and even illegal (p. 37) — and ultimately calls for accomplice feminism, emphasizing that these feminists "interrogate and challenge the cultural standards that underpin those [white supremacist views]. They don't just stand on the sidelines watching while marginalized people are brutalized for protesting, they stand between the white supremacist systems (which are less likely to harm them) and those that the systems are trying to harm... working against white supremacy in the same way that other marginalized communities do" (2021, p. 258). Thus, Kendall, hooks, Eltahawy, Collins, and Crenshaw reveal the necessity of intersectional feminism to develop a more just, more equitable, and blatantly better form of feminism.

Moreover, offering similarities to Kendall's accomplice feminism and Eltahawy's combative and liberatory feminism, Ahmed names and identifies the feminist killjoy:

> However she speaks, the one who speaks as a feminist is usually heard as the cause of the argument. She stops the smooth flow of communication. It becomes tense. She makes things tense... The problem is not simply about the content of what she is saying. She is doing more than saying the wrong thing: she is getting in the way of something, the achievement or accomplishment of the family or of some we or another, which is created by what is not said. (2017, p. 37)

Through this, Ahmed develops a feminist killjoy survival kit, including books, things, tools, time, life, permission notes, other killjoys, humor, feelings, and bodies. Of this, she claims: "We could think of this feminist survival kit as a form of feminist self care" (2017, p. 236). Within this survival kit, my personal favorite is the reclaiming of feelings — especially when women have long been told that they are too feeling, too emotional. Here Ahmed writes of the vigorous power and strength of that which is felt: "Our emotions can be a resource; we draw on them. To be a killjoy is often to be assigned as being emotional, too emotional; letting your feelings get in the way of your judgment; letting your feelings get in the way. Your feelings can be the site of a rebellion. A feminist heart beats the wrong way; feminism is hearty" (2017, p. 246). When we are encouraged to reclaim and acknowledge the power of feelings, we are encouraged to work against and revolt against a knowledge system and broader society that clings to the negative associations of feeling. My whole life, I have been told that in expressing my feelings (verbally and physically), I am making myself too vulnerable, diminutive, ditsy. I trained myself to hide my emotions in spaces and conversations when I felt that my feelings would be used as a tactic against me.[6] Moreover, women have historically been discredited due to their feelings for becoming "hysterical" and this constructed binary system that posits rationality and credibility against feeling and emotion.

Considering how emotions and feelings have been discredited in a world that prioritizes rationality and logic, Catherine D'Ignazio and Lauren Klein (2020) frame data feminism through intersectional feminism and develop seven key principles that are helpful even when not working with traditional instances and objects of data. To engage in data feminism, they encourage us to: 1) Examine power, 2) Challenge Power, 3) Elevate emotion and embodiment, 4) Rethink binaries and hierarchies, 5) Embrace pluralism, 6) Consider context, and 7) Make labor visible. As they write: "Data feminism is about power, about who has it and who doesn't, and about how those differentials of power can be challenged and changed using data" (p. 19). Additionally, data feminism, like the intersectional feminism it draws and relies upon, is about being better and kinder humans to contribute to more fair systems that benefit those who have been most disenfranchised throughout history to build a more equitable world.

Furthering the role of rebellion and subversiveness in a world that is without equity, Legacy Russell (2020) offers the conceptualization of glitch feminism — which subverts traditional understandings of a glitch to reimagine and conceptualize feminism: "Within glitch feminism, glitch is celebrated as a vehicle of refusal, a strategy of nonperformance" (p. 8). Especially in a capitalistic society that demands streamlined labor, a glitch represents a break in the system. As these intersectional feminists may remind us, the patriarchal system is one that must be broken — and may we all be a glitch that does so. With this framing, we can see how embracing emotion and feeling is an intentional glitch. Moreover, any opposition to the standard, powerful, and pervasive can be recognized as a glitch.[7]

---

[6] In a meeting about a programmatic problem, my classmates and I were told at the start: "Let's try to not speak from emotion. Focus on what happened." I ended the meeting wearing my glasses to try to hide my crying.

[7] As such, I would offer that this book was created with the goal of a glitch: working against the standard model of academic knowledge and producing knowledge in a form that might be deemed "wrong" or "insufficient."

While Russell focuses predominantly on the role of the body as a site of glitch across digital/virtual/online worlds (2020), Ahmed also aligns feminism with a body: "I think of feminism as a fragile archive, a body assembled from shattering, from splattering, an archive whose fragility gives us responsibility: to take care" (2017, p. 17). Ahmed's feminist body is one that demands attention and nurturing to best suit all. Similarly, Audre Lorde (2015) writes: "For women, the need and desire to nurture each other is not pathological bur [sic] redemptive, and it is within that knowledge that our real power is discovered. It is this real connection, which is so heard by a patriarchal world. For it is only under a patriarchal structure that maternity is the only social power open to women" (p. 95). Here, Ahmed and Lorde seemingly draw upon the exploited maternal care labor and situate it as a responsibility of feminism, but also an avenue through which power, knowledge, and care can be shared and found. As such, I see, as do many of these scholars, feminism *is* and *as* care.

Understanding feminism is care aligns with hooks's philosophy of love:

> When we accept that true love is rooted in recognition and acceptance, that love combines acknowledgment, care, responsibility, commitment, and knowledge, we understand there can be no love without justice. With that awareness comes the understanding that love has the power to transform us, giving us the strength to oppose domination. To choose feminist politics, then, is a choice to love. (2000/2015, p. 104)

Here, hooks emphasizes how love, as rooted in care, knowing, and work, is a critical method of feminism in pursuit of justice that can result in transformational change. Yet, this role and responsibility of care carries intricacies that intersectional feminism aids in teasing out.

While much of the language surrounding intersectional feminism does not invoke the word or process of "care," one must recognize that love and care have long been the underrecognized, underpaid, and under-celebrated labor of women. Yet, I identify care as a necessary and powerful vehicle of intersectional feminism that must not be discredited or disregarded due to its gendered lineage, aligning with Judith Butler's identification of vulnerability as strength

(2016), the love work of bell hooks (1999), and the care work of Nel Noddings (1984). Rather, intentionally evoking care for justice could be seen as a display of subversion.

These relationships between feminism and care and love are exemplified in Maggie Nelson's *The Argonauts* (2015), which offers a successful and poignant convergence of storytelling, theory, care, and learning. Nelson's work offers an analysis of gender and sexuality theory, through her personal memoir — her personal narrative. In doing so, she presents theory as coupled with her lived experiences, namely those with her partner and family. For example: while relaying a conversation with a friend, Nelson brings in Judith Butler: "Performativity has to do with repetition, very often with the repetition of oppressive and painful gender norms to force them to resignify. This is not freedom, but a question of how to work the trap that one is inevitably in" (Butler qtd. in Nelson, p. 15). As such, this text is an example of autotheory — a demonstration of the confluence of theory and practice, memoir and critical analysis to discuss and explore her experiences as a woman, a mother, a wife, and more.

And what I appreciate so much about Nelson's work is that it takes academic theory, yet applies it to what matters: life, love, family. It draws upon scholarship, without reading as such, to make it more readable and enjoyable. And this is a great fault of much academic knowledge.

For example, the care work of feminism has arguably been obscured by the veneer and inaccessibility of academia. In telling stories, we can make feminism human, accessible, real again. As Cherríe Moraga writes: "we have the rhetoric do the job of poetry. Even the word 'oppression' has lost its power. We need a new language, better words that can more closely describe women's fear of, and resistance to, one another; words that will not always come out sounding like dogma" (2015, p. 25). Likewise, Eltahawy expresses: "Words like 'feminism' and 'resistance' are being drained of their meaning when we offer them up as band-aids that offer temporary relief to women and girls against the vagaries of patriarchy" (2020, p. 13). In *Feminism Is for Everybody: Passionate Politics*, hooks writes of her goals with her book — which hold strong parallels to the broader issue of knowledge obscurity: "I want to be holding in my hand a concise, fairly easy to read and understand book; not a long book, not a book thick with hard to understand jargon and academic language, but a straightforward, clear book — easy to read without being simplistic" (2000/2015, p. xii). Moreover, hooks emphasizes that the world of academia has become a prominent sphere for feminist discourse, stating: "This trend has had positive impact for college students as it provides greater opportunity for folks to learn the power and significance of feminist thinking and practice, but it has impacted negatively on the work of broadening the engagement of a large public in feminist movement" (2000/2015, p. viii) and "[feminism and feminist thought] became and remains a privileged discourse available to those among us who are highly literate, well-educated, and usually materially privileged" (2000/2015, p. 5). Similarly, Kendall states: "I am not ashamed of where I came from; the hood taught me that feminism isn't just academic theory. It isn't a matter of saying the right words at the right time. Feminism is the work that you do, and the people you do it for who matter more than anything else" (2021, p. xiii). Here, Kendall illustrates that feminism and its work is not, and should not, be contained to an academic sphere — and hooks agrees in arguing that this has indeed harmed its utility and adoption across a far broader public. We can and should find feminism out in the world.

Summary

In relying upon Catherine D'ignazio and Lauren Klein's seven principles of data feminism[8] that outline how to perform more just and equitable data work and Legacy Russell's identification of glitch feminism as a subversive, multimodal, multidimensional means of leaning into the glitch (that which is seen or recognized as an error) to riot against normative and oppressive capitalistic structures, I define and situate intersectional feminism as a framework that prioritizes genuine equity and inclusion through instances such as subverting power systems (when one can), welcoming and prioritizing collaboration with and through community, and actionizing care while recognizing that our world is not experienced evenly or fairly.

In doing so, intersectional feminism looks to those who are most harmed, those who are most at-risk, and those that are most disenfranchised to empower and center, which simultaneously aligns with the work and principles of design justice. Design Justice can be understood quite

---

[8] 1) Examine power, 2) Challenge Power, 3) Elevate emotion and embodiment, 4) Rethink binaries and hierarchies, 5) Embrace pluralism, 6) Consider context, and 7) Make labor visible.

literally as designing justice — and when we understand design as any action done with intention (Costanza-Chock, 2020), we arrive at a framework of intended, purposeful action for justice. As such, intersectional feminism, too, can be thought of actionizing work in effort for justice to better care for our world and its inhabitants.

With these considerations of justice and because of the faults of a feminism limited and harmed by academics and scholarship, I lean on intersectional feminist thought and work to exemplify the need for knowledge sharing that is, as hooks (2000/2015), Moraga (2015), Kendall (2021), and Eltahawy (2020) call for, accessible and pointed — to be used, read, and understood. Such as Nelson does by drawing upon stories and theories (2015), I engage my killjoyness through autotheory and utilize intersectional feminist methodologies, namely centering lived experience and reflexivity, leaning into feelings and the role of emotion, and prioritizing that which has been deemed less useful and posited as invisible by society at large. As such, this work investigates the praxis and actionization of intersectional feminism, even and especially when it operates unnamed and unidentified as such. With goals (and actions) such as these, I am once more working in the fashion and goals of a glitch with this book to do the *work* of intersectional feminism, rather than just talking and writing of it.

critical pedagogy

Critical pedagogy is adopting a lens of criticality to strive towards radical learning in the fight against oppression — to provide the opportunity, tools, and space for radical agency and liberation.

Critical pedagogy can be understood as a framework for learning that adopts a lens of criticality, investigation, or examination. In *Pedagogy of the Oppressed*, Paulo Freire is concerned with the liberation of the oppressed, issues of humanization and dehumanization (as well as using humanization to fight against dehumanization), and the role of the oppressed to liberate themselves and the oppressors. As Freire writes: "The solution is not to 'integrate' [the oppressed] into the structure of oppression, but to transform that structure so that they can become 'beings for themselves'" (1985, p. 74). Freire offers insight to virtues and qualities of teachers (including humility, patience, impatience, tolerance, love, curiosity, a learner, demystified, passionate, and creative) while arguing against the education model of a teacher "filling" students with knowledge (1985, p. 71). Freire names this harmful, dehumanizing pedagogical process as the banking concept of education, which includes the mechanization of students and turning them into "containers" to be "filled" (1985, p. 72). Instead, Freire identifies that the pedagogy of the oppressed is "a pedagogy which must be forged with, not for, the oppressed... in the incessant struggle to regain their humanity" (1985, p. 48).

Freire further addresses a prioritization of the learner's ideas and thoughts over the book (1985, p. 19). Similarly, Peter McLaren situates critical pedagogy within the United States context as a means and a "hope" to "empower the powerless" (2015, p. 122) — recognizing how schools and the broader educational system are designed to support and uphold the dominant class and group, specifically white supremacy and cis-heteronormativity. McLaren addresses how critical pedagogy enables emancipatory/directive knowledge (2015, p. 134) to explore "the relationship between power and knowledge" (2015, p. 144). Through this, McLaren interrogates knowledge: "Critical pedagogy asks how and why knowledge gets constructed the way it does, and how and why some constructions of reality are legitimated and celebrated by the dominant culture while others clearly are not" (2015, p. 133).

Furthermore, Michael Apple argues against functional literacy and instead for critical, powerful, political literacy to "[enable] the growth of genuine understanding and control of all spheres of social life in which we participate" (1999/2014, p. 45). Apple explains that being critical "involves understanding the sets of historically contingent circumstances and contradictory power relationships that create the conditions in which we live" (1999/2014, p. 5). In *Official Knowledge: Democratic Education in a Conservative Age* (1999/2014), Apple analyzes the issue of "correct" learning, literacy, methods, and the issue of what is/isn't included in textbooks (as objects that are important due to their "content and form") that "signify more profound political, economic, and cultural relations and histories" (1999/2014, p. 49). Of textbooks, Apple argues that they serve as a curricula tool that is designed to reinforce colonialist and imperialistic norms that are reflective of the dominate group, and ultimately "participate in creating what a society has recognized as legitimate and truthful" (1999/2014, p. 49). These textbooks, that contain the dominant ideology of knowledge, demonstrate broader issues of what counts as knowledge: "What counts as legitimate knowledge is the result of complex power relations and struggles among identifiable class, race, gender, and religious groups" (Apple, 1999/2014, p. 47) and "All too often, 'legitimate' knowledge does not include the historical experiences and cultural expressions of labor, women, people of color, and others who have been less powerful" (Apple, 1999/2014, p. 52).

The work of Apple and McLaren align strongly with this book's efforts to investigate knowledge legitimacy and accreditation in avenues, forms, and constructions that are not seen as "official." As Apple illuminates the key issues of textbooks as a form of accepted legitimized knowledge, we can consider to what degree and how cookbooks are further differentiated from forms of knowledge that inherently uphold colonialist and imperialistic systems, while simultaneously becoming objects and artifacts with colonialist and imperialistic messages and biases. I wonder: By not being official, are cookbooks afforded the opportunity to be more critical forms of knowledge sharing? In this way, do cookbooks, intentionally or unintentionally, lean into an identification of illegitimate and a method of subversiveness to more effectively share the information, stories, recipes held within them?

Hilary Janks similarly addresses the power of critique while arguing for the need for critical literacy: "Critique enables participants to engage consciously with the ways in which semiotic resources have been harnessed to serve the interests of the producer and how different resources could be harnessed to redesign and reposition the text. It is both backward — and forward-looking" (2013, p. 36). Janks further declares that "critique is not the endpoint; transformative and ethical reconstruction and social action are" (2013, p. 36). As such, how might cookbooks present an alternative form, rooted in redesigning and repositioning, that better enables critique?

In defining and contextualizing critical literacy, Allan Luke (2014) aligns with Apple and Janks's critique of dominant knowledges and ideologies:

> These are the core curriculum questions: about whose version of cultures, histories, sciences, and everyday life will count as official knowledge. They are questions about pedagogy and teaching: about which modes of information and cognitive scripts, which designs and genres shall be deemed worth learning, what kinds of tools for use with reading and writing will be taught, for what social and cultural purposes and interests. (p. 20)

As such, critical pedagogy is not a method of exhaustive critiquing for critique's sake. Rather, critical pedagogy uses a lens of criticality to explore how and why things are the way they are, to investigate how systemic oppressors are being upheld, and identify opportunities to push and fight against these systems of injustice. Criticality is a method for striving towards justice.

In addition to fighting against injustice, Freire importantly posits human action as reflection and action, theory and practice (1985, p. 125) — while situating revolution as an act of love: "Love is an act of courage, not of fear, love is commitment to others" (p. 89). Freire's focus on the role of love in critical pedagogy aligns with the work of bell hooks. In *Teaching to Transgress: Education as the Practice of Freedom* (1994), hooks posits education as the practice of freedom (pp. 12, 207) with engaged, transformative pedagogy rooted in the "interplay of anticolonial, critical, and feminist pedagogies" (p. 10) and values in student and educator collective effort (p. 8), expression (p. 20), active engagement (pp. 11, 158), and recognition of multiculturalism (p. 44) to achieve an educational and liberatory experience, as well as a classroom that is a "radical space of possibility" (p. 12). hooks illustrates the benefit of "knowing rooted in experience" (p. 90), or the "passion of experience, the passion of remembrance" (p. 90), in our learning (and teaching). In doing so, hooks compares lived experience in our learning to use flour in a bread recipe: we need it, but not alone (p. 92).

Just as hooks looks to baking bread as an analogy for critical pedagogy, we can see how many of the tenets of critical pedagogy are ever-present in cookbooks, such as active engagement and experience, patience and humility, creativity and learning. Cookbooks are, of course, not an end-all-be-all solution to all learning and teaching, but rather present themselves as a unique case study in which we can consider more equitable forms of learning that rely on that which is not traditionally utilized.

This is further seen in Stephanie Springgay's work which explores the role of lived experience and feeling in pedagogy in *Feltness: Research-creation, Socially Engaged Art, and Affective Pedagogies* (2022). Here Springgay investigates and focuses on arts education and research-creation in Canada to draw a "connection between research-creation, socially engaged art, and radical pedagogy in different contexts, revealing how children, youth, and adults negotiate learning that disrupts and defamiliarizes schools and institutions, knowledge systems, values, and the legibility of art and research" (p. 4). Importantly, Springgay aligns radical pedagogy to feltness, which is radical, feminist, "relational, transcorporeal, and affective" (p. 5), to ask: "How are artists, in collaboration with students and teachers, understanding and materializing radical pedagogy?" (p. 7). I was initially interested in Springgay's work because I mistakenly thought feltness referred to the materiality of artistic crafting felt, and perhaps signified a pedagogy rooted in craft and cloth, but Springgay's framing is all the more poignant: "Feltness has various entry points, including the textile process of hand-felting; affect theory and feelings; the material and embodied experience of being in the world; queer-feminist theories of touching encounters; and feminist materialist conceptualizations of more-than-human entanglements. Intimacy conjures radical relatedness, reciprocity, and care" (p. 8). With radical pedagogy as feltness, Springgay identifies that "Radical pedagogy becomes a practice committed to working transversally, to resisting disciplinary categories and hierarchies, and to an ethics and politics of relationality" (p. 6) and "Radical pedagogy centers a subject's positionality to examine how it informs and shapes their opinions, reactions, and knowledges" (p. 23). While not using the terminology of critical pedagogy, Springgay draws upon the language of radical pedagogy, like Freire, and prioritizes the same critical lens and methodologies, namely that of emphasizing and centering lived experience in learning.

Additionally, as Freire emphasizes the importance of reflection and action and hooks and Springgay illustrate the value of experience in learning and knowing, Kiaras Gharabaghi and Ben Anderson-Nathe call for critical scholarship as "a way of thinking about research as a form of resistance" (2017, p. 97) and "a way of approaching knowledge that is inherently not certain, always fluid, rooted in the lived experienced [sic] of people with multiplicity of life-contexts and informed by dialogue, relationship, and connection with those who have a stake in the knowledge being generated" (2017, p. 97). This is the very manner in which this text is constructed and considered: fluid, reliant upon the collaborative participants and people involved, and rooted in conversation and connection. In doing so, this book, while exploring the application of critical pedagogy within cookbooks, is also attempting to perform critical pedagogy.

Summary

Critical pedagogy scholars and practitioners emphasize the capacities of critical pedagogy as a subversive method of learning and doing that prioritizes those who have been most harmed and marginalized by oppressors. Critical pedagogy relies upon a lens of criticality to ask the *who*, *how*, and *why* of the world around us to examine and push against systemic oppression and injustice. As such, critical pedagogy becomes a method for striving towards justice.

Critical pedagogy asks: Who constructed the knowledge that we must learn? Who is being centered in our learning? Who is left out of our learning? How are my experiences/the experiences of those around me/the experiences of those who are different from me dissimilar to those one might find in a textbook? How can learning reinforce a more authentic and just understanding of the world? Critical pedagogy offers a hope and strategy for betterment through liberatory learning. Yet, as hooks and Springgay demonstrate, critical pedagogy is also firmly rooted in lived experience — much like experiential inquiry.

experiential inquiry

Experiential inquiry is thinking and learning through the *doing* process. When we experience something, we learn through that experience. Experiential inquiry is the process of learning through experience. We learn to ride a bike, to make a paper airplane, to bake bread by doing it — and we learn to ask questions of these instances, objects, processes, and experiences by going through them.

(1916). "Fort Street Public School - [making jam]." Photographs by the State Archives and Records Authority of New South Wales. No restrictions, via Wikimedia Commons.

However, we all experience the world differently, unevenly, and without universality — such as intersectional feminism reminds us. Deanna Herst (2019) pointedly addresses this in exploring problems with universal standard design for those with disabilities and illuminates the capacity of the imaginary and collaborative making to aid in destandardizing design. As such, design justice, a framework focusing on design which centers those who are most often ignored, disenfranchised, and harmed in our world, is a helpful lens for further exploring the tenets and capacities of experiential inquiry.

Arguing and illustrating that design is political and exploring the relationship between design and power, Sasha Costanza-Chock's *Design Justice* defines and situates design as anything done with action — recognizing that not all design is celebrated or acknowledged as such: "However, inclusive visions of design as a universal human activity in many ways conflict with the realities of the political economy of design. True, everyone designs, but only certain kinds of design work are acknowledged, valorized, remunerated, and credited" (2020, p. 14). While recognizing that not all design is acknowledged as such, Costanza-Chock aims to "advance the growing conversation about the pitfalls and possibilities of design as a tool for social transformation" (2020, p. xviii) and "demonstrate how universalist design principles and practices erase certain groups of people, specifically those who are intersectionally disadvantaged or multiply burdened under white supremacist heteropatriarchy, capitalism, and settler colonialism" (2020, p. 19). As such, Costanza-Chock's work holds strong parallels to the work and framings of critical pedagogy as *Design Justice* offers a critical framework for analysis to think of how design distributes benefits and burdens between people of various groups and communities of practice.

Simultaneously, *Design Justice* is about a growing community of designers and practitioners, including the Design Justice Network and the Allied Media Conference, and how we can actionize the Design Justice Network Principles.[9] Established in 2016, the Design Justice

---

[9] As Costanza-Chock emphasizes, the DJN has 10 principles, including:
HEAL: "We use design to sustain, heal, and empower our communities, as well as to seek liberation from exploitative and oppressive systems."
CENTER: "We center the voices of those who are directly impacted by the outcomes of the design process."
IMPACT "We prioritize design's impact on the community over the intentions of the designer."

Network (DJN) argues that design can, and should, be used to explore how design impacts our daily lives — and how the harmful impacts of design tend to hurt those who have the "least influence" on said design. They envision design as a means to actionize and center joy, love, and care, such as many scholars previously mentioned, including Greene, hooks, Springgay, and Freire, identify the power of education. In doing so, the DJN "rethinks design processes, centers people who are normally marginalized by design, and uses collaborative, creative practices to address the deepest challenges our communities face." Therefore, DJN holds strong parallels to the pedagogical framings of critical pedagogists, namely hooks and Apple — the later of which argues for "the creation of the conditions necessary for all people to participate in the creation and re-creation of meaning and values" (1999/2014, p. 62).

As Costanza-Chock and DJN operate from a justice perspective to explore and investigate differences in experiences, Ty-Ron Douglas and Christine Nganga (2013) emphasize the importance of radical love in the education sector: "Radical love, as a theorization that privileges the voices and perspectives of marginalized voices and non-dominant positionalities/perspectives, allows us to recast power differences in our classrooms, even as it provides tools for dialogue, action, and hope" (pp. 65, 66). Like hooks's pedagogy and Freire's framing of love as revolutionary, Douglas and Nganga address how this love can be enacted and evoked through building community (p. 70), constructing dialogic spaces (p. 71), and facilitate critical reflective practice (p. 71), challenge fears (p. 76), and "learning from community-based pedagogical spaces" (p. 76).

PROCESS OF CHANGE: "We view change as emergent from an accountable, accessible, and collaborative process, rather than as a point at the end of a process."
FACILITATOR: "We see the role of the designer as a facilitator rather than an expert.".
EXPERT ON SELF: "We believe that everyone is an expert based on their own lived experience, and that we all have unique and brilliant contributions to bring to a design process."
SHARE: "We share design knowledge and tools with our communities."
COMMUNITY: "We work towards sustainable, community-led and -controlled outcomes."
NON-EXPLOITATIVE: "We work towards non-exploitative solutions that reconnect us to the earth and to each other."
EXISTING: "Before seeking new design solutions, we look for what is already working at the community level. We honor and uplift traditional, indigenous, and local knowledge and practices."

Through experiential inquiry, we once more see both a centering of experience and the opportunity for a more just manner of learning. As such, this work looks to experiential inquiry as a framework through which differentiated lived experience is a guiding factor in producing knowledge, in sharing knowledge, and being one of/with knowledge.

Summary

Relying on the benefits found in doing, experiential inquiry is rooted in the learning that occurs when something is performed, completed, or accomplished. In other words: in doing, we learn. In experiencing, we learn. And because of the diversity in our experiences (due to the diversity found among ourselves), experiential inquiry has the opportunity to place emphasis on the value in our individualized experiences. This is, indeed, what makes learning more meaningful, authentic, and oriented to the learner.

Johnson, G. N. & Eiler, T. (1978). "Carrie Severt milking cow, Alleghany County, North Carolina." Blue Ridge Parkway Folklife Project collection (AFC 1982/009), American Folklife Center, Library of Congress. Retrieved from the Library of Congress.

Critical making is learning through the process of *play*. I'm unsure sure if everyone would define it as such, but for me, critical making is the process of learning while playing through construction and craft. This prioritization on construction is seen in Seymour Papert's *Mindstorms: Children, Computers and Powerful Ideas* (1980), where youth learning is rooted in the real-world utility of playing, messing with, and working alongside technologies. This emphasis on process draws an immediate connection to experiential inquiry, which also looks to doing and experiencing. However, these terms and frameworks are distinctively different, namely due to critical making's roots in technology.

Matt Ratto (2011) defines and situates critical making as "a mode of materially productive engagement that is intended to bridge the gap between creative physical and conceptual exploration" where the end product is not as important as the critical reflection from "practice-based engagement." In engaging with critical making, Ratto expresses that we are enabling care work: "Our goal is therefore to use material forms of engagement with technologies to supplement and extend critical reflection and, in doing so, to reconnect our lived experiences with technologies to social and conceptual critique" (2011).

Like Ratto, Garnet Hertz establishes critical making as making with a lens of criticality and reflection with prioritization on the process and critique over the refinement and utility of the design (2016). Together, Ratto and Hertz define the critical making framework as "a conjoined pedagogical and research practice that [uses] material engagements with technologies to open up and extend critical social reflection" (2019, p. 18). While they explore critical making from an academic stance, and address the capacities of critical making to work against the confines of disciplinary knowledge-production, they simultaneously illustrate how critical making can enable unique learning and development opportunities by serving as "a non-disciplinary middle ground for different communities and groups" (2019, p. 21).

Charny additionally posits making as a liberatory means and opportunity to display "free will" (p. 2) and "the most powerful way that we solve problems, express ideas and shape our world" (p. 3). Through this, Charny argues for an increased recognition that we can all make, as well as why we all need to — paralleling Costanza-Chock's pointed claim that we all design.

Working from an architectural design perspective, Wim Nijenhuis analyzes the process of tangible making (and differentiates it from abstract design), arguing that making skips over thinking, and encourages folks to give voice to material — to "go along with matter" (2019, p. 129). Nijenhuis offers a valuable differentiation of design and making:

> Design sequence → "brain > hands-tools > eyes > drawing" (p. 130)

> Making sequence → "material > hands-tools > eyes > brain" (p. 130)

As such, making is an opportunity to work with and alongside that which is material to explore, reflect, and learn. In doing so, Nijenhuis sees making as "a means of personality transformation: by working materials, the maker remakes herself" (2019, p. 138). This draws immediate connection to making with food, as cookbooks teach us to do. We are not encouraged to really think of the ingredients within a given recipe, but to "go along" with the materials and tools to construct something. After a given recipe is complete, we may then think of how it could improve or change according to our taste, but this occurs as a reflectionary, post-making process.

Moreover, with a focus on transformation that we also see in critical pedagogy, this work also draws to attention how a lot of the scholars that talk about critical making focus on the materiality of critical making. In looking at the transformation of materials, if you see a child or an adult, or anyone playing with a set of materials and learning through interacting with them, learning by taking part, playing, constructing something through the processes of critical making, they are thus transforming the materials into something else as an object of learning, but also they are transforming themselves.

And while I draw connection to food, most critical making scholarship is firmly and historically rooted in the technological — as seen with many of the scholars above. Yet, more scholars are evaluating critical making's capacities and limitations. For example, critical making is not a flawless end-all-be-all methodology. Kelsey Cameron and Jessica FitzPatrick (2021) argue for attunement in critical making — or bringing back the importance of lived experience, as hooks calls for, to critical making in order to work against universalization (an issue that we also consider in relation to experiential inquiry): "Attunement helps bring equity into critical making, highlighting how larger systems shape individual acts of making." They importantly address significant concerns and tensions within critical making including how it "does not always structure [hands-on, academia] work in ways that are ethical, collaborative, and community centered." Through this, they ask comparable questions to critical pedagogists regarding which knowledge gets to count: "Who gets to make things and what modes of making are valued?"

Likewise, in an interview with Garnet Hertz, Natalie Jeremijenko illuminates key issues with critical making — and the broader maker movement (the cultural phenomenon of DIY making and creating in educational and learning realms): "the work [from the maker movement] needs to be about change, social innovation and political innovation — just as much as it is about technological Innovation. Social change has been excised from the discussion around making due to political views, and it's a tremendous, tremendous problem" (2012, p. 2). In specifically critiquing making-based learning through and alongside Legos, Jeremijenko states: "There's a way in which the maker movement or this kind of hands on education or this emergence of thinking of things has been co-opted and taken by this larger corporate interest and kind of very conservative pedagogical agendas" (2012, p. 3). Therefore, Jeremijenko calls for a critical lens in making — a greater prioritization of criticality.

Maya Livio and Lori Emerson (2019) also identify that:

> [the] increased prevalence of labs suggests that scholars and practitioners are actively pursuing new models for knowledge production, moving away from ideals of solitary work and towards collaborative, experimental and experiential, and interdisciplinary research approaches. However, despite the apparent

> newness of labs, their dominant lineage stems from a racist, sexist, and colonial past, bringing methods, infrastructures, and underlying assumptions along with it. (p. 287)

These lineages thus impact the knowledge that is cultivated and produced in these spaces. As such, Livio and Emerson "argue that contemporary labs, as spaces of collective and interdisciplinary thinking and doing, require their own consideration as sites for feminist methodology" (p. 287). All the more, they see the kitchen as an early proto-lab that illuminates significant tensions over making in relation to gender norms and expectations (p. 287): "With the gradual appropriation of the kitchen as a place for 'gentlemanly' experimentation over the span of the 18th and early 19th centuries, women were essentially given the bizarre and contradictory message that they belong in a kitchen, that the kitchen might in fact be a lab, but that a lab is not for them" (p. 287).

When the kitchen is framed as an early laboratory, a site of making and experimenting, greater knowledge credibility is associated with this place and space — as well as those who most likely occupied those kitchens throughout history, including women and people of color.

Further exploring the role of gender in making, Krystin Gollihue and Abigail Browning (2019) write of critical making: "As adult scholars, we have difficulty reconciling our curiosity in the masculine-dominated discipline of media and technology with our formative activities in more feminized fields" (p. 230). They share their project, [0U1JA], to "argue for more differentiated places of critical, cultural, and emergent making that come from our situated and lived experiences" (p. 228). Of this work, they write: "In creating a project that centered embodied, partial knowledges, mysticism, and technology, we also created a space for *feeling* inside of academia" (p. 233) and "For us, an intersectional feminist critical making must reside in what happens at the margins: play, feeling, space, relationships, and the unknown. This requires attention to embodied narratives: what makers experience outside of institutions, the pressures they exist within, the places they are kept out of, and the practices they find familiar and safe" (p. 235). In doing so, they demonstrate that an "intersectional feminist critical making praxis calls for us to create from our bodies, to invent in and with them, and to value that practice as knowing" (p. 236). In showcasing their project and process, Gollihue and Browning illustrate the capacity for learning from/with and generating knowledge from/with the body and lived experience — thus aligning with the work of hooks and Springgay. Moreover, their work emphasizes that intersectional feminist methodology in critical making strives to center the marginalized — placing emphasis on marginalized communities and identities, emotions, knowledges, and methods, much like design justice.

Marie Bjerede further illustrates the hypocrisy and gendered, patriarchal domain of technology and technologists — seen in how making with sewing, knitting, art, and families is not seen as technological, valuable, or innovative (2012). This is akin to McLaren's illustration of how STEM subjects have more popularity, priority, and support due to their technological knowledge and applicability in capitalistic economic gain, whereas other subjects "legitimate certain gender, class, and racial interests" (2015, p. 134). Yet, when we value making in its entirety, we support inclusion and equity. As Bjerede writes: "Kids who MAKE enjoy teaching and learning from each other more than beating each other, and together MAKE art, MAKE technology, MAKE friends, MAKE a community, and MAKE a future" (2012, p. 1).

Summary

Critical making, as a term and as a framework, has roots in making with and through technologies (imagine taking apart an old TV and playing with the circuit board and wires to see if you could make something new). But critical making, as a process, is something that has been around much longer — and is something that many of us engage with without realizing it. Moreover, while the making that is often performed through feminized modes of making is often not recognized as such, cooking and baking and making with food offer a full-sensory experience that is rooted in critical making — the process of learning and doing through trying to make something.

critical making + critical pedagogy + experimental inquiry + cooking = this book

In thinking of critical pedagogy, experiential inquiry, and critical making, I am reminded of micha cárdenas's conceptualization of the stitch as material and conceptual: "As sewing is a technique of making that has been used primarily by women throughout history, and continues to be primarily a task of women in sweatshops in the global South, this proposal of the stitch as a material and conceptual operation can be seen as a feminist proposal, a way of generating new concepts by learning from people who have been subjected to material inequalities because of their gender, race, and geographic location" (2022, p. 134). cárdenas expresses that the stitch "is an operation that involves using one entity to connect two formerly separate entities" (2022, p. 134) and enables transformation (2022, p. 135).

Perhaps critical making is the stitch that ties critical pedagogy and experiential inquiry together, demonstrating that these frameworks of learning, critical pedagogy and experiential inquiry, are more alike than they are different, and when they are brought together we are able to engage in a form of learning that draws upon both, as well as that which is material, in order to strive towards a more equitable form of learning.

I ultimately define critical making as the process of learning about and investigating the world through creating, through making, through doing. I see critical making as dependent upon critical pedagogy and experiential inquiry — it cannot exist without the radical pedagogy of love and hope and the drive for betterment, the centering of the oppressed and lived experience, and the emphasis on reflection of critical pedagogy nor without the emphasis on differentiated experience of experiential inquiry as the driving force of learning. I see that together these pedagogical framings and methodologies, critical pedagogy and experiential inquiry, enable critical making — forming a Venn diagram where critical making falls at their nexus.

This understanding of critical making as reliant upon critical pedagogy and experiential inquiry is best seen in instances of praxis. For example, over the course of a year, Giorgia Lupi and Stefanie Posavec (2016) exchanged 52 weekly postcards that contained and illustrated the data of their everyday lives (from compliments received, instances of physical contact, clothes in their closet, doors, etc.), all of which were then published in *Dear Data*. In doing so, they argue for, and literally illustrate, the humanness of data and its capacity to "become more humane" while bringing us to ourselves and together (p. xi). Their "data diary" (p. xi) demonstrates a sustained, experiential critique of society's identification of what counts and is valuable as data.

We work towards justice and equity when critical pedagogy, experiential inquiry, and critical making serve as the pillars and priorities of learning. When we prioritize and center lived experience, especially that of those who are most marginalized and underrepresented in our education system, and adopt a lens of criticality in our learning — we engage in a form of learning that is more accessible, relatable, and just. As this work illustrates, critical pedagogy, experiential inquiry, and critical making are invaluable frames of analysis for considering the role of making with food, or cooking, especially when we draw upon an intersectional feminist method which encourages us to consider forms of making, creating, and sharing which are historically feminized and discredited.

An example of such engagement through experience and critical making is the People's Kitchen Collective, co-founded by Saqib Keval, Jocelyn Jackson, and Sita Bhaumik. Based in Oakland since 2011, the People's Kitchen Collective offers recipes to dismantle white supremacy and, through the combination of art, activism, and food, aims to facilitate political education: "Feed the mind, nourish the soul, fuel a movement." These efforts are further seen with Earthseed Land Collective, a place and practice, which looks to achieve collective liberation, justice, and equity: "Earthseed is a center for community resilience through cooperative ownership of land and resources. We are a transformational response to systemic oppression, committed to centering People of Color and other communities pushed to the margins." Like Earthseed, Transplanting Traditions aims "to uplift food sovereignty in the refugee community through access to land, education and opportunities for refugee farmers to address community food insecurity and the barriers they face in reaching their dreams of farming. The farm provides a cultural community space for refugee adults and youth to come together, recreate home and build healthy communities, and continue agricultural traditions in the Piedmont of N.C."

I see an additional converging alignment of experience and criticality with The Food Youth Initiative in North Carolina further aligns justice with community work and the food system, but focuses on the work led by youth across the state. Similarly, Pupusas for Education works "to create solutions together by providing holistic support services that uplift our collective knowledge and manifest the healing and thriving of our communities" by providing scholarships to undocumented and DACAmented students.[10]

Ultimately, while critical making (much like many terms in this paper, including "pedagogy" itself) is a phrase belonging to academia, I believe that its healthiest, strongest, and most fruitful roots of this learning mechanism are to be found in the world. I see critical making when a child creates a new animal that can survive in our ever-changing ecosystem with playdough, sticks, and dried grass. I see critical making when cities adopt SPF dispensers for those that need to protect themselves from the sun and do not have immediate access to sunblock. I see critical making in street art and graffiti that critiques racism, inept government

---

[10] Beyond food (which this work is pointedly focused on), there is great work being done at the convergence of critical making, critical pedagogy, and experimental inquiry. Rita Raley explores how new media art projects develop political interventions and engage in "micropolitics of disruption, intervention, and education" (2009, p. 1). Raley emphasizes that tactile media, as rooted in tactics, produces and focuses on open-ended questions, performance, instructions, and that which is experiential with more weight placed on "viewer experience and engagement" (2009, p. 12). Many artists create from and draw upon a lens of critically to draw attention to and critique various issues — seen with the work of Hank Willis Thomas, Kehinde Wiley, Asma Kazmi.

Data for Black Lives brings together "activists, organizers, and scientists committed to the mission of using data to create concrete and measurable change in the lives of Black people." Furthermore, the work of Artists and Scholars in Public Life utilizes imagination and creativity as key facets of experiential inquiry to envision a more inclusive, equitable future to enact critical pedagogy: "The Imagining America consortium (IA) brings together scholars, artists, designers, humanists, and organizers to imagine, study, and enact a more just and liberatory 'America' and world. Working across institutional, disciplinary, and community divides, IA strengthens and promotes public scholarship, cultural organizing, and campus change that inspires collective imagination, knowledge-making, and civic action on pressing public issues. By dreaming and building together in public, IA creates the conditions to shift culture and transform inequitable institutional and societal structures" (2018). Likewise, "And Also Too" is a design justice studio that "[facilitates] the co-creation of art, design, media, and technology to support movements for justice and liberation." Their mission reads: "We are working towards a redistribution of power in design. We develop co-creation practices that center communities that have been systematically excluded from and harmed by conventional design processes. We do this in ways that cultivate care, deep listening, and joy."

policies and laws, and systemic harms. I see critical making when a young woman tells me that she has a group message with her friends to ensure they get home safely and her mom bought her a metal water bottle to protect herself. I see critical making when local communities, such as our own Raleigh, plan and actionize initiatives like Food Not Bombs to bring aid to those that need it.

I see and recognize critical making when people use their imagination (Greene, 2009) and draw upon materials around them (Nijenhuis, 2019) to build, create, or make something that helps them think through or process a problem or tension that they identify (DiSalvo, 2014). Perhaps what they make is sophisticated and distributed — actionized at a larger scale. Perhaps what they make instantly falls, melts, crumbles apart, but this does not matter if what they have learned is more likely to be retained. Critical making is a manner of learning to envision better.

I see critical making as a primary method through which I conducted my research — relying necessarily upon critical pedagogy and experiential inquiry to better investigate and interrogate the world around me. Moreover, as Costanza-Chock reminds us: "Stories have power" (2020, p. 133). As an English teacher, I knew stories were powerful with characters to move and change us, lessons to shift us, and themes to interrogate our own world. But our stories too are powerful — even more so. And these stories, unlike the ones I knew to teach, are not always bound to a book, to a text, to something written. Stories can be shared through something made, found, told — an experience. In doing so, they can encourage us to see the world differently, to learn and grow. Therefore, perhaps critical making can be storytelling and story sharing. Perhaps stories can serve as opportunities of critical making.

[Photographer unknown] (1940). "Butchering a buffalo." National Archives and Records Administration, Department of the Interior. Bureau of Indian Affairs. Pine Ridge Agency. Public domain, via Wikimedia Commons.

Chapter 3.
Conversion charts:
The methods

I am interested in how forms of making that are not usually thought of are those that are most vital to care, most typically devalued and discredited, and most traditionally gendered and feminized.

To explore this, I engage in a mixed-methods process to investigate:

1. How are equity and justice supported in the community through the process of making? What role do critical making, critical pedagogy and experiential inquiry play in supporting equity and justice?

2. In considering the role of care in reimaging power, who is responsible for the care, labor, and power of ancestral and community stories, histories, and affect? Moreover, how does gender intersect with care? What is the relationship between gender and care? Who is responsible for care (and all that is cared for/is made through care)?

3. As seen with the capacities of cookbooks, how can systems and manners of knowing more equitably and critically enable exploration, learning, and care to reimagine power (of care, literacy, and justice) and knowledge (production, recognition, and legitimacy)? How can cookbooks serve as a template for more equitable and better knowledge sharing?

More specifically, I engage in community-based and rooted work and draw upon archival imagery and photography from and about cookbooks and cooking to investigate the roles of equity and justice, the dichotomy between gender and care, and the value and utility of cookbooks in relation to knowledge sharing. In doing so, I am aiming to provide a more holistic and authentic perspective to then look through local application and utility.

As such, past scholarship, literature, and research has pointed me in the direction of intersectional feminism and critical pedagogy theory as frameworks of analysis here. Through this, I consider how an intersectional feminist and critical pedagogy research method may operate like in practice. As distilled from the previous chapter, these frameworks encourage one to practice:

Transparency in regards to both how research is conducted and the way in which it is shared and exchanged with others

Awareness of subjectivity, biases, and power — in relation to those that I as a researcher carry into and throughout the study, but also those that this work exists within (cultural, societal, historical)

Empower those without and with less power

Putting to action the theory that this investigation is rooted in, and looking to its application and utility beyond the classroom, academy, textbook

Centering the lived experience, stories, and knowledges of those who are most affected by the disenfranchisement and marginalization of the knowledge economy, capitalism, sexism, racism, classism, and other oppressive systems

Consideration of how different oppressive systems layer on top of each other to create compounding effects that affect different people in different ways

Critique and challenging of standards, power, domination, and that which is established and accepted

Transformation of the self as a learner, researcher, and practitioner, but also that of the research itself, to enable the research to follow and focus on that which the participants bring to the table, rather than what I want to bring or find on the table

Feel and work in alignment and acknowledge of one's emotions and feelings, knowing that this is not widely accepted or practiced in the pursuit of (academic) knowledge, or elsewhere

Embrace love in the name of justice and revolution

With, not for means of engagement and knowledge sharing

Working against oppression and injustice

While the practices and methods I have outlined above serve as a primary basis of purposeful action, I also look to Catherine D'Ignazio and Lauren Klein's *Data Feminism* principles[11] (2020), as well as those of design justice[12] (Costanza-Chock, 2020), to both assess how the various participants perform and enact care alongside and through food, as well as lead and guide my own investigative efforts — all of which intersect with gender, justice, and equity. In doing so, these established principles provided a valuable framework through which to develop these methodologies, as well as see them come to action and determine in what matter the findings were assessed. More specifically, I, as a researcher, strove to embody and prioritize the principles of data feminism and design justice to promote a more equitable, fair, and caring form of academic research and knowledge production.

interviews

This work relies on conversation. Here, I refer to conversation as a face-to-face exchange between myself and the collaborators, sometimes meeting me individually or in pairs, at an agreed-upon location where we speak together. While I selected this mode of communication in striving for a more equitable, respectful, and caring form of knowledge exchange, I cannot be sure that this was what was truly achieved. As much as my positionality is critically engaged

---

[11] 1) Examine power, 2) Challenge Power, 3) Elevate emotion and embodiment, 4) Rethink binaries and hierarchies, 5) Embrace pluralism, 6) Consider context, and 7) Make labor visible.
[12] 1) Heal, 2) Center, 3) Impact, 4) Process of change, 5) Facilitator, 6) Expert on self, 7) Share, 8) Community, 9) Non-exploitative, and 10) Existing.

with and ethical research is prioritized, power dynamics and systems of oppression are always at play.[13]

With this said and through this avenue of conversational communication, this work relied upon speaking and communicating with folks in my local community who work with a variety of materials, purposes, businesses, and avenues, but all seemingly actionize and perform care through their making work. In speaking with these individuals, I hoped to learn more about how care is achieved and prioritized (subversively, un/intentionally, commodified), how making (what academics call critical making) is an avenue through which this is elicited and achieved, and how we might all care better. By following this prioritization on that which is elicited through conversation and engaging with folks directly, I am emulating the process and methods of grounded theory, which looks to the qualitative data (and the identifiable patterns) that arise from such engagement as I strove to perform here and then looks to what that data may mean and can indicate. Because of this process, my methodology aligns with the practice of constructivist grounded theory, which engages participants to "construct meaning in relation to the area of inquiry" while the researcher "co-constructs experience and meanings with participants" (Chun, Birks, & Francis, 2019).

In the particular case of my work here, grounded theory seemingly lends itself to intersectional feminism and critical pedagogy analysis, which purport looking to those most affected and center their experiences. Here with grounded theory, the experiences of the participants and what results are elicited from that are centered and serve as the basis of analysis. We see an additional connection to critical pedagogy and intersectional feminism through the emphasis on "co-constructing" knowledge between the researcher and the participants, which parallels the collaborative, participatory, and inclusionary learning and research models with these corresponding theoretical frameworks. Grounded theory further acknowledges the role and participation of the researcher, which also aligns with intersectional feminism in being cognizant and reflexive about one's own biases, positionality, and influence on research.

---

[13] I address this limitation, among others, in Chapter 8. Cleaning the table.

In following the precedents of grounded theory, I identified participants, engaged in an interview-based dialogue, transcribed and edited the conversations, identified commonalities and tensions across the participants and their conversations, and then analyzed these points to answer the questions posed above.

Because this work was constructed through connection, conversation, and collaboration,[14] I reached out to local folks directly to see if they would be interested in participating, engaged in face-to-face conversations with them at their place of work, operation, or business, and then invited them to collaborate through the inclusion of recipes, photos, and media (and the conversations we had as well).

I found most of these businesses and individuals by patronizing their establishments as someone local to the community/ies that they serve. I knew of Videri Chocolate Factory, Wonderpuff, 321 Coffee, and Two Roosters through my many frequent visits to these establishments. Yet, others, I learned about by reaching local businesses and efforts that focused on food, service, and giving back to the community — such as A Place at the Table, Bee Downtown, and the Well Fed Community Garden. Once I identified an extensive list of potential participants, I began reaching out and inquiring if they might be interested or available. Many folks didn't respond, and many did. And of those that did, they enthusiastically wanted to participate and talk about their work. They also offered other names for me to reach out to and connect with, which is how I learned about the Root Cellar Cafe and Catering and Dr. Erin McKenney.

The participants included in this project include:

> 321 Coffee
>> Michael Evans, Sophie Pacyna, and Rene Grunow
>
> Bee Downtown
>> Leigh-Kathryn Bonner

---

[14] Known academically as semi-structured interviews with community partner participants.

A Place at the Table
    Maggie Kane and Andrew Gravens

The Root Cellar
    Sera Cuni

Erin McKenney

Wonderpuff
    JAC M

Videri Chocolate Factory
    Sam Ratto

Two Roosters
    Sarah Romeo

Because I sought out businesses and people connected to making with food in my local area, I was able to physically meet each of these individuals in their places of work — seeing their facilities, buildings, kitchens, employees, customers, neighborhoods. For example, in meeting with JAC M, the owner and founder of Wonderpuff, I was able to meet them at Wonderpuff's former storefront in Research Triangle Park and I was able to speak with Two Rooster's Sarah Romeo at one of their ice cream shops. By engaging in place and space alongside the participants, I was able to saturate myself within their places. Order their food. Eat their biscuits and drink their coffee. Sit in their offices or at their tables.

While meeting with them, the basic questions I strove to ask and have answered were as follows:

- What do you do? How do you do it?
- How does making inform your work?
- What role does care play in your work?
- Can you talk to me about the power/capacity of food in community?

Because these were informal, conversational interviews, the conversations were fluid and followed a near-unpredictable trajectory. For example, in my conversation with JAC M, we spent several minutes of our conversation discussing and thoroughly distracted by a dog near us. When speaking with Michael at 321 Coffee, we paused our discussion to move inside when it started raining. Other times we became fixated on a worthwhile tangent (about books with Dr. Erin McKenney or food allergies with Chef Sera). As such, each conversation with each person was different — not only due to their unique focus and work, but also because of the nature of the conversations that unfurled.[15]

With the ubiquity of where exactly conversations would end or explore, I lightly edited the corresponding transcripts and retroactively explored similarities, as well as points of difference, across the conversations. In doing so, I identified themes and tensions focusing on the roles of care, community, and making.

These themes and tensions then resulted in the data analysis, addressed within Sharing the table and Clearing the table. Across these sections, I present commonalities and patterns, points of dissonance (across participants and across scholarship in relation to the data), and centralized areas of investigation.

Perhaps most importantly, I have included the transcripts of these conversations and interviews directly within the middle of the book. Rather than including these materials within an appendix, where they would be less likely to be read and engaged with, I am situating them within the core of the text to reassert their importance as contributors to this exercise in knowledge creation and sharing in efforts to demonstrate their significance and legitimacy within a knowledge economy that would view and expect otherwise. Significantly, other scholars have showcased similar disruption to the genre — as seen with the writings of bell hooks in

---

[15] While what we usually see and recognize as research involves quantitative data, large and hard numbers, big charts and graphs — I am more interested in *data humanism*, as conceptualized by Giorgia Lupi. Lupi asserts that we need to refocus data to knowledge, behaviors, people — and, in doing so, embrace the messy complexity of data, the context of it all, and data's [and research's] imperfections. So, this work strives towards data humanism. Data humanism serves as a research framework through which data (and what kinds of data) are selected, codified, presented, and analyzed.

Teaching to Transgress (1994) and Georgina Johnson's *The Slow Grind: Finding Our Way Back to Creative Balance* (2020), where entire interviews (fictional and playful, serious and focused) are made central within a text for readers to engage with. Yet, leaning upon the interview in such a way as I do here is still highly atypical in scholarship. In pushing against the academic knowledge genre in this manner, I am also able to further put my work's argument into action.

Hill, Janet McKenzie. (1922). "Table laid for Sunday-Night Tea. 'Sunday clears away the rust of whole week.'—Addison." Public domain, via Wikimedia Commons.

images

"Eventually I want to write a cookbook. And I've been working on it forever, but I'm not very organized... But I have [the recipes] all like written down, but you have to have pictures and I'm taking classes and they're like: *You have to have a picture with everything you submit so that we can see what the cookbook could look like and everything like that.*"

— Chef Sera Cuni, the Root Cellar Cafe and Catering

As the data derived from and alongside the participants is reflected in the methodology of grounded theory, the photos included throughout this book are not. Rather, the images here offer a multimodal and supporting supplement to the narrative argument, while also serving as a facet of the overarching argument in of themselves. By including images in this way, the work aims to take on a more accessible and multimodal language, which in turn actionizes the advocacy of public-facing knowledge sharing.

While I took pictures throughout many of my visits with the folks I was able to meet and interview, I also looked to photos that many others have taken to supplement my own — and to supplement and enrich the conversations, ideas, and themes. For the purpose of this work, I utilized archival imagery and photography from and about cookbooks and cooking to provide a larger, big picture perspective of these practices to compare to/juxtapose/align with my own investigation in the local application.

I found these images through Wikimedia Commons and the Library of Congress, looking to openly available, public domain, or openly-licensed through Creative Commons licensing images. I selected these sources due to their democratized accessibility. Anyone reading this can find these images themselves and use the images themselves. They are not hidden behind academic paywalls or institutional regulations.

Throughout this book, I include many images that stand alone, embedded within and across the text, for readers to engage with independently (similar to those and the fashion one may find in a cookbook); however, at other times I include ekphrastic descriptions, where language is documented and given to an otherwise silent object, such as a painting (Milner & Milner, 1999, pp 162-163). Through these ekphrastic writings, I offer them alongside images where I put a voice, a story, an explanation to the photograph. Following a tradition of such writing, I lean into storytelling to emphasize an alignment between the visual and the textual components of the argument/s. As such, these images serve as visual contrasts to the modality of text, in which this book predominantly relies upon, but also reinforces the genre and interdisciplinarity found within cookbooks, which look to photos to help convey how to accomplish something. Similarly, along with the interviews and media incorporated throughout, the methodology of genre (Miller,

1984), of working in a manner to produce a product of a particular genre, also plays an important role in striving to emulate the form and function of a cookbook to explore its knowledge sharing capabilities in light of, and often against, the identified limitations of academic and legitimized knowledge practices.

Curtis, Edward Sheriff. (1927). "Drying Meat - Cheyenne." Museum of Photographic Arts Collections, No restrictions, via Wikimedia Commons.

Wtewael, Peter. (1620s). "Kitchen Scene." CC0, via Wikimedia Commons.

Surrounded by numerous carcasses of various animals, from roosters to rabbits to plucked birds, to the ribcage of a large mammal to more, the most unrealistic or gruesome facet of this painting are the two forced and dull smiles exchanged between the man and woman. The former holds a basket of eggs and a votive in one hand, while the other hand clutches the legs of a bird. Smiling at the former, the latter, the woman, is the focal point of the unsettling and macabre painting. Situated in the middle of the painting with rosy cheeks, a bright white blouse and a crisp, lace collar and bonnet, she stakes a featherless bird unto a metal pike that is already encumbered by a set of red ribs. One of her hands holds the metal with white knuckles, the other is firmly grasped onto the bird as it spears its naked body. Perhaps it is a chicken. Maybe the same chicken that laid some of the eggs that the man now has in a basket with straw and cloth.

Enveloping the couple are the bodies of other animals, in various states of butchering. Two limp rabbits lay perpendicular to two similarly limp birds, perhaps Long-Billed Thrashers. Between the two sets of animals lie a ball of twine and a knife. A rooster's dark feathers glisten against the dark background and scenery of the painting as it hangs upside down. Cold metal plateware adorns the back walls, nearly fading into the dark background completely. The muscular red of the animal ribcage and skull both feel less unsettling than the coral red of the string tied at the woman's throat; a small river of salmon that feels dissonant against the chalky body it lies against.

Circumventing these two people is enough meat to feed many for some time. Imaginably this is a depiction of the ill effects and fates of greed: to take and hold on to more than necessary is more grotesque than the dead bodies of the animals one may try to lay claim to.

Chapter 4.
Care materials

Throughout this section, I offer juxtaposing views of care as it is currently, and has been, studied and understood. In doing so, these Care materials, the different understandings of care, serve as the different building blocks and ingredients in which care is conceptualized and understood within this book.

The goals of this section are not to pit the different framings of care against each other or weigh their merits and/or faults, but rather to aggregate and present a differentiated and multifaceted view of care that is as complex and messy as it is in reality.

Bledsoe, J. T. (1959). "African American woman at refrigerator holding a pitcher as she pours out drinks for children, probably Little Rock, Arkansas / JTB." No known restrictions on publication. Retrieved from the Library of Congress.

Lee, R. (1947). *"Mrs. Elige Hicks and her daughter in the kitchen of the four room house which rents for $10.50 monthly. Mrs. Hicks' husband and son are now working in a coal mine in Virginia and are looking for a home to buy. Southern Coal Corporation, Bradshaw Mine, Bradshaw, McDowell County, West Virginia."* Public domain, via Wikimedia Commons.

care as cute

(1905). "A Kitchen Nymph." No known restrictions on publication. Retrieved from the Library of Congress.

I feel multiple spheres of responsibility in my arms at every moment. Most pressing and prioritized is that of being a mother. Then being an employee. My other spheres: being a daughter, being a wife and partner, mental and physical health and restoration, being a friend and sister, my dog, figuring out what to do with the praying mantis that I found by the laundry, etc.

Each enables and requires care, to varying degrees, and the labor associated with that care.

While holding each of these spheres, this looks like me raising and taking care of my son, responding to emails when he is independently playing (in chunks of five minutes), writing during nap time (in chunks of 25-120 minutes), doing work after my son goes to bed, texting my husband about meal plans and ideas and requests while nursing, folding cloth diapers (because I felt bad for the planet) during play time, going to the bathroom while tossing hairbrushes across the floor as distractions and a game for my son, it goes on.

I wear several t-shirts a day, each retired after I'm covered in enough food and spit up and boogers that the smell turns my stomach. My son rests his head on mine as we let our dog outside for a few minutes before anyone burns their feet in the heat of the Carolina summer. We share bagels and cheese and pickles for lunch. My stomach drops when I find more and more emails in my inbox. My son attends my Zoom calls, and my dog barks during them at the Amazon vans that drive down the street. I see texts from friends that also have young babies asking how I manage the guilt of working out of home (even though I leave the home as little as possible for work). I talk with my husband at night about how I need more help with it all. I think of how when I graduate it will be harder. I think of how it was all *designed* to be hard. I think how being a stay-at-home working (what I do/try to do) or out-of-home working (what costs no small fortune in childcare expenses) has been designed to be difficult.

I think of this as I see an article from *The Cut*: "Is Tradwife Content Dangerous, or Just Stupid?" by Kathryn Jezer-Morton. It's under a section called "Brooding" and another called "Parenting." Jenzer-Morton begins by identifying the usual tradwife content: "bed-making and bowl-stirring while barefoot in a floral dress, abundant sourdough, male dominion over women, and urgent warnings that the government is trying to disrupt the sanctity of the white hetero nuclear family."

Tradwife is shorthand for "traditional wife." I think. I refuse to look it up any more than I already have. But it is a social media movement, trend, phenomenon, niche of white women that showcase whiteness, heteronormativity, homesteading, childrearing, and a particular flavor of femininity that looks like elective 1800s farm life meets abundantly wealthy meets blonde. It's a performance and declaration of care, an aestheticization of care that is dressed in an apron with curled hair — a new iteration of the Stepford wife, the mid-century American housewife.

Jezer-Morton writes: "You could argue that by prettifying care, tradwives obscure how exhausting it really is and reinforce outdated gender norms around who does what kind of work. But honestly? Women have been trying to make care work cute since forever. We were making it cute for the fun of it, and to help cope with the work itself, and as art. Making it cute is not the problem." Making care cute is a form of coping, of survival, of subversiveness. And I see how care work can be cute and pretty. I think of how writing and creating Valentine's in elementary school with crayon and construction paper may be one of the earliest examples of purposeful care into craft for someone else that I can recall from my own life. And children's Valentine's are always cute. It can be pretty like when someone sent me flowers as a gesture when I had a miscarriage.

But the beautification of care perhaps further draws our attention from the issues that necessitate care in the first place. And it draws concerns as to who has access to and affordances for such aestheticized care.

While I worry of this, Jezer-Morton identifies that the real problem behind the tradwife movement and image is the "mommy wars" or women-against-women sentiment that ensues when one path of motherhood (because there are no traddads nor tradqueers that I know of) is posited as better, more holy, and right. When the reality is that you really can't win.

Wyeth, N. C. (1948). " The Ladies' home journal." No restrictions, via Wikimedia Commons.

Lee, R. (1939). "Kitchen scene in Spanish-American home near Taos, New Mexico, Taos County. Making tortillas." No known restrictions. Retrieved from the Library of Congress.

Rosener, A. (1942) "'Share The Meat' recipes. Braised stuffed heart. Fill hearts with stuffing and sew up the slit with coarse thread." United States Office Of War Information, Public Domain. Retrieved from the Library of Congress.

Atop a floral and checkered tablecloth, a plate and bowl are used for meal preparation — for stuffing hearts.

On a clear glass plate, one heart sits, plumped with filler and sewn shut with neat and trim stitches. Next to the tailored organ lies an open heart — not yet filled and appearing more like a wilting piece of lettuce. The third heart finds itself in the hands of our faceless woman, where her own unseen heart is concealed beneath a buttoned outfit and layers of intact muscle and anatomy. But of this third heart: a coarse string, threaded through the needle and held delicately in one hand, while the other cups the raw heart — slit and now stuffed, being sewn back together before braising. A lurid reverse operation.

The gilt of the needle matches that of the woman's watch, her buttons, and her wedding ring.

Rosener, A. (1942). "'Share The Meat' recipes. Braised stuffed heart. Make gravy of the pan drippings and serve the hearts piping hot, garnished with crisp greens." United States Office Of War Information, Public Domain. Retrieved from the Library of Congress.

care as labor

We know that women are posited as those who are most responsible for care — including its labor (physical, emotional, unpaid, often invisible). In looking to our job force, we see that women make up a larger portion of grade school teachers and nurses, both of which are underpaid and undervalued professions. Carolina Criado Perez's *Invisible Women: Exposing Data Bias in a World Designed for Men* (2019) examines the labor practices of women, particularly the "invisible" and unpaid labor, asking: "is women's unpaid work under valued because we don't see it — or is it invisible because we don't value it?" (p. 78). Importantly, Perez states: "There is no such thing as a woman who doesn't work. There is only a woman who isn't *paid* for her work" (p. 70) and "Globally, 75% of unpaid work is done by women, who spend between three and six hours per day on it compared to men's average of thirty minutes to two hours. The imbalance starts early... and increases as they get older" (p. 70). Perez's "The Long Friday," a chapter named after October 24th, 1975 when 90% of women in Iceland did no work, calls for radical uphaul and reevaluation of labor in the world, as well as systems that recognize, value, and pay labor to not be designed around the male universal (p. 91).

Statistically, this issue of care and labor is evident around the globe — demonstrating how "sexism and capitalism unite to make nothing of the work women do" (Morales, 2019, p. 30). Aligning with Perez's analysis of inequities in labor, Eltahawy writes: "No country has achieved political equality. Many countries have never had a female head of state. No country pays men and women equally for work they do. In every country it is fact that most acts of domestic, intimate-partner, and sexual violence pose significant threats to women and girls, and that the majority of such acts are perpetrated by men. Some religions still refuse to ordain women to holy orders. And men by and large control and are disproportionately represented in the media, the arts, and the cultural landscapes that shape our tastes and ideas" (2020, p. 5). As hooks reminds us, these systems of oppression and exploitation are the very reason that feminism is necessary. Correspondingly, Aurora Levins Morales states: "We can't live without feminism, any more than we can live without eating" (2019, p. 32).

Similarly, Marjorie L. DeVault (1994) focuses on the unpaid labor of feeding a family and how caring within the home and family unit is positioned as the responsibility of women — becoming "central to women's identity" (p. 4). This aligns with bell hooks's claim: "When women in the home spend all their time attending to the needs of others, home is a workplace for her, not a site of relaxation, comfort, and pleasure" (2015; 2000, p. 50). While recognizing that men also perform care work, but that women have culturally positioned to bear the labor and responsibility more, DeVault writes:

> In my analysis, the social organization of the family setting provides a way of understanding both how women are recruited into the work of feeding, and also how feeding work contributes to women's oppression. Women learn to 'care' because the production of a 'family' as a socially organized material setting requires particular kinds of coordinative and maintenance activities... By doing the work of 'wife' and 'mother,' women quite literally produce family life from day to day, through their joint activities with others. (1994, pp. 12-13)

Importantly, through this undervalued, unpaid, often invisible care work of feeding the family, DeVault pointedly argues that women participate in and reinforce their oppression: "by doing the [women's work of feeding], women are drawn into relations of service to others, subordination of self, and deference to male partners" (p. 30). DeVault also offers a critical analysis of care, which further illustrates complexities and limitations of Noddings's own analysis of such, identifying that care "has also been obscured by the organization of gender relations and their construction in terms of 'natural difference': by belief about women's 'disposition' toward care, by the trap of economic dependence set for women by barriers to labor-force participation and wage discrimination, even by language that discounts the importance of caring" (p. 3). Therefore, care prescribed as labor for women is a trap of oppression — one that exists due to patriarchal oppression, and is reinforced through its forced and expected participation, rather than an innate caring skill that is exclusive to women.

(between 1941 and 1943). "Madison County, Ala., --Mrs. Frank Jacobs likes to can fruits and vegetables." No known restrictions on publication. Retrieved from the Library of Congress.

care as radical intersectional feminist action

In considering the necessity of feminism and the power of care — care becomes increasingly complex when we consider its role in patriarchal and oppressive systems. Care is an expected output and responsibility of women — with men often situated as the consumers and recipients of this care. Nel Noddings (1984) offers a more traditional perspective on care, namely one that is rooted in and reflective of historically-situated gender expectations and roles: "An ethic built on caring is, I think, characteristically and essentially feminine — which is not to say, of course, that it cannot be shared by men, and more than we should care to say that traditional moral systems cannot be embraced by women. But an ethic of caring arises, I believe, our of our experience as women, just as the traditional logical approach to ethical problems arises more obviously from masculine experience" (p. 8). Furthermore, Noddings expresses that we care out of empathetic moral obligation and understanding for the one that receives/is given care: "Apprehending the other's reality, feeling what we feel as nearly as possible, is the essential part of caring from the view of the one-caring. For if I take on the other's reality as possibility and begin to feel its reality, I feel, also, that I must act accordingly; that is, I am impelled to act as though in my own behalf, but in behalf of the other" (p. 16).

Like Noddings's ethic of care, Collins offers an ethic of caring, which is dependent upon individual uniqueness and expressiveness, emotions, and developing the capacity for empathy (2000, p. 263) and hooks establishes a love ethic, which prioritizes nurturing and sustaining relationships with others out of care, rather than pursuing power (p. 88). However, hooks notably differs from Noddings by adopting a feminist stance on care: "Females are encouraged by patriarchal thinking to believe we should be loving, but this does not mean we are any more emotionally equipped to do the work of love than our male counterparts" (p. 154). In *All About Love: New Visions* (1999), hooks argues and calls for a return to love, and to see love not as a noun, but as a verb — a practice (pp. 4, 165). Moreover, hooks identifies the significance of truth as foundational to love, alongside "Care and affirmation, the opposite of abuse and humiliation" (p. 22). hooks emphasizes the importance of working with and through love: "we renew the spirit; that renewal is an act of self-love, it nurtures our growth" (p. 65). To work in love, one increases self-love — illustrating the cyclical power of love.

However, race, class, dis/ability, and gender further illuminate critical concerns regarding care and in/justice. Drawing upon Angela Davis and Audre Lorde, Hiʻilei Julia Kawehipuaakahaopulani Hobart and Tamara Kneese (2020) illustrate how care, which they define as a feeling with (rather than a feeling for), plays a foundational role in social moments (p. 1). Through this framing, they situate "radical care as a set of vital but underappreciated strategies for enduring precarious worlds" (p. 2) that is "built on praxis" (p. 13). Simultaneously, Hobart and Kneese acknowledge that radical care is not an exclusive good: "Because radical care is inseparable from systemic inequality and power structures, it can be used to coerce subjects into new forms of surveillance and unpaid labor, to make up for institutional neglect, and even to position some groups against others, determining who is worthy of care and who is not" (p. 2) and "Care is unevenly distributed and cannot be disentangled from structural racism and inequality" (p. 8).

Collins also investigates the problems with care-as-labor and addresses the racist and sexist perceptions of Black and African American women as caregivers: "The first controlling image applied to U.S. Black women is that of the mammy— the faithful, obedient domestic servant. Created to justify the economic exploitation of house slaves and sustained to explain Black women's long-standing restriction to domestic service, the mammy image represents the normative yardstick used to evaluate all Black women's behavior" (2000, p. 72). Here, Collins calls upon Black feminist thought and critique to assess care and motherhood.

Further investigating issues of injustice and inequality in relation to care, Leah Lakshmi Piepzna-Samarasinha (2018) writes from a disability justice lens[16] to interrogate care:

---

[16] Leah Lakshmi Piepzna-Samarasinha writes: "To me, disability justice means a political movement and many interlocking communities where disability is not defined in white terms, or male terms, or straight terms… Disability justice centers sick and disabled people of color, queer and trans disabled folks of color, and everyone who is marginalized in mainstream disability organizing. More than that, disability justice asserts that ableism helps make racism, christian supremacy, sexism, and queer- and transphobia possible, and that all those systems of oppression are locked up tight" (Preface).

> Are the poor and working-class disabled femmes doing all the work all the time? Care is feminized and invisibilized labor. Care is something that many (not all) poor/working-class folks do like breathing—we got time! It's just the right thing to do, right? What's going on with race and entitlement? Who feels comfy asking? Are the white queers, the pretty queers, the middle-class, relatively happy, skinny, normal queers getting much care? How many masculine-gendered people have I cared the ass off for, with no reciprocity? Talk about this stuff! It's really important! Disrupt it! Get the masc, pretty, abled people to put in time! (2019)

Piepzna-Samarasinha's critique of care's relation to systems of oppression parallels Ahmed's engagement of intersectional feminism through a critical analysis of care and labor performed by women — namely how white women hire women of color to perform labor for them and/or depend on their labor being completed at the expense of other women: "When being freed from labor requires others to labor, others are paying the price of your freedom. That is not freedom. A feminist army that gives life and vitality to some women's arms by taking life and vitality from other women's arms is reproducing inequality and injustice… We have to refuse to support the system that sucks the blood, vitality, and life from the limbs of workers" (2017, p. 86).

Care, like feminism, is not neutral. Yet, in enacting care, we actionize feminism. And when we prioritize intersectional feminism, we prioritize justice and equity. But if we understand feminism as care and the recognition of and fight against systemic oppression — I wonder: Why are more people not feminists?

Fleischhauer, C. (1980). "Making Lunches for School." [Thomas, Jean (Depicted) & Thomas, Cheryl (Depicted)]. Paradise Valley Folklife Project collection, 1978-1982 (AFC 1991/021), American Folklife Center. No known restrictions on publication. Retrieved from the Library of Congress.

In Matthew Booker's "Why Do People Care for Sourdough?" (2020), Booker shares the history and lineage of his sourdough starter, which goes back 120 years (and for anyone that has tried to maintain a starter, you will know how long this is — I couldn't sustain mine for even one summer). But more importantly and awe striking than the time involved is the craft and care of maintaining and producing sourdough. Booker states:

> Perhaps we care, all of us, for our sourdough cultures because we care for one another, and for the community that we are all part of. We have obligations, and we honor those in many small ways, including feeding those whom we love and passing along the cultures that fed us... Whether we know it or not, we are all part of multi-species communities that evolve over time, that incorporate us, and that carry on something of us even after we die.

Without stating it, Booker's identification of care and making with and from sourdough is a great example of everyday critical making as intertwined with care. Critical making is not about the end product, but about the learning process of doing. Moreover, Booker's work demonstrates how care and making and nourishment, as obtained through sourdough, are also important facets of care labor.

At the same time, some scholars have explored how the labor of care can be, or should be, organized to give aid to those who need it the most — enacting an intersectional feminist methodology. This is demonstrated in Leah Lakshmi Piepzna-Samarasinha's exploration of the practice of care webs (2018). Writing from a disability justice lens, Piepzna-Samarasinha asks: "What does it mean to shift our ideas of access and care (whether it's disability, childcare, economic access, or many more) from an individual chore, an unfortunate cost of having an unfortunate body, to a collective responsibility that's maybe even deeply joyful?" In care webs, the labor and demand of care is distributed and enacted by a collective — who then participates in (as able) and receives care (as needed). Importantly, Piepzna-Samarasinha reminds us that this is just one possible practice of actionizing more equitable and fair care labor:

> I want us to dream mutual aid in our postapocalyptic revolutionary societies where everyone gets to access many kinds of care—from friends and internet strangers, from disabled community centers, and from some kind of non-fucked-up non-state state that would pay caregivers well and give them health benefits and time off and enshrine sick and disabled autonomy and choice. I want us to keep dreaming and experimenting with all these big, ambitious ways we dream care for each other into being. (2018)

However, care is not limited to that which we extend to family, ourselves, or our companions — nor to humans. hooks begins "Touching the Earth" with the claim: "When we love the Earth, we are able to love ourselves more fully. I believe this" (2010, p. 363). hooks's piece and the pointed alignment made between the self, love and care for the self, and love and care for the Earth is ever important due to the role of intersectionality. hooks draws careful attention to race in relation to the earth: "From the moment of their first meeting, Native American and African people shared with one another a respect for the life-giving forces of nature, of the Earth… Sharing the reverence for the Earth, black and red people helped one another remember that, despite the white man's ways, the land belonged to everyone" (2010, p. 364).

Moreover, the most popularized association with care is that of "selfcare" — or care that we show to ourselves. Selfcare is a popular phenomenon — currently often including skincare, baths, relaxing/resting. However, care for the self is not exclusively this supplemental opportunity of pampering (which is also important and valuable in of itself, especially in systems that do not "pamper" or enable such for all). Often, care of the self is also a feminist opportunity to work against the patriarchy, such as Ahmed emphasizes with the killjoy survival kit: "This is why for [Audre] Lorde caring for oneself is not self indulgence but self-preservation. It is rebellious to fight for life when you have been given such a deadly assignment" (Ahmed, 2017, p. 238).

S.D. Butcher & Son. (circa 1908). "Pine Ridge Indians drying meat / photo made by S.D. Butcher & Son, Kearney, Neb." No known restrictions on publication. Retrieved from the Library of Congress.

In employing posthuman analysis and considerations, María Puig de la Bellacasa develops *Matters of Care: Speculative Ethics in More than Human Worlds* (2017) as "a speculative exploration of the significance of care for thinking and living in more than human worlds" (1). In doing so, Ballacasa explores care "as intrinsically involving an ethical and political intervention that affects also those who are researching care. Because speaking of "good care"— or of as- well- as- possible care— is never neutral" (2017, p. 6). Of care, Ballacasa emphasizes that there is distinctiveness with caring, especially when compared to concern, because it denotes a subsequent action: "This is because understanding caring as something we do materializes it as an ethically and politically charged practice, and one that has been at the forefront of feminist concern with devalued agencies and exclusions" (2017, p. 42). Therefore, Ballacasa identifies care as something actionable. Moreover, Bellacasa further argues that thinking and knowing about our relations (with each other, with other beings on this earth) are dependent on care — which in turn influence how we care (2017, p. 69). In doing so, Bellacasa writes: "Thinking with care as living-with inevitably exposes the limits of scientific and academic settings to create more caring worlds" (p. 92). Bellacasa further writes about the importance of care in relation to those that we may not usually consider our care to reach, including dirt, mud, plants, and worms, due to their role in our collective and collaborative experiences on Earth that are dependent upon each other (p. 147).

All the more, in assessing the destruction of the planet due to human in/action, Morales (2019) critiques the harmful effects of capitalism, greed, and monetary exploitation, emphasizing that "Every other system of oppression is at the service of this goal, the concentration of wealth. Every other systemic oppression exists to create and uphold that project" (2019, p. 5). Through this, Morales seemingly evokes Collins's framing of the matrix of domination to argue that the ecological disasters that our planet and its inhabitants face are "inevitably disasters of social injustice that flow along the existing cracks in our world" (p. 6). As such, Morales writes: "For human society to be sustainable on earth, it must become inclusive, must take into account the well-being of each one of us" (p. 4). In doing so, Morales calls for an intersectional feminism.

Writing from a similar position of concern for more-than-humans that we coexist with, Donna Haraway writes that of the Chthulucene, which "[names] a kind of timeplace for learning to stay with the trouble of living and dying in response-ability on a damaged earth" (2016, p. 2). Haraway explains that staying with the trouble "requires making oddkin; that is, we require each other in unexpected collaborations and combinations, in hot compost piles" (2016, p. 4). Haraway's work is significant here because, like that of Ballacasa, it de-centers the human and reinforces a broader interconnectedness across the earth — and purports a feminism that takes this into its fold. Samara Madrid Akpovo, Sarah Neessen, Lydiah Nganga, and Cassie Sorrells (2018) further extend Donna Haraway's call to "stay with the trouble" through a pedagogy of discomfort and by looking to the vulnerability of hope and the role of feelings: "our troubling is an act of inventive connections that stays with the discomforts of thinking long enough to conceptualize a critical hope in discomforting times." Through this, they emphasize that "critical hope is tempted to rely on a relationship to a futurism that exempts us from staying with the trouble, and learning to make with, think with, feel with." As such, we are once more reminded of the subversive power of feelings.

Porter, M. E. (circa 1907). "Baking Bread; Photograph showing two Pueblo Indian women baking bread in an oven." No known restrictions on publication. Retrieved from the Library of Congress.

United States Extension Service. (between 1925 and 1930). "Women Canning Food Outdoors in a Wooded Area." No known restrictions on publication. Retrieved from the Library of Congress.

I wonder at what time in history did a hoard of women in the woods not strike suspicion of witchcraft? When did a cauldron in the middle of them stop being associated with spells and was found instead with the use of canning? Did either of these ever really stop?

Their bodies standout against the grayscale of the forest floor, while their heads, all adorned with pinned-back hair, seem to fade away. Their individual personhood seems to fade, pressing us to see them as a collective league amongst the trees and dirt. Working together in their canning efforts, working across the forest-floor and across various tables, baskets, tubs, and jars, they are forever frozen in their photograph. Their arduous labor paused and everlasting. A carried sack, a hunched back, hands peeling and holding.

And observing these women in the wood, nearly all dressed in white, when does the surreal become the ghoulish? The hoard of women is watched over by two broad tree trunks, which become figures of their own as the leaves cascade over bark and shapes are made against the tree. These shapes take the form of watchers, guardians, protectors, or surveyors. (My eyes keep seeing a man with a top hat and cloak in one of the trees.) These trunk-figures are close enough to watch, but not enough to help a hand or be truly involved, much like us.

Chapter 5.
Staples

Throughout Staples, you will find transcriptions of conversations, recipes, photos, and more for each of the various folks and businesses that participated in this work.

Johnson, G. N. & Eiler, T. (1978). "Carrie Severt in kitchen, Allegheny County, North Carolina." Blue Ridge Parkway Folklife Project collection (AFC 1982/009), American Folklife Center, Library of Congress. No known restrictions on publication. Retrieved from the Library of Congress.

321 Coffee

"We get to see stereotypes and biases challenged all the time in person, which I think is super cool. I mean you see people that come in that maybe don't know what to expect or I guess, I would say, don't know what to expect and are, I think, surprised. And I think that they don't, people don't always realize what other people are capable of."

Michael Evans
Co-Founder of 321 Coffee

Personal photograph of 321 Coffee.

3 interviews with 321

Michael Evans

Kelsey   So, how did you go from statistics to 321?

Michael   We primarily were always working on 321 throughout school. We started it our freshman year. At that point we were just a student organization and we were just going and doing. We'd set up unfolding tables somewhere and serve coffee for two hours and then sort of be on our way to the next event. But we were doing that throughout school. And as we got sort of closer and closer to graduation, we started, Lindsay and I started, thinking about: *Okay, how do we do this like full-time after graduation?* So we never really, I never really pursued, anything in statistics, if you will, beyond just the degree. But we sort of got a double major and 321 Coffee and coffee and hospitality. Yeah, all that stuff. So we started our freshman year with mainly the student organization. Our sophomore year we did mainly the same thing, except that fall we got invited to be vendors at the State Farmers Market.

Kelsey   Oh, yes! I've been to that location.

Michael   So we sort of brought our folding table outside at first. And we just sat — they have what's called The Craft Shed. And we set up in The Craft Shed for... I guess it was probably for the whole fall. And then they had a spot open up inside and they said to us: *Oh, do you all want to move inside?* And we were sort of: *Meh, we don't really know anything.* We actually sort of thought that that spot was a little weird and we were like: *I'm not really sure about this.* But my freshman year roommate was a construction engineering major. Family owned a construction company. He was like: *Oh, I'll help you build it.* So we took some cabinets from an old project that they had and sort of repurposed. Threw some countertops on them. Bought our first espresso machine off Craigslist for a thousand dollars. And set up shop. And: *Oh, this will be... This will be fabulous*. Taught ourselves how to brew espresso the night before that shop opened. Ran out of coffee within, I don't know... two hours of opening. There were so many more people that came than we ever thought we're going to come. And we were completely not ready. [laughs] We were like: *Oh, we'll use these first couple of days to really learn how to do all this*. And that did not happen.

Kelsey [laughs]

Michael So we opened that shop. Ran with that shop — going on four years now. We've expanded it a couple of times. When we got to the first COVID summer, we had shut down for a while. Obviously, given that we work with a lot of individuals with disabilities — typically we see a more immuno-compromised population. So we had closed for a while. We weren't really sure what our path was gonna be getting back up and open. But we were worried that no one was ever going back to coffee shops as we knew it, like pre-COVID. So we started roasting our own coffee. We were like: *Oh well. If no one was ever gonna go back to a coffee shop, we'll get coffee to people*. So we bought a little two pound roaster. And set it up over at the shop at the Farmers Market and started roasting our own coffee.

Did that for a little while and then along the way got connected with Pendo. So Pendo reached out to us and said: *Hey. We'd love for you all to supply coffee to our office*. And Pendo's a big tech —

Kelsey [pointing over her shoulder at the Pendo building downtown]

Michael	Yes. Yeah right down the street.
Kelsey	Yeah, I was like: *I've heard of this place.* Yep. It's because it's everywhere.
Michael	Yeah. Big, big tech company. I think they now have over a thousand employees, but started in Raleigh.
Kelsey	Wow.
Michael	And so they reached out, were like: *Hey, we'd love for you to supply coffee to our office.* Well, they needed 40 pounds. And I mean we were working on this two pound roaster and we had the math down to a science as to like: *Oh, if we roasted Wednesday, Thursday, Friday while we were open, we had enough coffee to get through the weekend.* So then we started going after hours. And we were like: *Okay. We'll roast from five to eight at night. Roasting coffee in order to do Pendo's order, whatever.*

Then we got around the holidays and Pendo said: *Oh, we'd love to send all of our employees a 321 Coffee gift box.* Well, again at that point it was probably like 500 plus employees. We were like: *Okay. Math on that is roughly 375 pounds of coffee. Okay, we're not doing that on our little two pound roaster.* We were like: *We'll be here for the rest of December roasting coffee.*

So we got connected to the people that we were buying our coffee from — which was De La Finca Coffee Importers. He's a third generation coffee farmer from Honduras, but now in Holly Springs importing his family's coffee to the US. They had a big coffee roaster at their facility. They said: *Hey, we'll let you all rent space on that.* So at that point, we sort of made our jump to, call it, our first commercial coffee roaster, which was a great move. Really opened up the possibilities that we had in terms of roasting coffee. Let us take on, start to create an actual wholesale program and like that kind of thing. Coffee roasting was a huge step forward and that was probably around the time that Lindsay and I were starting to get into our junior-senior year and we were starting to think about —

Kelsey	You were all in college while doing all of this?

Michael	Yeah. We're still in college.

Kelsey	Oh my goodness. Okay.

Michael	So yes, so COVID was our junior year. So in junior year we had this, we had basically the shop at the farmers market for a year. We were about to celebrate a year when COVID happened and we sort of made the pivot towards: *Okay, we're gonna start to learn about coffee and roast coffee.*

And then we were part of the Andrews Launch Accelerator at NC State that summer. And that was when we started really thinking about: *Okay, how does this become a real business? Is there a path to Lindsay and I working on this after graduation?* All of those sorts of things.

We'd been a nonprofit for a while. So after... or sometime in our sophomore year, maybe, maybe right before sophomore year... We had made the organization a non-profit. As we got closer to graduation, we started realizing maybe that wasn't the right structure for us. So, essentially graduation comes, we bring the company private. Lindsay and I decide we're gonna work on this thing full-time. And our senior year we had sort of started to lay the groundwork for a couple of other cafes that we were gonna open that were gonna help us be able to work on this full-time. So Pendo had actually circled back around to us and said: *Hey, we want — we're looking to do we're building a new headquarters in downtown Raleigh.* [gesturing to Pendo] That's the building that you now see. *We're hoping to have a private coffee bar on the 19th floor. Would you all be interested in doing this?*

So we were like: *Yeah, totally.* And so we, February of last year opened, up a private coffee bar with Pendo that was shop number two.

Kelsey   Okay.

Michael   So at that point we had the Farmers Market and that shop. [gesturing to shop we are sitting at] This shop was basically under construction at that point. So this was going to be shop number three. This opened in August of last year. And then once we had signed the lease for this shop, the agent that had sort of brokered this transaction was working on a spot in Durham and said: *Oh, we're looking for a coffee shop in Durham. Are you all interested?* And we were always like: *We think Durham would be like a great market for this.* So we said yes to that and ended up opening shop number four in Durham last year.

Kelsey   That's amazing.

Michael   Yeah, so last year was a lot of —

Kelsey   [laughs]

Michael   Last year was a lot of growth. But we graduated May 2021 and sort of knew that the organization had to grow a little bit in order to really support us working on it full-time and it also just being a sustaining entity for those that we're trying to support and letting it create, like, real opportunities in that way. So it was a very cool year for growth.

Kelsey	Yes. Graduating. Opening up four coffee shops. That's amazing. I didn't realize that. I had been to the 321 at the Farmers Market and I've seen — I drive this road to get to school all the time, so I got to see this kind of coming to be. But I didn't realize that you all were in college this whole time too.
Michael	Yeah.
Kelsey	I just — I'm kind of speechless. That's incredible.
Michael	A fun journey, you know. There's lots of stuff that you balance and whatnot. And a lot of balls in the air at times it feels like, but I think it was a lot of fun. I think we got a lot of experiences that we wouldn't have otherwise had. Also last year, we opened our own roasting facility. So that was a really, a big step forward for us. So last year we had bought a roaster. It got installed. We also — we were on *The Today Show* last year. *The Today Show* actually came out to film and Sophie roasted on that machine for the first time on *The Today Show* because it was they were coming and it was just they wanted to show those sorts of shots of like production and whatnot. And so just Sophie went through a very brief training on how to use the roaster about an hour before *The Today Show* arrived to film and then filmed her roasting on it for the first time. But that's been like another huge upgrade and just terms of what we're able to do and offer because we now sort of control that schedule of roasting and we control how much we're able to output and whatnot. But Sophie in there is a queen roaster
Kelsey	[laughs] That's awesome. So like you have all these amazing shops, all these amazing machines and tools and resources — and you all are kind of, like, self-taught with coffee-making, which is really incredible. So how did you come

to coffee and come to this mission of working and supporting the disabled community?

Michael	Yeah, I would say that the mission came first. So Lindsay, who I co-founded 321 Coffee with, she grew up in Cary and in elementary school became really good friends with three girls that had different types of disabilities. Sarah, Grace, and Emma. And actually Emma and Grace work at 321 Coffee now, which is super cool. But Lindsay became super good friends with them. They were friends all throughout growing up. Did a lot of stuff together. But as Lindsay went off to college, Lindsay also went to NC State, it was like a really stark contrast that there were almost endless professional opportunities that she was able to explore or be privy to or whatnot, but for her friends those opportunities didn't exist at all in the same way. A lot of recreational opportunities out there, but not necessarily a lot of professional opportunities. And even some of the professional opportunities that people will finding weren't like what they wanted. Like it wasn't challenging or it wasn't right. It was — It wasn't about them. It was: *Oh, you can wash the dishes, but you're not allowed to be out front.* And so we wanted to create a business that was centered around: *Hey, look at everything that this community is capable of.* So I'd say the mission came first, coffee came second. It was just an easy — when we were freshman in college, it was an easy thing where, like, we could go to Starbucks and buy the little to-go traveler of coffee and serve that at an event. And so that was, probably more so than anything, it was just an easy means to the ends.

Kelsey	Right. That's incredible. Years ago, like my family lives in Jacksonville, North Carolina — I don't know if you know, it's on the east coast. So Wilmington is like the big city near Jacksonville.

Michael: Yeah.

Kelsey: So, I've been to Bitty & Beau's a lot —

Michael: Yeah.

Kelsey: — which is fantastic. And so when I saw 321 opening I was, like, very happy to see that there's something similar coming to this community.

Michael: Totally.

Kelsey: Especially since, like, Raleigh's so growing — there should be lots of opportunities for everyone. So it's really beautiful to see a business founded on inclusion.

Michael: Yes.

Kelsey: Versus, like, a lot of places add that on secondarily if, or, like even later down the road, so that's amazing. And so also you all make coffee and you work with a very specific community of people to serve a very specific community, like Raleigh and Durham, but so what have you learned about yourself and others whether that be the folks that you work with or the people that you, like, serve coffee to?

Michael: I think that... what we've learned about people. I think we get to see a super — we get to see stereotypes and biases challenged all the time in person, which I think is super cool. I mean you see people that come in that maybe don't know what to expect or I guess, I would say, don't know what to expect and are, I think, surprised. And I think that they don't, people don't always realize what other people are capable of.

And for us maybe it's like: *Okay, maybe we have to train someone in a different way*. But it's been seen everyone's capable of doing great things. You just have to find the right way to give people that opportunity.

But I think at the same time, we see the people whose expectations or biases or challenges they come in, but we also it's those people and it's others that are also super accepting and super open-minded. And I think that's a really great thing to see out of the Raleigh-Durham community as well is that I'd say largely we have been accepted with open arms and it's been like: *This is so cool to have in the community*. And so many people that have been such big supporters, advocates, and like part of our community, which is really cool.

Kelsey That's awesome and just thinking about the origin story, so you mentioned, like, Lindsay, noticed the differences upon high school graduation, it sounded like. So do you all do anything with children potentially? Like a pre-high school graduation?

Michael Not necessarily at this point in time. A couple of our current staff came to us very young. So we had a couple of our current staff that probably started with us at 14.

Kelsey Yeah.

Michael And so we had a lot of really young staff. It's something in our future plans. What we'd love to have almost like a program for a younger audience that would almost be like Intro to Hospitality or Intro to Food Service — almost like a class or like a camp or something like that. And I know also there's a couple of initiatives at the shops to do a couple more programs over the summer that are

	like a summer reading series or things like that. That would really be sort of targeted at that younger demographic.
Kelsey	Oh cool. Yeah.
Michael	That's the other thing that we see is, we do see a lot of parents and young kids coming in and like they want their children to see that this future exists for them and that there will be opportunities for them. Which is also a super cool thing to see because I think that's another thing that we've realized is there's also a lack of representation for this community in a lot of things. I mean in media and advertising and just across the board. There's a lack of representation. But to be able to see someone that represents you doing something is: *Hey, like I can do that too.* Or: *Hey, look. That's possible.* I mean, I know it's a big thing that we started to talk about also if it's gonna —
	[it starts raining] We can move inside
Kelsey	[laughs] Sure. Yeah. This is that *Twilight* weather.
Michael	Right? It's what we've been battling with all weekend.
	[Michael and Kelsey relocate inside]
	[telling the folks in 321 Coffee] It's drizzling on us now. It's drizzling out there. I know it's horrible.
	But there was a great *How I Built This* episode with Tristan Walker. He started a shaving company that was really centered around shaving for Black men. And he talked about, at one point during his interview he talks about going to Target with his son and like walking through the aisles of Target and his son, like, sees their packaging and says like: *Oh, look. That person looks like me.* And that was

like such a meaningful moment for him. Full circle. He was like: *Yes. That representation matters. When you walk into a store and you can say there's someone that looks like me and that represents me on this product.*

I think that's also a lot of the stuff that we've started creating that representation in stores and all that matters too.

Kelsey
And so you all make coffee and you're roasting beans and you're doing and making space for community and representation. So making so many things every day, but what role... I feel like it does play a big role, but in your own words... What role does care play in 321 Coffee with what you make, what you do, how you do it?

Michael
Yeah, I think probably primary. I'd say it's on one hand a big consideration of how we train everyone to interact with each other. Right? Like this is a space where everyone needs to be cared for and respected. We teach that between staff and customers. And then we hope that it's shown back to us from customers, but I definitely think in terms of our staff, right, it's that we want everyone to feel like this is a place where they are cared for and that you come here and it's a safe work environment and you know that you're going to be supported and you know, this is a place where you can grow and be yourself. And I think that's really important, too. And I think that then our staff does a great job of reciprocating that forward to everyone that walks in here and they make sure that everyone that walks in here feels cared for and taken care of. And I'd say hospitality and whatnot probably one of our real strong suits. We have some people that are just naturally really... caring is probably the right word. They're really caring people. And they'll come in and immediately: *Oh my gosh, I love your nails. I love your hair.* A great experience for people that way.

Kelsey	And that's so different then because you can go places — I'm thinking of Target. Like I go through the Target automated checkout and it's very transactional. I just think that comment — *Oh, I love your nails* — that can just make someone's day and it's just so nice. So that's really beautiful. And my last question, and then we can talk about whatever else you'd like to, is like what do you think is like the power or capacity of community with what you all do and like in your future trajectory?
Michael	Yeah. I mean, I think that it's exactly what you're saying, right? 321 was founded first and foremost on this mission and there are a lot of companies where it may be more like a secondary thought, but there's also nothing wrong with that, you know. That is how change is going to come about is that we need more people to get to that almost, like, second step. I hope that it challenges, what we're doing challenges that and challenges people to think about that. And challenges people to think about how they're hiring and where they're advertising jobs and who they're open to recruiting and interviewing and working with. And that people are also willing to realize how they are able to do that, right, and that you just really — honestly, I mean like you've just got to be able to listen to people and hear them out on what they need in order to be successful.
Kelsey	Right.
Michael	I hope that's what 321 challenges more than anything. I hope that there's people that see this and say: *Oh, we could do something similar, right?* That would be really cool.
Kelsey	Yeah, and I'm thinking now like Pendo — they physically built a coffee shop with you all in mind. Like that is something really fantastic where it's like — in

the structural Integrity of that building is 321 Coffee. That's really cool.

Michael	Yeah. I think the community there has been super cool. Not that it doesn't exist at our other shops. But in that one in particular, right, I mean it basically serves the same couple hundred people every single week.

Kelsey	Yeah.

Michael	So everyone there knows each other by name. Pendo employees walk up and it's: *Oh, hey, Christine. How's your day going?* But it's like they *all* know each other by name. They all know things about each other. And that's really cool too. I mean there will be times where our employees will go on lunch break there and they'll sit down at a table with a bunch of Pendo employees and eat lunch together. And —

Kelsey	There's just a little community there.

Michael	That's what we were going for. Yeah, right. But yeah, yeah. So Sophie and Rene both worked at the Pendo shop a little bit. But Sophie actually worked there when we first opened the shop, so she worked over there for a couple of months. But getting to see the relationships she got there was super cool. She was back there last week and it was like: *Oh, I get to go hi to all my friends and see everyone I haven't seen in a couple of months.* So seeing that kind of community actually form is super cool.

Kelsey	Yeah, and it's wonderful to see Pendo like demonstrate care too and that way that kind of like what you're saying is like really important — Something else that I've been wondering. And I was thinking of this yesterday as I was

	preparing to talk to you today is: Where did the name 321 come from?
Michael	321 represents Down syndrome, which is the third copy of the 21st chromosome.
Kelsey	Okay, that's what my mom maybe thought it was referring to but I wasn't sure.
Michael	Yeah, it's a very subtle nod. And then a lot — So it's a nod to down syndrome, but we work with people with all disabilities. Not exclusively down syndrome, but it was inspiration for the name and then even a lot of the branding components that we have sort of plays with like… [gesturing to the windows] This pattern that's like on all the windows is inspired by DNA mapping. Chromosome mapping, if you will. But if you look at like the test of chromosome, I don't know enough about biology, but that's like what it's inspired by — if you ever if you look like pictures of it, it's like very cool, but then done up in the 321 colors and whatnot, but it's represents like the uniqueness that like everyone brings and like contributes. It's a lot of, like, a subtle thing. It's subtly there and then in a couple of different ways.
Kelsey	Yeah, that's beautiful. I remember, so I drive past this and I thought it was like a stained glass design to juxtapose these very fancy glass buildings. It is so colorful and beautiful. That's incredible.
Michael	It is nice and colorful. What I also like is that it is very bright and colorful.
Kelsey	It is very bright. It's very lively. It feels very lovely. Very welcoming. It feels like a manifestation of everything that you've talked about. So that's very cool.

Sophie Pacyna

Photograph of Sophie. Photograph provided by 321 Coffee.

Kelsey	What are the best parts of the roasting process?
Sophie	So the roasting process is a lot more accessible now and a lot easier now because basically there's a lot more touch screens and vacuums and stuff like that.
Kelsey	Yeah.
Sophie	It's a lot more.
Kelsey	With the roasting process, what's your favorite part?
Sophie	I think my favorite part is when they are trapped in the glass — is the talking glass.
Kelsey	What does that involve?
Sophie	That involves the container and the touch screens. And that's one of my favorite parts.
Kelsey	I love how, I love how coffee beans smell. So like when you're roasting the beans like do you get a lot of the smell from the beans?
Sophie	Yeah, and that's one of my favorite parts too — smelling the coffee. The smell is like my favorite part.
Kelsey	Yeah. Yeah. And so what are some of your best memories with the roasting or with 321 Coffee?

Sophie	I think one of the favorite parts is being with my favorite boss, Michael. Yeah, because he's really fun to be around.
Kelsey	Yes. It's great having a very good boss. I think that makes a big difference.
Sophie	Yeah.
Kelsey	And so you work at this location. Do you work at any of the other coffee shops?
Sophie	I used to work at the Farmers Market and Pendo.
Kelsey	What is the — Is there a big difference between working at the different locations, have you found?
Sophie	At the Farmers Market and Pendo, I had to transition to wearing just a black apron and a pink apron and a key fob.
Kelsey	Right? Yes. Was that at Pendo where you had to wear the key fob?
Sophie	Yeah.
Kelsey	I've been to the Farmers Market location and that was like very blue. It's very pretty. That was the first one I went to and I think I had a hot chocolate and it was probably one of the best hot chocolate I've ever had.
Sophie	Yeah. I love hot chocolates too.
Kelsey	Yeah. Yeah, I love and this is like perfect hot chocolate weather. So what are

	your some of your favorite things about 321?
Sophie	I think one of my favorite things is the atmosphere. The atmosphere and the inclusion. I love it.
Kelsey	Yeah, that's amazing. And so how long have you been working with 321?
Sophie	Since like three years.
Kelsey	Three years? That's awesome. Yeah, and so you've been — What are some changes that you've seen over three years?
Sophie	Through the years, it's just an amazing family. They're very happy. And very fun to be around. I just really love the family. And just the best memories.
Kelsey	Mm-hmm. That's great. And I hear you're the queen of roasting?
Sophie	Yeah, I'm the queen.
Kelsey	[laughs]
Sophie	I'm the queen of roasting and the queen of espresso.
Kelsey	Do you have a favorite thing that you make here?
Sophie	Yeah. I like the lattes.
Kelsey	The lattes! I think you probably made my latte. It's very good.

Sophie: Lattes, hot chocolate, but anything that's hot or cold — I love to make.

Kelsey: Was it hard learning how to make coffee?

Sophie: Not really that hard. I actually know how to make it so it's just like a snap to the hand. It's really easy.

Kelsey: Yeah. I I sometimes mess up using coffee pot machines so whatever I see the espresso machines, like they feel so fancy to me. So they're all so like really beautiful machines that make like all that beautiful foam. It's just lovely.

Sophie: Yeah. I also make latte art. That's my favorite too.

Kelsey: Aw — That's my mom. She likes coming to Raleigh because when she gets a latte they have latte art and she thinks that's really cool.

Sophie: Yeah, I can make — I won a latte art throwdown in Portland.

Kelsey: What? What was that?

Sophie: So basically I made a speech in Portland. And they had a party one of the days and they had a latte art throwdown. And I won.

Kelsey: Congratulations! That's awesome.

Sophie: So yeah.

Kelsey: They had a latte art throwdown?

Sophie	Yeah.
Kelsey	That sounds super fun.
Sophie	Yeah, it's really fun. [laughs]
Kelsey	Did you do the heart design?
Sophie	Yeah.
Kelsey	Oh my gosh — that's amazing. And was this Portland, Oregon?
Sophie	Yeah.
Kelsey	That's so cool. Yeah, it's really cool.
Sophie	So yeah, so it's kind of fun. [laughs]
Kelsey	Sounds really fun. I'm gonna have to like look up videos of latte art competitions.
Sophie	Yeah it was kind of fun.
Kelsey	And is there anything else you want to talk about with 321?
Sophie	So, yeah — 321 is the best.
Kelsey	It seems like the best.

Sophie	Yeah, and as you can tell this store has the highest rating.

Kelsey	Oh, out of the all of the 321s?

Sophie	Out of all of the other 321 storefronts — the Farmers Market, downtown Durham. This has the highest rating. It's amazing and it's the best one to be around. The atmosphere here is the best.

Rene Grunow

Photograph of Rene. Photograph provided by 321 Coffee.

Kelsey — Let's see Rene. Is it R E N E?

Rene — Yes.

Kelsey — Okay. Awesome. How are you?

Rene — I'm good, how are you?

Kelsey — I'm great. So, can you talk to me about who you are and what you do at 321?

Rene — I'm Rene and I'm a barista — I started back in 2022.

Kelsey — Amazing. So have you always worked at this location or have you been to the other ones?

Rene — I've been — so I'm here for this home base. But now I'm cross training now with, between this store, Pendo, and now the Farmers Market.

Kelsey — Oh nice. Yeah, I was telling Sophie the location at the Farmers Market is the one I went to for the first time and it's so good. It's so like it's very different visually like it's a lot more blue and it's inside. But do you have a favorite location to be at yet?

Rene — Probably here. [laughs]

Kelsey — [laughs]

Rene — Pendo too. The Farmers Market…

Kelsey   Is okay? Yeah?

Rene   I'm just like…

Kelsey   That's okay! So what are your favorite things about 321 Coffee?

Rene   Probably the atmosphere.

Kelsey   Atmosphere. Yeah.

Rene   And getting to know new people. New faces. And not seeing the same people.

Kelsey   Yeah. Yeah, and I bet especially being like at this location downtown —

Rene   There's a lot of, like, the same people that come in every day. Like: *You were just here yesterday.*

Kelsey   You all have lots of regulars it sounds like. That's awesome. So you're a barista. What is your favorite thing to make?

Rene   I make the lattes. I'm actually a really good latte artist.

Kelsey   Yeah, Sophie was telling me she won a latte art competition.

Rene   Yeah.

Kelsey   That's incredible. That's very cool. I didn't know they had those things. But yeah, what's something that you've learned about yourself and working here at

                    321?

Rene   Probably getting the drinks on time. Because before I was just like: *Uh-oh*.

Kelsey   Yeah, was it hard learning how to make coffee?

Rene   It was hard at first, but now I'm an espresso queen!

Kelsey   Yes. Yeah. That makes sense to me.

Rene   You just pour the milk in and whatever flavor they want.

Kelsey   Yeah, is that like the most popular drink that you see people getting?

Rene   If it's warm. Yeah. And sometimes if it's cold too, they get cold.

Kelsey   I like hot coffee. And so one question that asking folks is because I'm making a cookbook for my dissertation because I'm really interested in how we make with food and how that plays in with care and so how do you see care in relationship to 321?

Rene   Seeing the smiling customers' faces and also enjoying their lattes that I make.

Kelsey   That's okay! We can still talk about some of your favorite things at 321. What's your best memory here?

Rene   Probably getting to know Sam. Like me and Sam have been friends for — when I went to go visit with my school at the Farmers Market and that's how I knew

	Sam.
Kelsey	Who's — I haven't met Sam. Who's Sam?
Rene	He's Sophie's boyfriend.
Kelsey	Okay got it.
Rene	I don't know if she told you —
Kelsey	No, but it's okay! That's nice. You're making lots of friends. And so it sounds like you have lots of great community here.
Rene	Yeah.
Kelsey	What is that like?
Rene	We get more people and I was like I'm not used to it but — This is actually my first real job anyways. Yeah.
Kelsey	Yeah, it seems like a great job.
Rene	And I love coffee so.
Kelsey	I know, I love coffee too — especially on days when the weather's like really gross like this.
Rene	And I'm just like: *Okay*.

Kelsey	Do you do anything with the roasting process?
Rene	No. I wish.
Kelsey	[laughs]
Rene	I wish.
Kelsey	So you do a lot of the barista work. Is there anything else that you really enjoy doing with 321?
Rene	Probably the events. That's like my most, most favorite.
Kelsey	Okay, what kind of events do you all do?
Rene	We go to the Western Wake Farmers Market over there by the airport.
Kelsey	Oh, I didn't know there was a farmers market over there.
Rene	Yeah, it's called the Western Wake Farmers Market if you look it up. Me and one of the managers, Tiffany, we always go there every Saturday morning.

321 Coffee's coffee beans. Photograph provided by 321 Coffee.

321's iced honey cinnamon latte

Here is 321 Coffee's recipe for an iced honey cinnamon latte! It was the drink that got Michael into drinking coffee. The very first one Michael had was from Global Village on Hillsborough Street, which is directly across from where he studied for college.

Ingredients

1 double shot of espresso
1 tablespoon honey

Milk of choice (8 oz. recommended) Sprinkle of cinnamon

Directions

1. Prepare a double shot of espresso.
2. Combine a double shot of espresso with honey and cinnamon. Stir until all of the honey and cinnamon is fully mixed into the espresso.
3. Pour the espresso mixture over a glass of ice.
4. Top off with milk of your choice (8 oz. recommended) and enjoy!

Bee Downtown

"And I deeply believe that food brings people together. The stories of food brings people together. Bees do that in a great way. You just have the ability to have that story. But all food does that. And care goes into cultivating it and growing it, but it also goes into how you prepare it and how you cook it and how you wash it…"

Leigh-Kathryn Bonner
Founder and CEO of Bee Downtown

Photograph of Leigh-Kathryn Bonner. Photograph provided by Bee Downtown.

Bees in the bee boxes. Photograph provided by Bee Downtown.

Bee boxes. Photograph provided by Bee Downtown.

interview with Leigh-Kathryn Bonner

Leigh-Kathryn   Any day I get to be out with the bees I am happy. [laughs]

Kelsey   That's perfect. I randomly have been taking beekeeping classes at the Garden Supply Center in Cary actually.

Leigh-Kathryn   Yeah? Amazing!

Kelsey   And it's very lovely and very sweet. And so that's just something I've been doing. But yeah —

Leigh-Kathryn   I love that.

Kelsey   It's very fun.

Leigh-Kathryn   And you get to, at the Garden Supply Center, you can host your hive there. Is that correct?

Kelsey   Yeah!

Leigh-Kathryn   Okay. Yeah, I get their like emails.

Kelsey   It's led by this very, very Southern, old school gentleman, who's just like a hobby beekeeper and he's just the sweetest man. So it's lovely.

Leigh-Kathryn   I love that. It seems like it from the emails. I've never met him. I think two of our beekeepers have gone one time to just introduce themselves, but he seems sweet and very invested in the program.

Downtown came to be? I think I saw you were in college and your landlord was like: *No beekeeping here.*

Leigh-Kathryn   [laughs] That's exactly how it went. I am a fourth generation beekeeper and that has been a gift to me because when I started Bee Downtown, I was not a good beekeeper. I don't even know if, as I look back on it — like I wasn't a beekeeper. I just wanted bees and didn't have anywhere to keep them. But I had generations of knowledge that I could just call up and they had an answer that I trusted and I understood. There's the saying: Y*ou ask three beekeepers the same question, you get nine answers.* And it's true. Like there's so many different ways to do things. People have so many different philosophies. And I trusted my family's philosophy and beekeeping and that helped me learn a lot faster in the grand scheme in the world.

I'm coming up on nine and a half years, nine years of beekeeping and I still know nothing compared to like my grandfather and my uncle, you know, or David Tarpy at NC State. Like I know nothing compared to them, but it's just like you can't rush knowledge with beekeeping. You have to see seasons and understand how things ebb and flow with good honey years and bad honey years. You just have to. Can't rush it. Just like nature. You can't rush nature.

So it started when I was in college — it was just meant to be a way for me to keep bees and learn about beekeeping. I was so intrigued by it. And then some of the first hives we put in were at Burt's Bees World Headquarters and media picked up on that and other companies in the area heard about it and said: *Hey, we're looking for a sustainability program.* It was originally just bees, but the minute the bees came... It was just these magic boxes. So people were like: *I've always heard about beekeeping. Can you bring me a suit? I want to try.* I was spending like all of my time showing people bees and talking to the companies about bees and their employees wanted the honey. And then it was like: W*ait this can't just be putting bees on campuses. It's a whole program.* But it's been a natural progression. And because we've taken on money once and our investors are amazing — they just want to see us succeed however the best way for Bee Downtown to succeed is. They don't push their own agenda at all. We've gotten to grow and develop the company that is the right company to build and I'm very grateful for that.

Kelsey	Yeah. I have a lot of questions about a lot of those businesses, but I still want to learn as much as I can about you first. You mentioned that you were spending all your time doing this, which is really wonderful, that then, not organically but through a lot of really hard work, you then we're able to pour yourself into this and so were you studying beekeeping or animal life science at NC State? What were the steps that kind of led to this? And why did you then decide to kind of pursue this full-time as your career?

Leigh-Kathryn	Yeah, everyone always thinks I studied entomology or animal science and I like to think that I am an honorary graduate of the College of Agriculture because I love it so much and I'm so supportive of that college, but I graduated from the College of Humanities and Social Sciences and had an international studies degree with the European concentration and then a double minor in Spanish and nonprofit management. So, nothing to do with what I do all day every day today.

Except for what I tell people is: *If I'd been an entomologist, Bee Downtown would never have been here.* Because I would have been a really really great scientist, but the fact that my entire education in college was built around: *How do you build authentic relationships? How do you write well? How do you use what resources you have and figure out how to move forward? How do you quickly problem solve? How do you build relationships with people that have different viewpoints and mindsets from you? How do you storytell in a way that brings cultures and people together from different backgrounds to one common good? And how do you listen to other people's thoughts as well?* And that was what I studied. And so it was like this beautiful marriage of the two things. There was no marketing department. There was no, you know, copywriting. We still don't have that. I still have to do a lot of it. [laughs] But that's because my education gave me that and then my family gifted me the just depth and breadth of knowledge with agriculture and bees that allowed me to be good at both of them. Far from great at either, but at least good enough to like pass a sniff test with a Fortune 500 company. That's like: *Yeah, go put bees on our campus. Sure. Why not? That'll be fun and we'll pay you to do it.* I'm very grateful that I studied what I studied in school and that both the College of Agriculture and CHASS have been so supportive, even past when I graduated.

Kelsey — Mm-hmm. I'm also in CHASS. I'm a big fan of CHASS. I remember my very first day at NC State someone asked like: *Oh, are you in CHASS?* And I said: *Yes, why?* And they're like: *Well, you just give CHASS girl vibes.*

Leigh-Kathryn — [laughs] I love that. You're like: *Thank you.*

Kelsey — Another question I have, a little bit more about the context of this place, is what have you learned about yourself and about others — whether that be for the Porsche and all these really fancy and expensive companies that you work for or even just like your family. What have you learned about them by doing Bee Downtown and also the folks that you work with every day?

Leigh-Kathryn — Yeah. Oh that's a loaded question. I think from the corporate perspective that it's easy to think that big corporations don't care about anyone about themselves. And that is just as far from the truth as we at Bee Downtown could experience. Like people care so much about what the impact they're making is. They want to do good. They want to find ways to use money and budgets to make a difference and to make people love where they work and invite people to be part of something bigger. And I think that narrative gets lost a lot of the time where people say it's fake... it's just greenwashing — and it's not. Like we had a woman email me the other day who, they don't even have bees on their campus yet, and we've been emailing with her for a year and she was like: *I'm getting ready to get married. I just want to let you know my China, my wedding China just came in and it's bees. It's bee plates.* I was like: *Excuse me?! We would like to send you a gift for your wedding. Could you give me your address?* And she sent me a picture of her address stamp and it has a bee on it. And, like, they don't even have bees yet and she's already like that invested and ready to get bees. I'm wearing Bandwidth bee socks. Those are their socks that employees get now. So they genuinely do care.

I think for me as a founder and starting a business as a female, learning to use my voice and to be confident in who I am. And I talk a lot about that with everyone on our team because it's a young team, but especially the women — use your voice and don't apologize for great ideas or belittle them before you even speak them. And know that you have a team that's willing to support you and is here for you. And that's a huge thing about the culture for us as I have very very low tolerance for somebody's not supporting a teammate in the way that they should. And that just doesn't fly because it's not the kind of business I want to build.

I've learned so much about my family and my family's history and agriculture and just a genuine respect for it that I didn't have before this was my day. My cousin is literally outside in the back. He works for Bee Downtown now. He's in school at State and he's working. He works during the school year and he's working the summer. He's proud of it too because it's his family's legacy also. It's from that side of the family. And it lets me... My grandpa, I don't think still fully understands what I do. [laughs] He's still a little confused. My mom shows some pictures and she shows him videos of things like our warehouse and my grandpa's like: *What is that? There's so much stuff in there!* That equipment, for him, is wild in that we would have that much. To him farming is on a farm on a tractor. And that's not what we do, but we're still farmers and I get to honor my family's legacy and history in a way that is really special to me. My dad's family is super entrepreneurial, that's his grandparents. And so it's fun for me to get to take both sides of my family and mix it into something. That's, I think, quite magical.

Kelsey — Yeah, I would agree. It's very magical and I feel like you're so incredibly humble, which is really beautiful. And as you're speaking I was reminded of how NC State is a very entrepreneurial, very innovation-driven university, which is wonderful — and at times the drive for innovation is very pervasive over a lot of things that maybe aren't done in the name of innovation, so they get a little bit buried under all of that. And so I think it's really wonderful that you have brought together folklore, family beekeeping alongside entrepreneurship. And I'd love to hear more about what it's like to work in a field that does a lot of innovation, but isn't electronic. It's not engineering. But then working with companies that do those things.

Leigh-Kathryn — Yeah. Yeah. I like to say we're like a new twist on an age-old tradition, you know. Those bee boxes out there have not been redesigned since the 1800s. Like there is a lot of things in farming: *Well this works so this is what we are going to use.* [laughs] And those bee boxes work great. I'm sure there's so many amazing things that could be done. The highest grossing Indiegogo campaign of all time was a new version of the beehive. They tried to get, I'll get these numbers wrong... I'll butcher them, but like $75,000 and they ended up raising like 12.2 million and they're like: *Whoa!* But 90% of people that bought it were not beekeepers because of the way it was shown, which is not good because then all these people thought that they could keep bees and get honey for their pancakes. And it's not how it works. And they just weren't expecting it to take off like that. They didn't take the time to tell people you have to know how to keep bees to get this beehive and they tried to revert back, like: *Hold on. Wait, you need to be a beekeeper!* It had gone way past that.

But I think for the corporations they... Well a lot of people ask: *How has Bee Downtown gotten these corporations on board? How have you gotten in the room with these people?* I think a lot of it is like sheer dumb luck... that and like being in the right place at the right time. I think a lot of it is that I did understand the importance of relationships and speaking with people and I could hold conversations with people as a young college student that I think impressed people and we were there like: *Okay. Send her up to the CEO. See if she can hold her own. Like gosh. I think she can. Let's try it.*

But in the world of startups, like we're young in the world of corporations. We're a super young company. But whereas, you know, some startups are trying to sell something that nobody knows anything about — everyone has a memory in agriculture. Everyone's grandfather or grandmother was a farmer or gardener. Everyone grew up with a farm or, you know, wanted a horse when they were little. And people today, they want land and they can't afford it yet, but they have this dream of living on the land in a way that the bees make it nostalgic. And so it's like safe to them in this way, because it evokes memories in a really beautiful way. And then everything we do is storytelling. It's just the core of who we are and what we do. We find ways to tell beautiful stories and help corporations tell their stories in relation to the bees as well. And that makes me happy — like finding how the stories fit each company because every company is a little different and the story we want to tell is a little bit different, but once we find it — like it's so exciting to help them tell it.

Kelsey	Right. That's incredible and I can't imagine the portfolio of stories that you all have. That must be incredible. And so with working with all these companies and working with folks in community and all over the place, I'm wondering... Like my own work is focusing on making. So like the bees make honey, you all are making bee boxes and making these stories and making these relationships. So how does making and then how does care, how do those together inform your work?

Leigh-Kathryn	Oh. Yes. And care in regards to what piece?

Kelsey	I feel like care is a part of a lot of what you do.

Leigh-Kathryn	Yes.

Kelsey	Like care for the bees.

Leigh-Kathryn	Yup.

Kelsey	Care for the environment.

Leigh-Kathryn	Yup.

Kelsey: Care for each other.

Leigh-Kathryn: Yup.

Kelsey: Like you have that Care Bingo.

Leigh-Kathryn: Yup.

Kelsey: So there's no limit to what you can talk about with care.

Leigh-Kathryn: Yeah, one of my core values is intentionality and I think that that ends up being a lot about care. Seeing what people need and how to… One of the things we say is: *Surprise and delight*. One of our beekeepers coined the term the *joyness* and the *joyous* and I really loved that. Just caring for people. And my favorite word is cultivate. Because the root of the word "cult," which, you know, positive negative whatever people want to say, but it means a deep sense of adoration. So the fact that cultivate is the word we use when we are raising bees and we are farming and we are growing crops and we are maintaining our farms and our livestock and we cultivate our land… It means to deeply adore something to the point where you will nourish it and care for it and take it from seed to harvest and make sure that it's fed and it's watered and it has the right sun and it's got shade when it needs it and that, you know, it's not too cold in the winter. And I think that that word cultivate is very much care at the end of the day.

We work hard. I mean people are pulling 60 hour work weeks right now. Multiple of us pull 80 hour work weeks right now. And if we don't care for the people on our team that are building this company, and I try to go above and beyond every year for those people that do put in that many hours every year, then they can't and they won't stay. We'll burn out. So self-care bingos like the prizes at the time of the year where you're exhausted and burned out. We do it every quarter, but this quarter's quite easy. It's like write a haiku for a teammate, you know, like sit in the sun and do nothing for 15 minutes. In the winter, it's like more honestly more workout related because people need to be in shape for bee season. So it's a little harder in the winter.

But we have competitor companies that will put a beehive anywhere. Anywhere. In Kalamazoo, Idaho and one company will be like: *Yeah, we'll put bees out there*. And they train people for honestly, like a couple of days and then they give them these beehives and they crash. They're going to. You don't know what you're doing. And, one — you're putting them on corporate campuses where people could get hurt if they don't have the right genetics, but two — you're killing bees. And I have a fundamental distaste for that being the way you try to build this industry because you're harming the bees that you're trying to take care of. And you can do everything right and things still go wrong, but care, concern, understanding, respect, and fairness are what creates trust. And the bees have to trust their Keepers. So we go out and we work the hives every two weeks throughout the year. It's a ton of work. Our competitor companies do it once a month, if that. But if we don't, we mess up and the bees die. My uncle likes to call what I do Boutique Beekeeping. It's like high-end... like just so much care. We don't just say: *Well, that hive's not gonna make it. Like, whatever*. We have the, I will say we have the privilege to be able to say: *No, let's nurture it. Let's get it back*. Some people just don't have the ability to do that at the time that they've got to make their honey for the year. They can't do it. But we do, so we we do it. At the end of the day, I just wanted to leave the world better than how I found it. And this felt like the best way I knew how. [laughs] Might not be.

Kelsey	No, I completely agree. And I mean, I first really got into bees when teaching. My background is in English education. So I was teaching a literature course at NC State as part of my grad program. And I teach Sylvia Plath and she was doing agro-therapy with bees and so she became a beekeeper and she was writing all these bee poems. And so she writes about the boxes and showing up to learn how to beekeep in a T-shirt and everyone else is in all the garb.
Leigh-Kathryn	[laughs]
Kelsey	Like she has a whole poem about it. And so all my students always love these bee poems. I think it speaks to that nostalgia, but also like she was writing poems about caring for her family, but also caring for bees and students really love that and like I think that care for something so small that's so important really resonates with people because it's also caring for the world. And so for you, as a beekeeper, what does it mean to care for something so precious that like our whole ecosystem is so incredibly dependent upon and then to care for yourself and what is that like?
Leigh-Kathryn	Yeah. We like to say there is a difference between beekeepers and beehavers. Beehavers have bees, and then the bees die — and they don't fully understand that their impact or actions or inactions caused that to happen. And it's like: *Oh yikes, you know. Mother Nature.* Beekeepers — like it hurts and it's painful and you can do everything right and you know, my mom told me — so when I started this company she said: *Please don't do it.* And she's the ag side. And I was like: *Mom. This is like I'm trying to honor our family and I want to make a difference and I want to honor Pawpaw and your childhood and growing up.* And she's like: *Just don't do it.* But why? She said: *Because this is the only industry where you can do everything right and lose everything in a minute.* And so I don't wish that on my worst enemy,

much less my daughter. And she's right, you know. Farmers, they're gamblers. And they are gambling against Mother Nature and betting against the house and the house always wins at the end of the day. And so they can put in an entire year's worth of work and lose it in a night. And that's so scary and so sad and I don't think people fully understand that because grocery stores always have food. It's always there. And farmers don't set the prices, the grocery stores do. You don't see the price fluctuation like you should during certain years, but we just don't. We just have Farmers aging out and people aren't replacing them because it's too much work. And so for me, a big piece of Bee Downtown was I wanted there to be stable, great paychecks for people coming in. And these beekeepers do work wild hours this time of year, but I try to pay them in a way where it's worth it to them. That's my whole hope — to build a business where young people in agriculture can say: *I can do this for the long haul.* If their bodies are like, you know worn out, I try to find, you know, self-care Bingo.

Our principal beekeeper, he's got a newborn and he's exhausted. And so I told him the other day, I was like: *I need you to tell me this time this time or this time on these three days. I need you for two hours.* He's like: *What are you doing?* I'm like: *You just got to tell me the time and yeah give me a time.* I'm gonna send him to go get a massage because, like their bodies break this time of year and they're exhausted and they're lifting thousands of pounds every day of honey, and they deserve that, you know. Like they have far beyond earned that. So I think trying to build a business for people to understand that if you need a day, take a day — or how can we reward surprise and delight teammates too?

Not typically does a farmer get a Thai massage scheduled for them in the middle of the day, but they should 'cause they're exhausted and their bodies hurt and they, of anybody to get a massage in the middle of the work day,

	they should be a farmer at the end of the day. [laughs] We just haven't gotten that progressive yet in the farming world. You know, we're like: No, no. We don't know about massages yet. One day the farmers will. [laughs]
Kelsey	Yes, my mom's family are dairy farmers from upstate New York. Yes, and so like when you're talking about how things can just all vanish completely in a day — they were hit by a hurricane last year. And so they have all the dairy cows and they have fields of produce. And so all the produce —
Leigh-Kathryn	Just gone.
Kelsey	Just gone. But yeah, so it's interesting. Like, every summer we go up and see all the cows and it's very interesting then to talk to people that don't have that relationship. Because my mom was drinking unpasteurized milk her whole childhood and that was just normal.
Leigh-Kathryn	Yeah.
Kelsey	So there's such a beauty of farming and like that connection/care to land too. But there is a gap between, like, the reciprocity of everyone else then giving care back too so I think it's beautiful that your business is trying to teach that care. That's wonderful.
Leigh-Kathryn	I always tell people: *We have to be sustainable to be sustainable*. And that comes from one — we do have to turn a profit in order to be here long term, but two — we have to keep the people here that have the, you know, like elder wisdom that have helped build this company... and what do we need to do to make sure that that intellectual, you know, property of theirs that

they've built this company with this stays.

Kelsey	Right!

Leigh-Kathryn	The turnover's expensive and it's a lot. And there's very special people that built this company with me and I want them to stay as long as they can. And then if they ever decide to leave, we'll cheer them on. But I'll do everything I can to keep 'em for as long as I can. [laughs]

Kelsey	Yes, and I love that idea of intellectual wisdom and elder wisdom. Part of my work's looking at the difference between, like, academic knowledge and also kind of like more personal, family knowledge. A lot of, like, feminized knowledge is not often credited or valued as much and so when you're talking about like how you don't have as much beekeeping knowledge as like an academic professor, but it's like your knowledge is still very valid important — as is, like, your grandfather's and uncle's... and how if you would have studied entomology you wouldn't have created Bee Downtown. So I just wanted to know if you could speak a little bit more about how you experience the legitimacy of beekeeping and care knowledge in what you do and how you either work with that or against that?

Leigh-Kathryn	Yeah. I mean, there's so many different ways people keep bees. So there's no... there's a couple wrong ways.

Kelsey	[laughs]

Leigh-Kathryn	There's a lot of right ways and then there's a lot of ways where you just have to learn, you just have to get it wrong in order to get it right. And it doesn't matter if everybody tells you the right answer, if you don't have the skill to do it — you just can't do it.

Yeah, so I think for me... Can you repeat the question?

Kelsey　　I was just wondering if you'd speak to what it's like to work with or against legitimate, like socially accepted forms of knowledge or those that are more celebrated, taken more seriously, credited versus maybe like learning with your hands.

Leigh-Kathryn　　Yeah. I have ADD. I never did well in school when you had to sit still. It was always kinetic learning. We built our Leadership Institute off of kinetic learning because that, one — we know is the best way to learn and retain knowledge. But two — it's just how I learned and I felt like adults sit still so much. Like: *Why? Let's not have them do that. We're gonna build a Leadership Institute that's like the absolute opposite of what I want people to do.* And I started the company because I don't want to sit at a desk all day and, you know, like I've been sitting at a desk a good bit recently — so I'm out of here, going to pull some honey today. I was talking to a principal beekeeper about it, like I will have so much more energy this entire work week because I got to pull honey for half a day. And yes, if I did it all day every day for three weeks on and on, I'd be freaking exhausted but I got to get out there. And learned something today, you know? Like I got to remember: *Okay, how much time does it take to pull honey?* I can read about it all the time. I can listen in on their meetings all the time. But until I do it and I watch it and I see it. You don't feel it the same way. Understanding, though, new papers that are coming out, new studies that are coming out, is what keeps you a good beekeeper because bee keeping is very different now than when my grandfather kept bees. There's so many more diseases and if my grandfather didn't keep up with it, his bees would just be dying left and right. He wouldn't know what to do. But I think it's all about balance at the end of the day.

And I will say a lot of times you have the ability to read a lot and think you know a lot about beekeeping and then we can put someone in a beehive and in three minutes know if they can keep bees or not. They might be able to answer every question we could ask them about what to do right. But can they actually do it is completely different. You know? Like once you're in it with 60,000 bees flying all around you and they're starting to get pissed off because you've been in there too long. How do you do it? Yeah, that is completely different than writing a paper about how to do it. So I don't know if that answers your question.

Kelsey	No, it does. Absolutely.
Leigh-Kathryn	[Leigh-Kathryn notices that her overall strap has broken]
	We are officially — This is like a totally random thing, but for my 30th birthday, I have a very supportive husband and he, for my 30th birthday, wrote to Carhartt and told Carhartt how much my team loves Carhartt, really how much I love Carhartt. And we are officially like sponsored by Carhartt now as a company.
Kelsey	That's incredible! Congratulations.
Leigh-Kathryn	Thank you. So everyone's stoked because we all have a ton of Carhartt now. But yeah, I need to tell them that my overalls broke! The second time.
Kelsey	Oh, no! I'm a big believer in bad sewing and hot glue, worst case scenario.

Leigh-Kathryn   I just married a man who can sew.

Kelsey   Oh, well, there you go.

Leigh-Kathryn   [laughs]

Kelsey   Congratulations for your birthday and your marriage!

Leigh-Kathryn   Thank you very much. I'll fix this later. It's a shoulderless vibe today.

Kelsey   That's fine.

Leigh-Kathryn   [laughs]

Kelsey   Um, so another thing with bees too, you've mentioned being a woman business, a woman in beekeeping. Do you have any thoughts at all, and if not, that's okay, about bees being feminist symbols?

Leigh-Kathryn   [excitedly whispering] Oh yeah.

Kelsey   Can I hear them?

Leigh-Kathryn   I have a whole keynote about it. Well, when I got into the *Inc. Magazine* "30 under 30" — there's a quote in there that I freaked out a little bit when it came out, and so did my mother. You know, people will say: *Like she can't do this and you can't lift a hundred pounds worth of honey.* And the quote says: *Yes, I can and I can do it in high heels and a dress coming out of a meeting with the New York Stock Exchange if I want to.* And my mom was like: *Leigh-Kathryn. What if the Stock Exchange sees that? Like they're gonna think you're so full of it*. And the Stock Exchange did see it and reposted it on every platform that they could and it was a reminder again of like: Be bold. Stand proud. Speak up if you need to.

And yes, I was pulling honey with, you know, over six feet massive like one of our strongest beekeepers today. He's moving two boxes for every one of my boxes. But at the end of this day, I could still do the work. It just might take me twice as long and I think that's something that's important for people to remember — that especially in agriculture, like, women can do the work. We're hard. And my uncle says, you know, when you try to get bees to do something, you can lead them in the right direction, but they're still going to make their own decision. No matter what. And my uncle, his response is: *Yes, because it's all women and they're going to do what they want to do, when they want to do it*. And I always appreciated that because it's true. You can try, you can try to tell a woman what to do. But at the end of the day she's gonna do what she wants to do. And the colony of 60,000 of them, they're really gonna do what they want to do. But there's a reason why honey bees have been around for millions of years and there's a reason why one of the most efficient and effective super structures that we have is female lead. There just is. I deeply believe that.

And women work together really well. Women understand what it means to be on a team really well. Women understand if you go to villages, remote villages in Africa — the Grameen Bank in Micro Financing, they finance 10 women to become beekeepers right and all 10 of them, they only get paid if all the hives are taken care of the right way. So one female beekeeper might end up becoming allergic and not able to take care of her hives. Well, these women say well our profit sharing needs to be for these hives. So we'll pick up the slack. Or you look at when they want to put wells into villages in Africa, if you ask the men — men want it as close to their house as possible.

If you ask women, they'll put it in a centralized place where it's easiest for children to get the water. And there is something to that that just, it translates in nature as well in a really beautiful way.

They're super high functioning. And we do say, you know, we teach a lot about how you build high performing teams — it's not that it needs to be all women on the team. [laughs] Not everything translates. But you do need a balance of it as well. And I think a lot of our corporations are trying to get there, but they're still not quite there yet. But I don't think it can be rushed either. If you put a woman in a position of power in a corporation because you need a woman in that seat and she's not ready — I personally think it does more harm than good, where a woman can drive the price of a sale of a company down if she's not qualified. So can a male who's not qualified. But if you're doing it to put a woman in the seat to say you put a woman in the seat and she's not ready it harms everyone.

Kelsey   Right.

Leigh-Kathryn   And again, just like in nature, like some things you can't rush them, but you can backfill things so that when it is time, you've got so many women ready and capable of taking the next step and becoming the CEOs and C-suites of these organizations. But if you rush it, just like in nature, it just — it doesn't work.

We're learning that with our team right now with all the managers. They all got promoted to managers because they're good at their jobs. But we failed them in teaching them how to manage and make sure that they were going to be good managers. And so they had really hard years last year because all of them did not have the skill set they needed to be a manager yet. They were great at their job and then all of a sudden they had to help other people be

	great at their job and make sure they were getting their jobs done and that was...We didn't set them up for success.
Kelsey	That's a very wonderful reflection though. And I think I agree there has to be a system and culture in place that allows for, like, women to succeed because if that is also not existing, it's not gonna work. That's that's just feeding them to a shark, unfortunately. But I also wanted to know if you could explain what a Journeyman beekeeper is and how that's different than like maybe other forms of beekeeping.
Leigh-Kathryn	Yes. So there are, all over the country, there's different levels of beekeeper. In North Carolina, you have: Certified, Journeyman, Master, Master Craftsmen.
Kelsey	Okay.
Leigh-Kathryn	North Carolina is one of the only states that has Master Craftsman. And you're like participating in research studies and writing papers and so it's a whole different level. There's like a handful of them in the country. There's not many. Journeyman is certified. You have to take a test, written and practical test to become certified. My role here is if you have a full-time job at Bee Downtown, I don't care what you do, you must take the introduction of beekeeping class and you need to become certified as a beekeeper because, no matter what people do on our team, they have to know bees to understand how to make decisions properly or talk to partners who are saying like: *What's going on with my bees?* They need to know what swarm season is and here's what happens when colonies swarm. And then you stay a certified beekeeper for a certain number of years. And you have to have a certain number of credits. Those are public speaking credits. They are volunteer credits. They are continued education credits. And then you can test for

Journeymen. And you test in front of a Master Board and you have a written test too, but you also have, like, a verbal test you have to do. There's eight sections you have to do for Journeyman. You have to pass five, I think. And then you have to be a Journeyman beekeeper for a certain number of years. Get all of your prerequisites done for Master. All of mine are done. I'm just too scared to take my test. [laughs]

Kelsey — I'm sure you would do incredible!

Leigh-Kathryn — Those tests are hard and they're not necessarily... it's the, like, academic knowledge versus the applied to knowledge.

Kelsey — Right.

Leigh-Kathryn — Like the academic knowledge is you know, this study that came out and you know, blah blah blah. And like: *What is the chemical compound in this medicine?* I know this medicine works and I do know the chemical that's the active ingredient, but I don't know why or like I don't know the specific date that this law was passed for beekeeping in the state.

But I know that I'm allowed to keep these in this area and how many hives because I've written the paperwork for it. Um, so that is where — it's like you start to lose some beekeepers where, you know, fantastic beekeepers that aren't Master Beekeepers. And you'll have not great beekeepers that are actually Master Beekeepers because they know how to test.

Kelsey — Right.

Leigh-Kathryn — Which is pretty interesting.

Kelsey   Yeah, I was going to ask if your grandfather and uncle, if they're on that scale at all.

Leigh-Kathryn   Yeah, so my uncle is I think he passed the first half of his Master and then he was like: *I'm not gonna finish.* Yeah, so he's like partially finished with his Master. And there's a lot of, like, old school beekeepers that got a little bit frustrated with the testing system and said like: *No, I've got more than enough knowledge. I don't need this so.*

I like competitions. I want the Masters, I want Master Craftsman. Why would I not? Like that's awesome. So Journeyman is where I'm at now. If I can muster up the courage to test, I will do that this fall. I keep saying it. I keep pushing it off and they happen in like six months intervals. [laughs]

Kelsey   Fall sounds good. I mean that's after the busy beekeeping season right?

Leigh-Kathryn   Exactly. I'll get there one day.

Kelsey   Is there a limit to how many times you can take the test?

Leigh-Kathryn   No.

Kelsey   There you go!

Leigh-Kathryn   It's one of those weird things though that I'm, like, I am young. I had to earn my place with the Beekeepers Association. I did. There's a lot of people at the beginning that we're like: *You're just gonna be like a blip on the radar and you're rocking the boat and you're trying to put bees on campuses. If you mess up, you're gonna mess this up for us to keep bees in cities.*

There was a good bit... Now given, they would hear: *Oh, you're Jerry Flanagan's niece.* And they'd say: *Okay.* And they'd, like, pause. But they pause on his reputation, not mine. And that took a while, but like we're here now and I've been fully embraced by so many amazing beekeepers and Beekeepers Associations across the country as: *Okay. They're here and they're here to stay and they're good beekeepers.* Because, again, when I started out, jeez. I wouldn't have given myself a second interview here. I'd be like: *Yo, this kid cannot keep bees. Absolutely not.* But it is nice that we have earned that.

But it's this weird thing for me because if I fail the Master test, I don't want people to think I don't know what I'm doing. And yeah, they're like: *Well, she's building this business. She can't even pass the Master Test, you know.*

Kelsey
Well, like you said — The Master test is like all of that textbook knowledge. And the textbook knowledge you were saying if someone could memorize all the things and you put them in the beehive and they don't know what to do in three minutes, you wouldn't hire them. So you would hire you and that's all that matters.

Leigh-Kathryn
That's fair. That's fair. It's that weird piece of it though. I think men are way more likely to say, like: *Oh, yeah, I'll get it wrong.* But women are like [whispering]: *I don't know if I'm gonna pass. They are gonna think I can't do it.* You know, it's weird like...

Kelsey
Oh I had a high school history teacher, and I always think of this, he always told the girls in the room, because we were all like 16: *When you take the like tests tomorrow, if you mark your answer don't change your mind. Just keep going because statistically girls are far more likely to change their mind*

and then second guess themselves and then choose the wrong answer because we're used to being told that we're wrong or to double think ourselves. So versus like men are and boys are better test takers.

Leigh-Kathryn   You're yeah, correct 100%. Yeah. [laughs]

Kelsey   So some of that institutional sexism just that's very infuriating. So I think even if you fail the test, you took it and that's great. So.

Leigh-Kathryn   Okay. Okay. I appreciate that.

Kelsey   [laughs] Not that I have anything to do with the test.

Leigh-Kathryn   I'm gonna do it this time. I will.

Kelsey   I'm sure you'll be great. Yeah, um. But I just wanted to know… I know I've taken up so much of your time, but is there anything else you want to speak to in relationship to care or food or making with bees?

Leigh-Kathryn   I think, just in regards to food, like I grew up in the South and that is what my family was built off of is food. Is cattle farm. My mom is like: *We're quite poor, but we ate well because we had a cattle farm.* And my whole life has been built around that because it was such a big part of my mother's life and my grandmother's and my great grandmothers' on both sides. My great grandmother on my dad's side, she and my great grandfather ran a bar for shift workers in Philly and she was up every day, like, you know 3am cooking and stayed up till almost midnight. Like she didn't sleep. My dad's like: *I don't know when she slept.* Like she must've slept under like a table to just, like, get a couple hours because she cared so much about providing food for the people that were getting off their shifts that she was just there constantly because she wanted to be able to have food.

And I deeply believe that food brings people together. The stories of food brings people together. Bees do that in a great way. You just have the ability to have that story. But all food does that. And care goes into cultivating it and growing it, but it also goes into how you prepare it and how you cook it and how you wash it and how you, you know, dry different things and can things and preserve things.

I have a friend who owns a farm, it's actually my husband's friend, and best corn I've ever had in my life. Like it is unreal. And they time out perfectly so that they're picking the majority of it the week of Fourth of July and they sell most of their corn on Fourth of July. And the first year he gave us two bushels of it. I mean just amazing corn and I did not take the time or have the care to blanch all of it and freeze it and bag it and freeze it — and a lot of that corn went to waste. Just soured so, so much faster than I thought it could. And the next year I told my husband: *Archie's gonna give us two more, I know he is. We're gonna go to buy one and he's gonna give us four. But we will not waste his food this year.* And having the care for that. And I think, as a farmer, one — I should have had more care the first go around and I still hate that I did that, but for everyone with food once you start to grow something, even a little something, you know tomatoes in a pot in your backyard. Once you realize how hard and how long it took to grow those tiny little freaking tomatoes, you're like: *I'm going to wash this. I'm not going to bruise it. I'm going to lay it. I'm going to cut it so carefully. I'm not going to, like, lose any of the juice or the seeds, and if I do I'm gonna, like, put it in a bowl and I'll figure out a way to use it.*

Like once you've done it, then you understand the importance of it.

Kelsey	Yeah.

Leigh-Kathryn	I think so. I don't know if that is on track with what you're, you're working on, but it's from start to finish. There's, there should be and there's the ability to have care in all of our food. And I think, you know, women especially in the South like that is, for so many of them, that's their legacy. *How do you bring your grandchildren to the table?* My grandmother when she first found out she was sick and she had dementia.

Kelsey	Oh, I'm so sorry.

Leigh-Kathryn	It was she you know, like she always cooked. I appreciate it. She always cooked. We always cooked. Yeah, she made a cake. Granny's chocolate cake. But when she got sick, she told me, she said: *I'm gonna teach you how to make my husband catchers.* And that was, like, what she wanted to teach me how to make. She wasn't gonna be here and so she's like: *Well, I need you to figure out how to catch a husband.* So I was like: *Okay, Granny.* Like: *Let's make husband catchers.* And she's like: *Great!* So we start cooking and all this stuff and I'm kind of looking around like: *Oh, Granny, what are we making?* She said: *Sug, I told you husband catchers!* And she said: *Cuz then you gon catch yourself a husband.* I was like: *Okay.* I said: *Granny, are these Hush Puppies?* She's like: *Mmm and if you can make 'em like I can make 'em, you're gonna catch a husband.* And she wanted me to learn how to make husband catchers and she wanted to pass on that, you know, knowledge.

And like recipe books, old southern like, they're such a special thing to have in your, like, family members' handwriting. But it's like it's... there's so much care that went into the food that was prepared by women for families for so many generations. And I think that that's a really special part of, as a storyteller, like... It's just... You can't... It comes with a feeling attached to it that makes you like happy and warm and fuzzy inside, you know. A meat, a carb, and a vegetable. Like that's a southern meal. Meat carb vegetable. That's all you —

Kelsey   That sounds delicious.

Leigh-Kathryn   [laughs]

Kelsey   And that's exactly what my work is about. I was inspired by a lot of cookbooks. And how I far rather read a cookbook that I've written in and spilled olive oil in and egg in —

Leigh-Kathryn   Oh, yeah.

Kelsey   — versus an instruction manual. Every time I have an instruction manual, I throw it away. I can't even read it. It stresses me out —

Leigh-Kathryn   Oh, yeah.

Kelsey   — how boring it is. But a recipe and the cookbook, especially one that was written by someone else or if I write like: *Oh, I made this for Christmas this year and it was really good.* Or: *Leave out all the vinegar. That is trash. Like, yeah do not do that.* That's far more interesting. It's a lot more human.

Leigh-Kathryn   Yup.

Kelsey   So all these cookbooks and recipes are often done by women and it's all this making with food and care. And so I just love all of that and I think it also speaks to the joyness that you were speaking about.

I have a baby and he's eating food now and, like, the joy he has with food. He just loves to play with food and eat the food. And it's like food is really fun. And I think we forget that like in addition to it being really nourishing and like caring for ourselves and for the food that makes it — there's just a lot of joy in it too. Yeah, when he gets to splash Greek yogurt everywhere. He loves that.

Leigh-Kathryn   It is like his favorite thing.

Kelsey   Yes. The best thing!

Leigh-Kathryn   I love that. We do something called Honey Camp that we built during COVID and people get to try — so there's over 300 types of modern floral honeys in the United States. They try three of them in Honey Camp. And we call it Honey Camp because it's meant to be fun. Like a wine tasting can be so serious. We wanted Honey Camp to be exciting for employees and in companies. So they get tasting wheels and color charts and they get to smell everything and taste everything and try to build the true profile together as a team. But it's fun because, most of the time, you say food is good or it needs salt or it's too salty. Like those are the three things. I like it. I don't like it. It needs more salt. It's too salty. Like that's typically, like, the area we stay in with food. But these wheels are fun and I always encourage people: *Keep them in your cabinets and your kitchen so that you can play the game with your family at night. Like what did I cook with tonight? What spices? What things?* Because it just, it trains your brain and it's challenging to your brain in a completely different way than anything else is. Like [whispering]: *What does paprika taste like? What does it smell like? Did you use paprika?*

	[speaking normally] *Like let me go let me go smell paprika. Let me smell the dish.* You know, like and really fun — super fun ways. So the tasting meals I think are a great way to help people learn to have fun with food.

Kelsey · And to take time with food too! Because, like you're saying, like we spend so much of our adult lives sitting and we don't, I think, we're just going through a lot of things really fast. So sometimes we eat really fast and so we don't have the time to enjoy the food. I do that all time. I was just watching my son eat you Greek yogurt for an hour and then I'm eating a bowl of pretzels in two minutes. Like: *Well, this is not good.*

Leigh-Kathryn · [laughs]

Kelsey · Yeah, but thank you so much for talking with me. This has been wonderful.

Grandma's apple and honey muffins

From the Children's book *The Beeman*, written by Laurie Krebs and Valeria Cis. Makes about 18 muffins.

Cook time: 18-20 min

Prep time: 15 min

Ready in: 40 min

Ingredients

2 cups sifted flour
3 teaspoon baking powder
1 teaspoon salt
½ teaspoon cinnamon
¼ teaspoon nutmeg
1 cup whole wheat or bran cereal flakes (or instant oatmeal)

¼ cup finely chopped walnuts (optional)
½ cup raisins
1 cup grated apple
2 eggs
⅔ cup honey
½ cup milk
¼ cup vegetable oil

Directions

1. Sift flour with baking powder, salt, and spices
2. Add cereal, walnuts, raisins, and apple
3. In a separate bowl, beat eggs well; add honey, milk, and oil
4. Add liquid mixture all at once to flour mixture, stirring just to blend
5. Grease muffin cups and fill ⅔ full. Bake at 400F for 18-20 minutes on the middle or top rack.

Leigh-Kathryn Bonner's easy honey garlic chicken

"The perfect meal to have when you feel like eating something sweet with a hint of savory!"

Prep time: 15 min

Cook time: 35 min

Ready in: 50 min

Ingredients

6 chicken thighs, bone-in or out with or without skin
⅓ cup honey
¼ cup water or chicken broth
6 cloves garlic, crushed
2 tablespoon rice wine vinegar, ACV or white vinegar

1 tablespoon soy sauce
2 teaspoon garlic powder, to season
Salt and pepper, to season
Parsley to garnish

Directions

For oven-baked, bone in thighs: Preheat oven at 400F or 200C. Sear chicken in a lightly greased pan skin-side down first for 3 min. Flip and sear for another 3 min. Bake in the oven for 20-25 min, until completely cooked. Continue directions starting at Step 3.

1. Season chicken with salt, pepper, and garlic powder. Set aside.

2. Heat a pan or skillet over medium high heat; sear chicken thigh filets or breast filets on both sides until golden and cooked through. This is about 6 min per side, depending on the thickness.

For bone-in thighs: reduce heat after searing on both sides. Cover skillet with lid and continue cooking until the chicken is cooked through, white turning every 5 minutes until done. Alternatively, see above note for oven method.

3. Drain most of the excess liquid from the pan, leaving about 2 tbsp of pan juice for added flavor.

For the sauce

4. Arrange cooked chicken skin-side up in the pan (if cooking with skin).

5. Reduce heat to prevent burning garlic and add crushed cloves between the chicken and saute until fragrant (about 30 seconds).

6. Add honey, water (or broth), vinegar, and soy sauce to the pan. Increase heat back up to medium-high and continue to cook until the sauce reduces down and thickens slightly (about 3-4 min).

7. Garnish with parsley and serve over vegetables, rice, pasta, or with a salad.

Bees. Photograph provided by Bee Downtown.

"'Cause for me, I'm trying to make biscuits like my grandma. That's exactly what I'm going for."

Andrew Gravens
Director of Operations at A Place at the Table

a chat with Maggie Kane and Andrew Gravens

Kelsey — So, Maggie, I saw that growing up you worked a lot with soup kitchens and you saw that there was a big deficit with food and making so I was just wondering what have you most learned, both of you learned, and working with food to foster community, to foster those relationships, and foster trust for all these things.

Maggie — Food's a tool. It's what we all share. It's what we have in common. When you said trust, it's what builds trust here. Our mission is: Community and good food for all, regardless of means. So using good food to create community by eating together, in having the tables like this so people can sit together or sit right next to each other, but also volunteering together. So creating space for people to do dishes together, to run food, and to build relationships. Food is kind of that thing that breaks down walls here and allows people to be together and and have that commonality — That common thing they're doing.

Andrew — Yeah, and I think it also connects people with their food when they're part of the preparation in some aspect. So here, not only do you eat the meal but then you may get up and go help clean up the meal, go help out with the dishes in the dish room. And it's very much like — It makes me think of Sundays at Grandma's where you went, larger than usual, maybe some cousins, maybe some people from church or whatever were there and you had this big meal and then afterwards everybody — People chipping in beforehand and most of the times those people chipping in beforehand are sitting afterwards and talking while the people that didn't chip in before are now cleaning up and taking everything to the room. And I think that's really what we do here, but it's inviting the entire community — Our entire, you know, extended family of

Raleigh in here to be a part of it with us. Just inviting everybody to, you know, Sunday supper.

Kelsey   Yeah, when I sat down I wrote: *In here it feels like a Christmas holiday kitchen where there's so many people in here and there's lots of people kind of commingling together.* So it feels that way.

Andrew   Top compliment. We had someone, less than month ago someone wrote on Google and they said: *This place feels like Mom's house.* Something like that. I was just like: *Wow.* Sometimes someone will eat like the biscuit or something and be like: *Oh, this reminds me of my grandma's food.* Top, that's top compliment. 'Cause for me, I'm trying to make biscuits like my grandma. That's exactly what I'm going for.

Personal photographs of A Place at the Table.

Personal photograph of A Place at the Table.

The Root Cellar Cafe & Catering

"And it's good in this town because there is a community. And I always tell people like: *This store is a restaurant and it's a community center.*"

Chef Sera Cuni
Chef and Co-Owner of The Root Cellar Cafe & Catering

Sera	I love this idea. I think it's a great idea.
Kelsey	Thank you.
Sera	So like my family revolved around food. So like that's where my stories came from as a kid. And then, you know, like a lot of families pass down recipes from generation to generation. And I feel like it's losing it's traction in the world because people are so stuck on social media things nowadays. Maybe my generation or maybe the next generation is not gonna pass on these — They're not gonna pass these things on anymore. We don't cook anymore. You know, like we grew up, we ate dinner together. We never had these like pre-made meals. We never went to fast food restaurants. That was like a treat. *Your father is out of town. Hey, we're gonna get you a McDonald's Happy Meal.* That kind of thing. And I think that a lot of times now that that is just gone by the wayside and kids eat in front of TVs and that's why I think it's really important to preserve those things.
Kelsey	And for you, so since you grew up with that, why do you think it's so important to preserve?
Sera	I mean, that's my family like the history and like that's the good times of my family. And like Thanksgiving's are big — Any holidays. Like we always had cookouts in the summer and all the neighbors would come. And it was always there's always food. Or anytime we had like anything, we always sat in the kitchen. Like still to this day, we sit in the kitchen —

Kelsey — That's the heart of the home.

Sera — Yeah. We sit around the kitchen table. I don't know why it is, but, you know, there's always something there. There's always snacks there. I just think that we need to get back to that.

Kelsey — Yeah, I think there's something really grounding in being around food. I think there's something so grounding like playing with food and making —

Sera — And growing your food or —

Kelsey — Yeah!

Sera — I've taken my niece and nephew to the Farmers Markets when they're with me. I'm like: *Okay, I gotta go to the Farmers Market to pick up produce. Do you wanna come with me?* And they're like: *Wait. This is where an apple comes from?* And I'm like: *Yeah, not Harris Teeter.* And they're like: *Can we have an apple?* I'm like: *Yeah, whatever.* They just are like: *Wow.*

I mean Farmers Markets weren't so big when I was a kid, but I grew up in part of Florida for a bit of my life and there's always fish people on the side of the road. Yeah, so my parents always bought that kind of thing.

But I just think that now everybody thinks it's from Harris Teeter or those kinds of places and they're like: *Oh, well I can get asparagus any time of the year.* But let's only eat it these three months out of the year.

Kelsey — In thinking of how you know, the farmers, the legacies, how they're all treated, all the animal products you are getting, everything that you're sourcing. Can you speak to the relationship between food, like making it and also seeking it out to make it, and the role of care?

Sera So I like to have that relationship with the farmers. I like them to say: *Hey, Sera. I know* — Because I change my menu in Pittsburgh every week. So, you know, there's a local meat farmer, pork and beef and chickens. And he'll be like: *Hey, Sera. I have a ton of pork cheeks that nobody's buying and they're in the freezer. It's like do you want this week?* I'm like: *Sure, like yeah.* He's like: *They've been frozen.* I'm like: *That's fine because you got to cook a long time.* But it's like I know that he had it. I know they were treated well. He *loves* those animals, you know. And then he's like: *Okay.* and I'll go and pick them up. You know, like I buy my sausage for breakfast every week from him. He's like: *I have so much because it's all the little trimmings, it's the easiest thing to turn them into.*

And it's just nice to know that here's this guy in my community. So my money is staying in the community, his money is staying in the community. So it's also helping our community, you know. And then he has a food truck that he serves, he makes food and it's all his food. So, you know. It's really nice that way. And it's nice them to say: *Hey* — Like this week. I was like, they bought a new fridge. I was like: *Dude, why did you buy a fridge? I have one sitting in storage. We could have made a trade. You know, like I would have given you the fridge if you wanted to give me like pork loin or something like that.* I was like: *Damnit.* Like that kind of thing.

I think that's what makes it nice, it makes it old time-y and like barter system. And it's nice that when somebody comes in it's like:

Oh, where did this pork come from?

Oh, Lillington! Like I see them on Thursdays at the Pittsboro Farmers Market.

Oh, we're gonna start going.

And then they buy there, you know, so it's like this whole like circle kind of thing.

Kelsey	And with community, I saw on y'all's website that you do like a lot of support for, like, trying to combat hunger and supporting local groups that support LGBT rights. And like can you speak to a little bit about that and like what it means to use food as a vehicle for community support?

Sera	So. We are supposedly in the greatest country in the world. In Chatham County one in eight are hungry. It's one in eight. They don't know where their next meal is coming from. That hits so hard for me that I am like: *That can't happen.* You know like that. So then I'm on a board that we're doing a pay-what-you-can restaurant, so kinda like the one in Raleigh.

Kelsey	A Place at the Table!

Sera	And there's one in Boone kinda like that. So that really speaks to me. Like I don't think anybody should not have a warm meal. I don't think anybody — You know, we give things when they get mac and cheese, when they get Ramen, they get stuff like that.

Kelsey	It's all one color on the plate and it's not —

Sera	I mean, I understand that it's food and it counts and they need nourishment. Whatever. It's so part of a human right to be able to sit down and eat dinner with somebody that they shouldn't have to worry. Kids should never have to worry about that. Um, so it really bothers me.

	I am in the process of starting a community fridge program for Chatham.[17] So it's kind of like those lending libraries but with food. And it's to also combat restaurant waste. Because we have a lot of waste. You know, we put soup out — At the end of the day if it doesn't sell, I can't do anything with it. It goes in trash or staff can take it home. But I can put it in a community fridge. I can't give it to the shelter because it's been out and it's not labeled and they're very particular now that it has to be like a package. But I can take it to my community fridge, put the major allergens on it, sell by date, and anybody can take it.
Kelsey	Oh, that's incredible.
Sera	Yeah, so I'm working on putting them throughout Chatham because we have such food deserts there in all the little towns. And then you have like a lot of the Latino population, they are too proud, you know, and they don't want people to know might not have enough. So these fridges are "come and go as you please." Like, let's say you forget your lunch and you're like: *Damn, I'm hungry today. You know, let's go see what is in the fridge.* There's ready-to-eat meals. They'll be frozen, you know. Like that kind of thing. Um, and I just — It just bothers me that you know, we live in this country that it's waste. Like...
Kelsey	And that's the norm too.
Sera	That's the norm and nobody thinks of it. You know, you go to Harris Teeter and it's, there's always "buy two, get six free" on things. I don't need 8 boxes of —

---

[17] To learn more: https://www.feedwellfridges.org/

Kelsey	It's like ice cream!
Sera	Whatever. So that could be another thing. I don't want people stocking the fridge, but it'll be like: Hey, you know, you bought at Harris Teeter and you bought this because you needed one ice cream. Here's the place, drop it off at the retailer, and I will put it in the fridge.
Kelsey	That's awesome.
Sera	You know. So that I don't have to worry about people doing it. And then obviously my wife and I really care about the LGBT community. You know, we did a Drag Brunch here. We did one in Pittsboro. We did — We were part of the Pittsboro Pride. So it's the first ever Pittsboro Pride in Pittsboro.
Kelsey	This past June? [2023]
Sera	This past June. We had over 750 people and it wasn't like people coming from Raleigh. It was people of the town. And there was a little boy that came up to my wife and he said to her: *I'm out! I'm out! My parents!* She was like in tears. He was in tears. And she's like: *I'm so happy because you had a safe place to come.* So it meant a lot to her, to the kids. It was really cool that way.
Kelsey	Aw, that's amazing!
Sera	Yeah, and there was little kids and little kids in dresses and there's dads with nail polish and makeup on and they're just really cool. And it meant a lot to

the community. So now we have planning already on next year. So the drag queen that we had at our Drag Brunch has already said: *Listen, I'll do one next year, you know for you guys at the drag, at the Pride.* Like we could do either a drag walk, something. Like she's like: *Yeah. Yeah, this is great. This is what needs to be because I grew up this way — All these things.* So it's really cool to see in such a rural, rural rural community that the community supported. I mean we do have [whispers] Confederate's, you know.

I think it makes it easier for the kids growing up in these towns. That they don't have access. Like yeah, Pittsboro's not far from Chapel Hill, but they don't really do that much here. Like there's no Pride Parade or anything. They do a few little things now, but, you know, you go to Raleigh. But now every — Like Apex has one and it's just really great for these kids. Like I didn't have it growing. And then I have friends who have like... I think he's eight or nine? And he has a Pride flag. He's like: *It's my pride flag!* And he knows it, but he doesn't know it. And like: *Why are you taking that away?* He's like: *It's got to stay up all the time.* He's just like a nine year old boy. He's like out of his flag.

Kelsey	I love that. It's incredible. It's exciting to see like that's the generation that's coming up.
Sera	Hopefully.
Kelsey	I... love it so much. Amazing.
Sera	Yeah, that there is no he her. It's just people. I mean in *Star Trek*, Captain Kirk, like they don't — They're just, they're just humans or they're earthlings or whatever. Like why do we have to have all these things?

Kelsey	Absolutely. And so it's great to see how saturated y'all are in the community — And also like the in and out process of everything. And so what do you think is like the power and capacity of like food and community and like making with food learning with food and care?
Sera	Um, I think we have to teach the younger kids about food, you know. Like they're so used to just boxed food or chicken nuggets. You know? I mean I have a niece and nephew and they, they love to bake and they love to make food with us. They'll come to the restaurant and I'll be like: *What do you guys want to do?* They'll come and stay and I'll be like: *Okay, let's go. Let's go make something.*

So they'll be like: *Can we do this?* I'd be like: *Okay, but we're gonna start from here. We're gonna go to here.* You know, like it's hard to show them and I'll show them like: *Hey, when I was little kid, this is what your daddy and I used to do.* And we'll do that kind of thing and then we'll just kind of keep going and then I'm hoping those things, like as they have families, they're like: *Hey, I used to do this my aunt. Oh, let's do that.*

I'm kinda lucky with them because they're growing up in this — Like they come to the restaurant. They hang out in the kitchen. They think it's theirs. Like we bought them aprons and it's just really cute to have them. And oh they're always willing. Like they'll be like: *What is that?* Like they'll see me cooking a little bit. I was like: *Oh, it's, you know, trout. Would you like to try it?* Okay. And they'll be like: *Can we help?* And I was like: *Yes.* So they come and stand and I was like: *Okay, but remember it's hot.* It's in the middle of service. And they'll be like: *Okay.* So I'll cook them a piece and he's like, my nephew's like: *Don't put black pepper on it.* Okay so we put salt on it. And he'll try. He'll tell me: *No, I don't like it.* Or: *Okay, it's good.* And that's the only way they're gonna learn. Like I feel like we're so used to making kids happy. Like: *Here's your chicken nuggets. Here's your Mac and Cheese.*

        I mean I sat at a kitchen table for hours until I finished my food.

Kelsey   Yes, we were not allowed to leave the table until our plate was cleared.

Sera   And I didn't get a special meal.

Kelsey   No. And we had to help clean up. But that's amazing that you're so involved and it's because we learn better — I'm thinking a lot in traditional teaching models, you have a kid at a desk with a piece of paper writing down things and like just being fed information that they have to memorize. But like so where you have your family in the kitchen and they're like watching you and they're tasting and they're like helping like that's such a more enriching way to learn.

Sera   Well also because this is how they do things now. They don't comprehend and they have that goldfish, 30 second thing. They sit there and they write and write, they don't — They might just memorize it, but they don't understand it. But when you sit there and you show them something like: *This is how you make a muffin.* Like: *It's egg and it's milk. And then you take it and froth.* And then they're like: *Wow, that's really cool.* We're just like, I mean — Even science things. Like, you know, like we grew up making volcanoes and all those kinds of things and these kids they don't. They learn how to do, I don't even know what, from YouTube.

Kelsey   [laughs]

Sera   Because I don't like it. But they're really like, when you give them a hands-on thing — Like my niece wanted to make cupcakes. So we made cupcakes. It took us, you know, six hours, but you know, she started it to finish it. She was proud of her cupcakes. I just think that the more we show everybody how things are made and like *why* we do this — Otherwise restaurants are all gonna be fast food restaurants, you know?

Like I was at Wake Tech a couple weeks ago doing a competition and I was talking to the chef instructor and I said: *Oh, you know, how it's — How's it going? How're students?* And she said: *I have four.*

What?

I have four students this year.

I'm like: *You have four?*

She's like: *Yeah. I don't know what's gonna happen to your industry, but nobody wants to do this anymore.*

So nobody wants to do this anymore. We're gonna run out of these independent restaurants. We're gonna get all the Chili's, MacDonald. It's: *Here's your burger patty out of a box, frozen. Put it on the grill.* You know, like: *Here's your whatever. Okay, put it in. Put it in the microwave. There you go.* Like we're gonna run out of these things because they don't want to do it anymore. You know, just like farming — There's no young farmers. We need more young farmers. Farmers are so old we're gonna lose 'em.

Kelsey	Yeah, and it's like every possible obstacle that they could put in front of farmers is there. So like our family — The state of New York is starting to switch to electrical vehicles, which in theory very good, will be very hard for farmers. Right?

Sera	So what happened?
Kelsey	I'm not sure if their tractors have to be adjusted. My mom was stressing out for them. So.
Sera	What's the year that has to change?
Kelsey	I think she would know better than I do. I think it's not immediate, they have several years.
Sera	It's like California is like 2030.
Kelsey	Yeah, but it's like on paper: *That sounds great.* Like this would be so good for the planet. The planet desperately needs love and care and that is one way to do it, but it's like... for me it's —
Sera	COVID was so good for the planet. Like we stopped driving, we stopped doing things.
Kelsey	People stopped littering
Sera	Yeah! Except for the masks.
Kelsey	But thinking of my dad — So when they left New York and everything, he joined the military. And a lot of military towns have only restaurants that are those big chains, like Chili's, Logan's, Outback because it's like you can find them anywhere. So like no one wants to go to a small, independent

restaurant because they're like: *This isn't what I have in my hometown, Ohio.* And it's always really sad because it's just a void of any kind of character, personality, or community. So like here [pointed to The Root Cellar] like it's so deeply enriched in the community and like you're so saturated community and like Logan's is not doing anything for the community.

Sera Yeah. I might give to the local soccer team that's, you know, like sponsors a little soccer team that's here. Like that kind of thing and then maybe someday like my son would play for some local soccer team, like that kind of thing. Like TGIFridays doesn't care. They're making their money. They might put it on there because they're told they have to. But we as independents, we're like: *We need to support them because they're gonna support us.* You have Roots on the back of your shirt because you just played and the parents are like: *Come on. It's time to go have lunch after the game. Let's all go to there.* That's what — It's all about the community.

[people laughing in the restaurant]

And it's good in this town because there is a community. And I always tell people like: *This store is a restaurant and it's a community center.* Like there's a meeting right there.

Kelsey Yeah, I saw that.

Sera When UNC is in session, we'll have like School of Social Work sittin' over here having a meeting. We have School Government over there having a meeting. And you know, like the police chief eats here on Thursdays with one of his officers every Thursday. Like it just one of those things that it's like nice, you know.

But in big places or places that don't have that, nobody's gonna know that's the police chief eating dinner. They don't care. But here I'm like: *Chief Blue, how you doing?* He's like: *I'm good. How are you? I saw this about you.* It's nice that it's so community-based. And I'm worried that we're all are gonna lose that because we go to places that nobody cares.

Kelsey | That's making me wonder, too, because like if food preparation is historically feminized, like how much of like the responsibility of maintaining community is also.

Sera | But also, it's so, you know women traditionally cooked in the house for, you know, like families. But there's no women in the profession. Like we don't get that, we don't get gratitude and all that for being in the restaurant.

Kelsey | Why do you think that is?

Sera | I think it's just that you know, it's everything is male-based, you know. Like everything. Like there's, you know, your mother might have cooked for the family down the street and then you know this and this and this. And then like so, you know, my grandmother might have done this and I'm like: *Well, I'm gonna be a chef.* And they're like: *Why?* You know, like I went — One of my first jobs I went and I interviewed, I was out of college, hadn't even gone to culinary school. And I said: *I want to do this.* I had worked in a pizza restaurant making pizza so it wasn't like I didn't know anything. And he's like: *Well, I would hire you, but you're never working in the kitchen. You could be a waitress.* And I was like: *I don't want to be a waitress.* He's like: *Well, no woman's ever gonna work in my kitchen.* I was like: *Well, this woman is not working for you.* And I left. But like that was 30 years ago, and I'm still telling the story.

Like I'm a big proponent of teaching women. In Pittsboro, I have two — an 18 year old and 17 year old girl that I have trained to work on the line. Like, you know, they're high schoolers. But they show up and they've watched *The Bear* and they're like [serious voice]: *Yes, Chef*. I'm like —

Kelsey [laughs]

Sera It's adorably cute. It's horribly annoying because they have to have an emotion board. So when they get told something and they aren't happy they go over on the emotion board.

But like I taught them to do this and I'm like: *Guys. You might want to do this, you might want to do this in your life and you go and do it, but with these skills you can go anywhere and pick up a job*. Like one of them, she doesn't know what she wants to do. She graduated high school. She's like: *I'm just gonna be here*. I keep showing her things and I'm like: *Listen. If you want to go live in a van like you want to and travel the world, you can roll up to any town and be like, "I can cook. I can do that."* Because she'll cook brunch with me and like she took on to cooking eggs. Not everybody can cook eggs.

Kelsey Yeah, I cannot.

Sera Yeah, and she cooked — She took it on and she figured it out and I'm like: *This skill right here can get you a job anywhere*. Because nobody wants it and they'll pay you for it. She's like: *Really?* And I was like: *Yes*. So she's like: *Oh, okay*. And I'm like: *Go to the community college and take the culinary classes. Like go. I'll pay for them*. You know, like I will pay for them because you're, *you're helping yourself, but you're helping me.*

So, you know, like those two have been great. And I think the problem is women in kitchens, they either go on and become pastry chefs or they're like a bitch. Like guys don't want to work for them, you know. Like that kind of thing. But I think it's changing now. Like because more women are entering it and more women are like: *I'm gonna be a line cook. I don't wanna be a pastry chef. I want to cook on a line and that kind of stuff.* So I'm hoping that as things change and guys learn that they can't treat people the way they do — And women who treat people the same — That it will get better as long as people still go into it.

Kelsey	My mom always loved Rachel Ray — But I remember something about Rachel Ray was that she always said like: *I'm not a chef, I'm just a cook.* I remember thinking like: *Oh, because men see themselves chefs and women will most often see themselves as cooks.*
Sera	Yes, and they need to say: *No, I am a chef.* You know, it's like some people who get like doctorates. They're like: *Well, I'm not really a doctor.* No, you have the PHD.
Kelsey	So say you are a doctor.
Sera	Say you are a doctor.
Kelsey	Stop discrediting yourself.
Sera	But a man is always like: *I'm a doctor!*

Kelsey	I think of how a lot of making stuff that women do is called crafting.
Sera	Yes.
Kelsey	And a lot of making that men do is called engineering.
Sera	Yeah. Yes. Totally.
Kelsey	One makes a lot of money. The other one makes no money.
Sera	And stays home. And so my good friend, she's Indian and she was born in India and her parents moved here and her mother cooks, like every dinner, everything like that. To my friend, I'm like: *Do you know how to make the food?* She's like: *No, my mom… No.* I'm like: *Well, you need to learn. Like go watch your mom.* She's like: *Yeah, but she doesn't write anything down.* I was like —
Kelsey	Go write it down.
Sera	*Then record her.* I was like: *Can I go?* She's like: *She'd probably love to have you.* But it's so funny like, you know, her mom cooked all this stuff and like she doesn't know how to do it. And I'm like: *But you need to know how to do this for your child. Like someday Sophia's gonna come to you and be like: "Mommy, how did we make grandma's, you know, butter chicken?"* And she's gonna be like: *Uh…. Let's look up a recipe.* I was like: *Get your mother's*

recipe!

You know, I have books like my grandmother would write recipes. You know, one side of my family is Italian so they're always very good about, you know, making sure everybody knows how to do everything. And my grandfather was a president of an Italian American Club, so they would put out a cookbook. So this cookbook I found moving. I found it all dirty and stuff. So I scan into my phone. I scanned every page. And then I printed it so that my aunt could have it and everything like that. But it has, it'll say things like: *Don't use this, don't use it.* Like my grandmother would write: *Don't use this. This was Eleanor's recipe and it doesn't work.* But it's so great.

Kelsey   And it's so much better than a manual!

Sera   Yes!

Kelsey   And I love seeing like olive oil —

Sera   Oh my god, it's so dirty! Even like my scans have like the coffee stain on the cover and everything like that. But eventually that paper is going to deteriorate. And I have it now. And my grandmother, my mom's mother, wrote everything on those little index cards. So I've been scanning all those in because, like, eventually I want to write a cookbook. And I've been working on it forever, but I'm not very organized... But I have them all like written down, but you have to have pictures and I'm taking classes and they're like: *You have to have a picture with everything you submit so that we can see what the cookbook could look like and everything like that.*

But like the whole idea of the name Root Cellar was to take — like this used to be Foster's Market. We just take her root, my family's roots, my wife's family — Like the whole idea of roots.

So it's like that is like my idea of a cookbook like I have all these little cards that are weird like... something you might not eat, but you ate in like the 30s, but things are coming back. It's coming back because people my age are like: *Wow, I remember this.*

Kelsey — Yeah, it's nostalgic.

Sera — So I just think that we can't lose those things. We're so stuck on the *new* trend, that maybe let's go back to some of the older things. Like fried chicken has been around forever. It ain't going nowhere.

Kelsey — It's so good.

Sera — And it's so good. Let's stop making it so fancy. You know, like all of those things that we need to make readily available and not cheap: *Oh, I went to that place and got it.* You know that like, things — We need to see those things in finer dining versus at just like a mom and pop or something.

But I know that it's there and there's a small amount of people preserving those things. So I have faith that we won't lose all those things.

Kelsey — Because those are things that matter too. Like, that's the stuff that matters — the legacies.

Sera — I use my wife's great, great aunt's Chow Chow recipe, but I've changed it a little and made it mine. But her family, and they're Southern, so, you know... Like I changed it and I asked — Like they did not want to give it to me for the longest and finally did. I've changed it to my own so that I'm not — But they're like: *Ohh.* Because she's been gone for so long and nobody was doing it. So, you know every summer I make a bunch of it like give it to her and then she gives it to her mom and her mom like gives it to the rest. And it's like: *Wow, it wasn't — She wasn't stealing something. She was doing it to preserve something.* You know?

Kelsey   It's cool to think of food as like preservation and recipes as preservation.

Sera   Yeah! I mean that's my fondest memories going up, were with food. Like eating something or doing something or going somewhere with food. I mean, still to this day, when we go on vacation I make my wife go to grocery stores. So you go to Seattle and I'm like: *Wanna go see this grocery store?* Or: *What days are the farmers market?* You know, we like always look for those things. Because something in another place or another country, they might still be doing it that way, whereas we have gone on and never look back to those things. I mean, I bring food home. Like that's my thing.

And everybody's always like: *Well, what kind of food do you cook?*

I was like: *Well, I cook American.*

What do you mean by that?

I was like: *American is Chinese. American is Korean. American is, you know, Filipino. Like that's American food.*

And they're like — Because there was, you know, New American, which was like beef and I'm like: *No. Now American is like this melting pot of everything. Because if I wanted to make American food, it would be Native American. Like that's the traditional American food.*

And they're like: *Uhh.*

So it makes people think. Like American food is not hot dogs and hamburgers, like it's Americana. It's not America.

I mean if you look at it, like we're trending Mexican like and all this stuff. Like that's American food now. It's not... Like when I was a little kid all we had was Taco Bell as Mexican, you know? But now you have 52 million individual Mexican foods — And that's what American food is now.

I think that's also where it has to change.

Kelsey	Yeah, across... beyond food, too.
Sera	If you want to say you're an American, then you must be Native American because that's the only way you were here. We all came on a ship sometime. And I don't think until that changes, that American will not change. But I feel like given the younger and younger and younger, they don't see it as that. Like animals don't have a nationality, like they go past borders without anything. Like birds fly. And so eventually that happens to us, too.

Well-Fed Community Garden

I visited the Well Fed Community Garden on Athens Drive in Raleigh, North Carolina in July. It was hot, but it was prime season for the 1.5 acre garden. I brought my mom and my son, who walked around the garden exploring during my chat with Lilias Pettit-Scott. Lilias runs the business and community space, which first took root in 2012 when it originally grew produce for Irregardless, a local restaurant, and has since transitioned to focusing on its surrounding community.

Now the garden relies on care, including that from Lilias, students, apprentices, and volunteers who offer and craft a hands-on connectedness to the space. In doing so, Lilias has seen how care grows — there's a cyclical effect between care and growth, where one expands, as does the other. They necessarily ebb and flow into each other. One asks "What does the flower need?" more than one might wonder: "What do I need from the flower?" And in doing so, care is directed towards that which is environmental and put into a position of giving (and receiving) through problem solving, exploration, and design. Moreover, Lilias has been able to teach how to share, make, and nourish others through the value and interest in food

Moreover, the garden explores how to "share the harvest" — how to share the bounty of the produce, crops, flowers, lessons learned. 20% of crops are donated back to the community, whereas those that are sold go back to supporting the operation of the garden.

If we could have such a garden in every neighborhood, we could perhaps find ourselves better connected to food and the Earth, alongside the boundless benefits of curiosity in learning.

Personal photographs of the Well Fed Community Garden.

Personal photograph of the Well Fed Community Garden.

Personal photograph of the Well Fed Community Garden.

Personal photograph of the Well Fed Community Garden.

Personal photograph of the Well Fed Community Garden.

Personal photographs of the Well Fed Community Garden.

Personal photograph of the Well Fed Community Garden.

Personal photograph of the Well Fed Community Garden.

Personal photographs of the Well Fed Community Garden.

Personal photographs of the Well Fed Community Garden.

Personal photograph of the Well Fed Community Garden.

Microbiomes and the science we eat

"The idea that there is this commonality and potential for community around food. And that hopefully also could provide a way to empower people instead of estranging them around science."

Dr. Erin McKenney
Researcher and Professor

Photograph of Dr. Erin McKenney. Photograph provided by Dr. Erin McKenney.

a conversation with Dr. Erin McKenney

Kelsey — Well, first things first. In my brain you are a sourdough scientist. Would you agree with that? Or how do you describe what you do and who you are?

Erin — I identify as a microbial-ecologist. Mostly in guts. So the sourdough and anything else fermented foods I did in my postdoc with Rob Dunn, which was amazing and very rewarding. And it's the perfect conduit and framework for citizen science and outreach because it's countertop science, right? Flour and water and a spoon are generally much more accessible than like sequencing materials or any guts and poop. I cannot take into classrooms. Right? So it's awesome to like — There's also a social equity side of it that like while we are mixing these basic food ingredients that are safe, we are also preparing something that can feed a child and their family. But that's amazing. Right? And what if, you know — So if we teach kids how to make sauerkraut and cabbage is like, what, 79 cents a pound or something? That's awesome. And if you ferment it, you get more nutritional bank for buck. So to me, it's like very heavy layered —

But as far as like how I identify: as an ecologist, a microbial-ecologist, mostly as a gut microbial-ecologist. But I do also love sourdough and fermented foods.

I just, as a tenure-track teaching faculty, I don't have a research lab — Like I don't have a lab. So most of my publications and research these days are collaborative projects and they do tend to be more guts. But I do still get invited to the International Bread Symposium at Johnson & Wales — Like every two years when they have it, they bring me in. And I just did the Asheville Bread Festival with Jennifer Lapidus[18] and that was the weekend of Earth Day.

---

[18] Jennifer is the founder and principal of Carolina Ground Flour Mill in Asheville, North Carolina.

Kelsey	Aw, that's so cool.
Erin	My partner described it — He's like: *It's like they've latched onto you as a celebrity scientist.* And I'm like: *Yeah, I know.* And it feels so bizarre because, you know, in the academic space, I'm an educator. I do research on the side, but it's like it's kind of a fringy fit of overlap. You know? Yeah, I'm like queer in my personal and professional lives, you know? In that it doesn't quite fit. Yeah, and I have no boundaries. So. [laughs]
Kelsey	I love that. That's awesome. So like how does that — So you do all of this outreach work and then you focus on a lot of different things, and you're a celebrity scientist. How does that then relate to being a teacher at NC State? Like —
Erin	Yeah, I was just thinking about this yesterday, because I'm reading this book for this workshop I'm doing next week on story collider and like how we as educators can tell stories.
	So I'm reading a book written by The Moth. It's like: *How to Tell a Story.* And they have all these like insert boxes or like different applications of stories. Like: *On the job, how do you, when you get asked about your CV or your job experience?* It's like, that is a story with a narrative arch if you take time to reflect on: *What did I get from each different position? And how did that position me for my next move?*
	So I was thinking about that like: *Oh, right. Okay. I was a pre-vet hopeful in undergrad. I did not get that.* I did go to Disney's Animal Kingdom for a six-month internship where I learned about gut microbes and nutrition and how we cobble together captive care and management for animals that do not live here or eat local foods, right? How do you translate what is locally or

commercially available into a diet that supports this creature that is not from round here? So that's when I like discovered about gut microbes. And then I came to NC State for a masters. Was doing the old school sanger sequencing in Colonel Libraries during that summer of research when I was collecting most of my data. That's when like next gen sequencing hit.

So then I'm like: *I want to keep doing stuff with gut microbes.* I love the idea of these processes and how do things change and like the very broad comparative realm. Like, I'm gesturing at you a little bit hand wavy because it's big, busy systems. And I love looking for patterns in that noise. So I got a PhD at Duke studying gut microbial succession — Like after birth, from birth to weaning, which is hugely relevant, like as a mother with a young child, right?

Kelsey	Yes.
Erin	I think a lot about like: *What are the foods that I will introduce first?* You know?
Kelsey	Yes! It's so fun!
Erin	And it's like feeding the microbiome. And then I'm like: *Your poops! I'm so proud. They are so beautiful.*
Kelsey	[laughs] It's like: *Wow, good job.*
Erin	Such a good job.
Kelsey	And some yogurt and chia seeds, and it's like: Good job, little buddy. I bet you feel better.

Erin	Yeah. And they eat diverse whole foods. Um, and then trying to balance that philosophically — We're diverging out. |//

Erin: Yeah. And they eat diverse whole foods. Um, and then trying to balance that philosophically — We're diverging out.

Trying to like balance that philosophically with like: *We do live in a world that is fraught with empty calories and processed foods.* And as a person who struggled and still struggles with like the hoard and binge tendencies. It's like processed or junk foods were not available or an option for me. It's like: *Oh, you will find a way.* And if you don't have a supported structured environment to practice responsible intake, then, you know, you're just gonna continue with the binge and board. So it's like, you know, we do treats. We have processed foods at home. It's like: *I want you to know how to navigate diverse nutritional landscapes including the junk.* And we have conversations with our four year old about real food and, you know, and she knows about nutrients, like: *Why do we need protein? Why do we need vegetables and fruits?* You know? She called me on it the other day because I said something about cucumber is a vegetable. And she was just like: *No it is not. It's a fruit because it has seeds.* I'm like: *You are correct. You are correct. I was botanically inaccurate.* And it's like: *What a little nerd.* [laughs]

Kelsey: That's so cute.

Erin: She knows. *I would like to eat —* Whatever she requests like spinach or brussels sprouts or whatever. Last 4th of July we made kimchi to celebrate.

Kelsey: Amazing.

Erin: So all that to say it's like there's this philosophical debate that, you know, and gut microbiomes in those thought processes and ecological processes kind of underpin so much of what I consider for myself in my lifestyle. Like: *How do I burn the candle at both ends and not feel like total crap?* I don't drink alcohol or like an ounce at a time, right? And I try not to eat too much of the junk. Or when I do I'm like: *Okay, I know this comes with the risk and I probably won't eat it after a whole meal or something.* You know? It's like: *What are those things that induce the haze of mental fog?* And trying to look for those. And knowing about the microbiome, it's like: *Oh, right. I get it. These macronutrients are causing this metabolic cascade inside of me all by themselves and they are favoring the growth of microbes that are not anti-inflammatory or that are more opportunistic or are more likely to potentially make me sick if I have an illness.*

Yeah, so like yeah. So anyway. PhD. Lemurs. Thinking about these complex processes. And then got a postdoc working with Rob Dunn. I did a lot of training in grad school on how to teach because every summer of my PhD, from 2011 to 2016, I was teaching at the North Carolina Governor School. So I taught natural science. I was the lead instructor for like — I was the department head in my summer life. As a grad student. Like super bizarre.

I taught a lot of seminars, which are interdisciplinary. And I did the tie-dye thing.

So I was teaching in the summers and that was great. There are no strings attached, right? It's not part of the public school standardized system. It was like: *Okay, great. Congratulations. You're hired. Make a class. No assessments. It can be whatever you want to do.* And I'm like: *Cool. What are all of my favorite things from undergrad through masters that I learned about?*

For me, it's like this holistic, like broadly it's evolution in ecology, but it's stories from how are our bodies built — And what are the variations on that general plan to, you know, including like skeletal systems, but also the gut, to what communities of creatures do we tend, you know, like animals and plants, do we tend to see in different habitats?

Just thinking about the world around you and why it is that way. It's all in response to distinct evolutionary environmental pressures, right?

Yeah, a bunch of thinking. And it became more and more microbial as we went. Especially then as a postdoc with Rob. So he was looking for somebody to kind of take Julia Stevens' place. She got a job with Monsanto and she had been on the Sourdough for Science Project, I'm pretty sure. And the Sourdough Project hadn't totally gotten off the ground yet because there's so much pilot work with, like, having people from 17 countries and 4 continents around the world send their starters in the mail to Tufts University. [laughs]

Kelsey   That's so cool though.

Erin   So they did pilots and all this stuff. And they were collecting for like a year or two. And then all the sequencing and culturing started. So he needed somebody there and he — I still sit with a little bit of tension or discomfort just around like rolling into a project because he would say: *Oh, this is Erin. She leads the Sourdough Project.* I'm like: *Woah, woah, woah. I joined your lab in 2017.* But people, like, came up with the idea and actually started piloting things in 2016. And like I am not the only lead — Like all the data production took place at Tufts University. That's all Liz Landis. And then Angela Olivero is the one who analyzed the most of the sequencing data and you know, like she and Liz are the co-first authors on the paper. I don't feel like I lead anything.

I had the idea of, like, where all the pieces were and I tried to, you know — I organized our Sourdough Summits so that we can all come together from these diverse places. Angela is at UC Boulder. And, you know, so we're coming from all over so that we could talk through like: *How do we even muddle through these data?* It took us three 10 hour days to wrangle just the participants survey data into a format that was consistent, cohesive, and that R would read.

Kelsey   That's a lot of work.

Erin   It was so much.

Kelsey   I feel like you're incredibly humble.

Erin   Well, but like, did I lead that? No. You know? I got to be — For me it was like this incredible opportunity to be one person on an all woman group of researchers. I mean the PIs[19] are men. It's certifiable. [laughs] The PIs are all men. All of the researchers who actually, you know, like the boots on the ground like were women.

Kelsey   That's amazing.

Erin   It was like: *Wow.* We had never had that opportunity before. We were all like: This is what our bosses feel like all the time, if they even notice it.

Kelsey   They probably, a hundred percent, do not notice.

Erin   Right. It always feels like such a gift to be in a space of women.

Kelsey   Yeah, especially in science like because I'm more in CHASS and it's, like, very common — My background is in English education and most teachers are usually, and most predominantly in the same North Carolina, white women. And so if you have like one male in your classroom, like: *Wow, this is noteworthy.* So

---

[19] Primary Investigator

but then everywhere else on NC State's campus is the inverse of that. My husband was in the College of Engineering — He said in a seminar 200 people there would be one woman and he said like he couldn't imagine how uncomfortable it is. So that's amazing that you had a team of all women.

Erin

Yeah, it was. It was awesome. It was a very complex system and it was really a chance to think about the microbial aspect for sure. Like: *Why does a sourdough do what it does?* And I'm thinking: *Oh my God, it's acidic. It's a simple microbiome. This is a stomach in a jar. That's really cool.* And at some point Rob said like: *Nobody thinks like a sourdough like you.* And I'm like: *Oh, interesting.* Well, I'm a universal empath. Like I love people but if it's alive, there's a chance I can relate to it. Like it just makes sense to me.

So, like what does that community want? What do each of the microbial players in that community want? They just want to live. And if we provide enough nutrients or, you know, complexity then there's space, niche space for everybody. But like if there are limitations, that's when we start to get more toward opportunistic competitive microbes and that's a lot of what's in a sourdough. Yeah, it's really really fun to me to think through those dynamics.

But it's also with sourdough. Especially in the context of Students Discovered Grant, which was engaging with the public with citizen scientists to amass these huge data sets to answer a scientific question, but then there was the added level to translate and return the results or translate and return the question and methods to the public in the form of teaching modules aimed for middle schools.

Kelsey

I love that.

Erin

So that's where Sourdough for Science came from. And then someone drafted the first version of Grow Your Own Starter using the King Arthur instructions online. So I partnered with — I kind of refined that and partnered with Boulted Bread because they have their own mill. So Josh Bellamy[20] gave me like 10 different flours that were milled on site at Boulted. And at first I piloted it at Exploris Middle School — And thank goodness because they're a charter school. So they have more flexibility. So when those quart-sized jars overflowed and they have a huge mess to clean up, anybody else would have just thrown everything away because they have to get on to the next thing. They cleaned it up. They emailed me and we talked about: *Okay, how do we, how do we fix this?* And so I scaled it down. Because it was also a realization like: *A quart-sized jar? If you're feeding that starter a cup a day, that's a five pound bag of flour for a starter. That's a lot of money.* So it's like: *How small can we make this where it's feasible and reasonable and that it is still charismatic?* Also, like a quart-sized jar is really tough for spoons to reach. And for small hands.

So I went to half pint and started it. That's why it's two tablespoons of water, two tablespoons of flour to start.

Kelsey   That's the entire starter?

Erin   To begin with. On the first day. The next day you measure it, you know, you measure the height. You smell it. You mix it up. You measure the ph. Then you scoop out a tablespoon. Right, so that backslop. Then you add one tablespoon of flour and one tablespoon of water. Do it again for 10 or 14 days. That requires like a rounded cup of flour for 10 to 14 days. So a five pound bag can do, what? How many cups of flour in a five pound bag of flour, you know? A dozen?

---

[20] Co-owner and co-founder of Boulted Bread in Raleigh, NC.

Kelsey   Maybe?

Erin   Something?

Kelsey   That sounds right.

Erin   I should know this.

Kelsey   [laughs]

Erin   So it made it so much more feasible and accessible.

Kelsey   And that goes back to like what you were saying at the beginning with the equity issue too —

Erin   Right.

Kelsey   Because when you were saying how you weren't exposed to a lot of processed foods and I was thinking like my mom's a teacher and her students, a lot of them get the school based lunch and I just I've gone with her school and everything on the tray is just a shade of light brown, like applesauce, the bread, the corn, the chicken. Like everything is brown. So then they gravitate towards the more sugary thing, right?

Erin   The Green Jell-O.

Kelsey   Yes, and then it's also like those things are often — Green Jell-O is far less expensive than buying a bag of apples.

Erin	Yes.
Kelsey	That's really frustrating. It's like systematically it's not designed with equity in mind. And so I think it's really amazing that the Sourdough Starting project, it just lends itself to that.
Erin	And it's an option at the end, they can take it home. And I always give out recipes and I actually scaled the recipe — Worked with another citizen scientist baker in Chapel Hill or Carrboro? You know, we're emailing for a while and he said: *You know, do you have a recipe? I just want small buns. Like a small loaf.* And so I ended up working with him to, like, scale stuff down for that one tablespoon of backslop. How much flour and water would you need?
Kelsey	To make, like, one bun?
Erin	Yeah. Because he wanted to bake like one roll for his sandwich at lunch and I'm like: *That's really it and you could actually do this every day with your backslop and see it is rock cake on the first four, five or ten days — that way you're not like baking a whole big loaf of bread that's a huge disappointment and a waste of material.*
Kelsey	Yeah, but it's a big time endeavor too.
Erin	But if you wanted, you could take a little bun. If it fails, that's okay. Pitch it into the garden.
Kelsey	I found making a sourdough giant loaf very stressful and then I remember thinking: *The bread can tell I'm stressed. So now it's gonna be stressed bread.*

So a stressed bun... I feel like that'd be fantastic.

Erin — It's low stakes. So we called it Tiny Loaves for Little Hands. And we actually released that through 4H, because it was like a big 4H push to do sourdough with everybody. And that was really fun because then it's like: *Yes, and now it's all scaled to be your size.*

My elementary school's Montessori. So I'm not an expert on Montessori philosophy, but I am a fan of, like, follow the child and make things accessible so you learn how to navigate the world. Right? So, like, that's what we try to do at our house. And making this sourdough accessible, like, you don't have to be an expert baker. Because I didn't ever really make bread, and like I have made bread before — And I started two sourdough starters the week I started my postdoc.

Kelsey — Do you still have them?

Erin — No. I have a different one now. My current one is named David Doughie and I've had it for years.

But yeah, I distinctly remember like day three when I was growing my starters. I wanted to take them to Governor's School. I was revamping my course. I had students that summer, in their welcome letter like: *Congratulations. Can't wait to work with you, you know. Here are the things you'll need: a notebook, a calculator, a pen or a pencil, blah blah, and, you know, a quarter cup of flour that you use at home. It could be like the thing you most loved to use or it could be the thing that you most generally use.* And they were all like [squeaky voice]: *I have my flour.*

And I'm like: *That's awesome.* Because we plated the flours to figure out what are the microbes in the flour. Because if it matters what order of microbes get in there for the final community, then it would matter what microbes are in the flour to start with. And that blew the students' minds — One, because they were doing real science. They were like: *Is this what I'm supposed to find?* I said: *Well, let's pause everybody. Stop what you're doing. What does the word* supposed to *mean and imply?* And they're like: *Uhhh.* I said: *Okay, it means that we expect a specific result. It implies that we know what is happening. We don't know what's happening. Right? If you don't remember, I've never studied this before.* And they're like: *What?* I'm like: *Come on up with me. Let's toe up to the edge of the abyss of unknowing in life. This is actually science. I know you all qualified to come to this amazing program because you're like know all the answers in school and that's how you get good grades. To do science is to have no idea. You learn as much as you can and then the whole point of viewing science — The scientific method was developed to approach ignorance.* And they're like: *Woahh.*

And then I had students, at that point the term was, you know, they had Asperger's and they're like: *I am not comfortable with this.* I said: *That's great. Thank you for sharing. Like I'm just so glad that you are aware of that discomfort and that you were able to articulate it. Right? Because a lot of people would be too scared to say that out loud.* Like that is the source of imposter syndrome all by itself, never mind all the societal stuff. Like just the nature of science is not knowing. You know. Like: *Welcome to your deprogramming. We are addressing a real question that nobody has ever asked before.* And it was really fun. And then I had the starters. I said: *So based on what you know about what microbes grew on your different plates. I have now baked bread* — I baked so much bread and so many sourdough waffles that summer. It was unbelievable. So we would spend the first week growing the microbes and categorizing them and then the next week we would talk about, you know, bread and gut microbes. Like bread and then food and gut microbes. So it's like microbe palooza. And the first thing I would do on that Monday morning is bake bread. So I said: *Based on everything that y'all found out that grows in flours, I want you — You get a taste test. Each of you gets one slice of bread from each level. They're marked A and B on your plate. One is wheat and one is rye. And based off of what you know about what microbes are growing and what we know what bacteria versus yeast do in a starter, you now have to tell me which one is wheat and which is rye.* And they guessed correctly every time because they have put together the ecological functions of those microbes and matched it with the aromas and the flavor profiles.

Kelsey	Which is so fun. And so different than the science — I remember the science I did in high school was like: *All right, we're gonna look at —*
Erin	Cookbook. Follow this, you expect to get this. And if you don't get that, then it's wrong. You messed up. But they don't even tell you how to troubleshoot it, right?
Kelsey	That's true. Right.
Erin	It's just: *Well you did that wrong. Here's what it's supposed to look like. Go look at Jackie's.*
Kelsey	Yeah, well with a cookbook, at least you get to make in a place that you feel safe and comfortable in with things that you probably somewhat used to.
Erin	This is like alien.
Kelsey	Yeah, like when you go into a science lab it often feels like: *You got your*

goggles, you got your gloves, you have an eye wash station in case you accidentally like get really really hurt.

So like working with the sourdough and like looking at the microbiomes and flours —

Erin — We even, we spent an entire class period walking through the protocol. I said: *First you just read it and write down what questions you have about every step and then I'm going to answer it for you. Next I'm going to demonstrate for you. Next you do it. And I get to walk around and state,* "No, don't turn your pipette upside down" *and* "No, don't cram your L-spreader onto your petri dish because you just burrowed a furrow."

Kelsey — So cool. I wish I had been in Governor's School to take that class.

Erin — It was so fun. And very cathartic for me in many ways. Because, one, I got to talk about things that I've been passionate about — Like all the fun stuff, right? Two, I got to, in my own small way, address issues with the system. Like the grumpy professor stereotype. Like: *Ugh, students. I can't believe they don't even know how to insert skill or something.*

Kelsey — It's very prescriptivized.

Erin — Well, it's very gripey and... A...

Kelsey — Old school?

Erin — There's a word that I'm looking for... It's a model of lacking. Anyway.

Kelsey — Deficit?

Erin — Yes. Thank you. It's a deficit model thinking about students, right? My automatic response internally, if not also externally, whenever I hear that is: *When do they learn? When did they get a chance to practice?* Right? So a lot of that was, you know, for every student who hasn't in high school already started to think about research opportunities or do it, because some of them, you know — And there's so much privilege just associated with who as parents and who as students have the time or, you know, have access to these opportunities. Who knows how to navigate the system. It is scary to cold call somebody and ask for a volunteership. My mom set it up with our veterinarian when I was 13 because I wanted to be a vet. And that was its own tunnel vision issue because there are more ways to work with animals.

But so that's been like — In reading the book by The Moth and in reflecting on, like, my scientific practices and growth and different systems that I use to study science and microbes, right — Like there is the equity thread and there's also the like filling gaps in training thread.

Kelsey — Yeah, and I — A lot of what I'm looking at now too is the deficits of academia, being very performative, being very gatekeep-y.

Erin — Yes.

Kelsey — And inaccessible in every regard. I'm looking at that especially in regard to feminism. Feminism is often a, it's an academic term and so like my mom probably —

Erin — And there's such a reflex against it.

Kelsey	Yes.
Erin	It's like: *No, actually it means everyone equal. All we want is for everyone to have —*
Kelsey	Rights.
Erin	*The same.* And then it's like: *Oh, you mean communism? Or socialism?*
Kelsey	Something completely different.
Erin	*No, I just mean everyone should be treated... There shouldn't be any, any one portion of the population that is afraid.*
Kelsey	Completely agree. And when we look at this country, it's very very scary to see. Like I went to Target yesterday and I remember seeing our Target still has the Pride collection up and I'm like: *Oh, like good for you, Knightdale Target.* Because I see so much about how other Targets have taken down their pride collection.
Erin	Really? Like it's only allowed during the one month. This makes me want to check this out.
Kelsey	I know some Targets were receiving like threats of violence and it's just like: *Where do we live where.... ?*
Erin	Like there was a point in history where Christians were persecuted in different parts of the world. Like that is why we have such a strong Puritan and whatever background because Christians were persecuted. Like how quickly people

forget. Just like everyone has been on that end of the stick.

Kelsey   So then this is all to say it's wonderful how food and working with food and making with food elicit considerations like that.

Erin   And I think there's — Because it is a basic need, right? Like we all have to eat. We don't, we can't all eat gluten, but we all have to eat. And so for people who can engage without a visceral reaction, food provides such a fabulous opportunity to bond. And it reminds me of different peace efforts like Community Gardens in Israeli and Palestinian communities, right? But like: *You can grow a garden together.* And you realize slowly: *Oh, right. They have to eat too. Oh, because we are all humans.*

Kelsey   It's a unifying factor.

Erin   In Northern Ireland — I can't remember the name of the speaker, but he came to Governor's School in 2006 when I was a TA and the director at the time said: *You just got back from Ireland?* And he just talked about it because they had The Troubles. Right? And so their big thing was cleaning up the river in Belfast because there hadn't been salmon in it for decades because it was disgusting. It had all the industry outputs into it. It was so polluted. So they put together this huge initiative to clean up the river. And the salmon returned. And it was like this mighty victory, no matter what sect you belonged to. I get choked up.

Yeah, the idea that there is this commonality and potential for community around food. And that hopefully also could provide a way to empower people instead of estranging them around science.

Like when I talk to the bakers, I've told them: *I feel a little nervous because I don't have a lab. So at some point I'm gonna run out of new stuff to say.*

> They're like: *No no, no. You're amazing.* I'm like: *Thank you, but also y'all are the experts. I need you to remember that you are the experts. That you can ask me questions about the microbes and I won't have all the answers and I can speculate and like maybe we can think of ways that we could study it. But like none of this makes sense without you.*

Kelsey   I think that's a beautiful display of teamwork too. I feel like oftentimes we think of knowledge as very individualized, like it's one person.

Erin   Or it's siloed.

Kelsey   Yes, it's siloed and one person's gonna get the credit. And like you think of Apple: it's like the one white man that's in charge or like Steve Jobs. So I think it's wonderful to think of knowledge sharing and creation as much more collaborative.

Erin   And reciprocal.

Kelsey   Yes, which it should be. It shouldn't be like caught up in one person's name on a paper or in a book or something.

Erin   Right. So I have a paper that's in review right now with Peter Jay and four of the authors are middle school teachers. And like that was the point. But we also had a discussion. They got paid for that work to come in and over the summer. And we had this whole discussion of like: *In this broader sourdough effort, what is helpful to you?* Like publications are the currency of academia, but not —

Kelsey   For grade school teachers.

Erin	Yeah, is that gonna help you at all? And for one of them, they said: *Yeah, I want to go back to grad school. So it'd be awesome to have a publication.* That's great. For everyone else, like: *Where is the value in what we are doing?* And we also put together this entire curriculum handbook around the Sourdough Project. But now I feel like I really need to dig that out — I'm sure it's on the Sourdough For Science page. But there's a reading of a poem and then they translated it into Spanish, you know. And they got paid for all this time. And we put together like: *How do you use Excel to put these numbers in and can we make a graph?* So it's like we had maximal alignment across disciplines for their curriculum. And we had alignment with the learning objectives for six, seven, and eighth grade.
Kelsey	That's amazing.
Erin	So it's like, you know, sourdough as a unifying framework for middle school education. With a focus on STEM, but also there was, you know, some literacy there. And when you read something, we have guided reading questions for —
Kelsey	Yeah. It's informational literacy. Media literacy. Data literacy. And also I think it cannot be understated the value of socio-emotional literacy wellness if —
Erin	Well that's where the mindfulness of keeping a sourdough, tending it, and making the bread. I haven't baked bread in a few weeks and I will see if I can this weekend.
Kelsey	So my favorite bread to make is focaccia because I feel like it's not stressful.
Erin	I have not made it before.

Kelsey	Oh, it's so easy. I've tried making sourdough and I found that too much of an emotional roller coaster, but focaccia is an emotional coaster in just like a few hours so I can handle it.
	And it's also like even if you mess up, it's covered in olive oil and salt so it's still good. And that's like my favorite thing whenever we have family around I always make focaccia.
Erin	Well maybe I'll do that.
Kelsey	It's so good. I like Claire Saffitz's recipe.[21] I'll send it to you. Sooo good. Very easy.
	But yeah. No, bread is great. It's very fun. Like yes, we all eat and that's such a unifying thing. And it's also unifying in that, like, there's a lot joy with food too. And I remember a teaching icebreaker for the first day class that was justice and equity oriented was to ask your students: *How did you grow up eating rice?* Because everyone eats rice, but like the way we all eat it is so different. So I think about that a lot.
Erin	Yeah, black eyed peas or black beans.
Kelsey	Yeah, and then for me — My mom learned how to make a lot of rice when we were stationed in Japan. So we always had rice and soy sauce. But culturally my parents are like from Upstate New York. So like none of their relatives can relate to that at all.

---

[21] Claire Saffitz's Focaccia Bread Recipe: https://www.bonappetit.com/recipe/focaccia-bread. I first worked with this recipe when I found it in: *Dessert Person: Recipes and Guidance for Baking with Confidence: A Baking Book* (2020).

Erin Yeah, I think of Indian food. I love it. I've done a working date — Well, the last one was with myself, but my favorite things are like you find somebody else who loves Indian food and you go to Kabab and Curry on the patio for like two hours, that way you actually get like two plates in. [laughs]

Kelsey [laughs] I need to do that.

Erin My inner grad student is still really really strong. I'm like: *Fru-gal-ity*.

#TINY LOAVES4TINY HANDS *Finally, a way to bake with your* **backslop**! **Backslop** is the sourdough that you would normally discard (throw away) when you feed your starter. Dr. McKenney offers many thanks to Joseph Monast for rigorously testing and tweaking this recipe to its current, optimized version. This recipe was developed specifically for children and young bakers.

Dr. McKenney's easy sourdough bread recipe

Total time: 2 days

Ingredients

1 cup all-purpose flour
⅓ teaspoons salt
½ cup water, room temperature

1 tablespoon mature sourdough starter
Vegetable oil
Cornmeal or rice flour

Materials

2 mixing bowls
An electric mixer*
A lid
A baking tray

Pot holders or oven mitts
A baking tray
A sharp knife

*If you don't have an electric mixture, you can use your hands to **knead** the dough. **Kneading** is a special kind of mixing for bread dough. Ask your adult helper to show you what kneading looks like. Kneading by hand takes longer than using a mixer, so plan appropriately.*

Directions Day 1: Making the Dough

1. Mix the flour and salt in a large mixing bowl.

2. Mix the sourdough starter and water in a different bowl.

3. Pour the wet ingredients into the dry ingredients and mix for 10 minutes (until the dough is smooth-looking). In the mixer, a "just right" dough will form a ball that "self-cleans" the sides of the bowl.

4. Turn the dough onto the counter.

5. Coat the inside of the bowl with oil.

6. Form the dough into a ball and put the dough ball back into the bowl, rolling it in the oil to coat the entire surface of the dough ball.

7. Cover the bowl with a lid or tea towel and let it sit on the counter for 12 hours.

8. Transfer the covered bowl to the fridge to continue fermenting overnight.

Did you know? Even the most experienced bakers find that the exact same recipe can yield a different dough from day to day!

Here, we have provided a starting place to get you close to where you need to be. The end goal is a dough that is *loose enough to form a pliable, stretchy/elastic dough* – but not so wet or sticky that it clings to your hands. You may need to add a bit more flour or water to get the consistency "just right."

Directions Day 2: Baking the Loaf

Make sure you have your adult helper with you.

1. Preheat oven to 500F, with a baking sheet inside. The baking sheet will get nice and hot inside of the oven.
2. When the oven has preheated, take the bowl of chilled dough out of the fridge.
3. Gently run a spatula around the edge of the dough ball, to separate it from the wall of the bowl.
4. Sprinkle rice flour or cornmeal on the top surface of the dough ball. 6. Use potholders or oven mitts to remove the hot baking sheet from the oven. **Your adult helper may need to do this part.**
5. Turn the bowl upside-down over the pan so that the dough ball falls out (flour-side down) onto the hot pan.
6. Quickly **score** the top of the loaf: Use a sharp knife to cut slashes about ⅛ inch deep across the top of the loaf. **Your adult helper may need to do this part.**
7. Place the pan (now with the scored loaf on it) into the oven on the middle rack.
8. Close the oven door and bake at 450F for 10 minutes, then turn the oven down to 350F for another 15 minutes.
9. Take a photo of your Tiny Loaf and share it with your agent. **#tinyloaves4tinyhands**

Did you know? Scoring helps the bread expand without splitting the crust as it rises in the oven.

You can experiment with different scoring patterns:

    || long straight parallel lines
    // slanted lines
    # a tic-tac-toe pattern
    () curved lines
    Or any other pattern you can think of!

Dr. McKenney's easy sourdough bread recipe for one loaf

Ingredients

3 ⅔ cups all-purpose flour
1 ¾ teaspoons salt

1 ½ cups plus 4 teaspoons water, room temperature
⅓ cup mature sourdough starter

Directions

Note: You can mix the dough 24 hours before baking.

1. Mix the flour and salt in a large mixing bowl. Mix the sourdough starter and water in a separate bowl. Pour wet into dry, mix for 10 minutes (until the dough is smooth-looking).

2. Turn the dough onto the counter, coat the bowl with oil, form the dough into a ball and put the dough ball back into the bowl, rolling it in the oil to coat the entire surface of the dough ball. Cover the bowl with a lid and let it sit on the counter for 12 hours.

3. Transfer the covered bowl to the fridge, to continue fermenting overnight.

4. *When you are ready to bake:* Preheat the oven to 500F, with a baking sheet inside (to get nice and hot).

5. When the oven has preheated, take the bowl of chilled dough out of the fridge. Gently run a spatula around the edge of the dough ball, to separate it from the wall of the bowl. Sprinkle rice flour or cornmeal on the top surface of the dough ball.

6. Remove the hot baking sheet from the oven, then turn the bowl upside-down over the pan so that the dough ball falls out (flour-side down) onto the hot pan. Using a sharp knife, quickly score[22] the top of the loaf. Place the pan (now with the scored loaf on it) into the oven on the middle rack. Close the oven door and re-set the temperature to 475F.

7. Bake 20 minutes at 475F, reset to 350F, and bake another 20 minutes.

---

[22] Score the loaf by using a sharp knife to cut slashes about ⅛ inch deep across the top of the loaf. Scoring helps the bread expand as it rises in the oven, without splitting the crust. You can experiment with different scoring patterns.

Wonderpuff

"Magic is also hope. You know? Hope for people who are truly in the dark and they can't come out of it. You know, and that's also magical, coming out of that darkness. Because at the end of the day, human beings are resilient. Even when we don't want to be. Even when we don't have to be. It's just in our nature and that is also magical. And I take magic, my magic, very seriously."

JAC M, Co-Owner and Founder of Wonderpuff

I had met JAC once prior to our conversation for this project when I invited her to come speak at North Carolina State University and share their experiences as a woman of color, as a small business owner, as an entrepreneur and creator. To a room full of students, staff, and faculty, JAC spoke of the dangers of white supremacy and capitalism, the beauty and power of vulnerability and healing, and the magic of cotton candy. Many students came to the event because they could smell cotton candy throughout the library.

But this time I met JAC at their shop. Before closing just a few months after we spoke, Wonderpuff was surrounded by other small businesses taking up space in container units in Research Triangle Park's Boxyard. There were lots of people. Lots of open air. Lots of khaki pants with collared shirts and others in Birkenstocks (including myself). For the unfamiliar: Boxyard is a funky mix of business and professional food and fun court. And JAC's shop was noteworthy in this space because it was not a restaurant, not a bar, not an escape room — but also because among the crowd of khakied folks at Boxyard for their lunch break, JAC dressed in a bright colors, Hawaiian shirts, sunnies, and gemstones.

Personal photograph of Wonderpuff's storefront at Research Triangle Park.

talking with JAC M

Kelsey   So. We've met before and you're —

JAC   Yes, we have. You hired me to speak. No, that's just amazing.

Kelsey   And almost a year ago.

JAC   So much life has happened since then.

Kelsey   Yeah, and that was such a great time.

JAC   Yeah.

Kelsey   That's probably my favorite thing I've done with NC State — Is having you come.

JAC   Yeah! I really want to do more of that. And it's like from then to now, so much has happened that I feel like I would be able to execute what I need to say a lot more truthfully and honestly. Because I was so shy. It was my first, like, grown up speaking.

Kelsey   You did amazing. And I mean it was just — So many people came and like it was amazing. I learned so much. It was great. It was perfect. You do so much amazing work with community. Like I look at your Instagram stories and like it's just so beautiful to see how much love you have for Durham and how much love you give to Durham.

JAC		Yes!

Kelsey		Can you talk about that?

JAC		Yes! Yes. Yes. Yes. I just — I just love good people. I just love good people. And I grew up in South Florida where it was very hard to find like-minded radical thinkers, like myself. And it's nobody's fault. It's just, unfortunately, we as a society — we've been conditioned and programmed, thanks to white supremacy and capitalism. And when I moved here seven years ago with my family, I found people who thought just like me and I'm like: *Okay, there are Freedom Fighters everywhere and North Carolina has so many.* I mean this entire land of ours has so many Freedom Fighters, but something about Durham, North Carolina — I think it's because when we started Wonderpuff six years ago, I wanted to be where the Black people were. And I wanted to be where the queer people were. And I just literally stumbled on Durham and Durham stumbled on me. Durham found me and changed my life and found — I found people like yourself, radical lovers and radical thinkers, who want to create safe spaces who wants to dismantle white supremacy and dismantle capitalism and create a world that is safe for us and that can give people the opportunity to live.

You know? Because at the end of the day, none of us really didn't ask to be here. [laughs] But we're here and we have to make the best of it. And when you know better you do better. And Durham is, is a part of that wave. And outside of Durham — the Triangle. There's a lot of amazing, wonderful folks. And so yeah.

Kelsey		And it's so cool — you've told me the story of how Wonderpuff came to be, where you and your husband bought the cotton candy making machine.

JAC	Yes.

Kelsey	And kind of started following that dream so boldly. So can you talk about — So cotton candy is so spectacularly beautiful and magical. Like you have on your door: *Magic lives here.*

JAC	Yes.

Kelsey	I just love the role of magic in your business because we often don't think of the space for magic in capitalism.

JAC	Right.

Kelsey	So you have made that space very pointed and like a priority, which is just amazing.

JAC	Yeah. That is so wonderful. That's a beautiful way of saying it. I love magic for so many reasons. I actually grew up with magic. My dad used to do fun — He's an artist. He's a hard worker, first and foremost. Growing up, I saw my father, you know, from Haiti and a lot of his siblings — A lot of people from Haiti, they're just born in color and also born in magic. There's a lot of magic history in Haiti, you know, when it comes to practicing the voodoo spirituality of that part of magic. But *my,* my magic I was introduced with my father doing lots of magic tricks. And I am just like: *This shit is amazing.* You know here is this awesome Haitian dad with his tattoos and his, he had these big rocker boots and this tight white shirt, typical Miami style, lots of tattoos, and playing — Just doing magic tricks in front of his kids when he wasn't working so hard to provide a safe life for us. And that's when I tapped into magic and color and vibrancy. And just like, I don't know Even the word *magic* is beautiful. You know, it's the G that sounds like J. It's the C that sounds like K. The mm. The ma.

Kelsey   It has good mouth feel.

JAC   It does. It does. Magic. Magic. Yeah. I don't know. Magic is also hope. You know? Hope for people who are truly in the dark and they can't come out of it. You know, and that's also magical, coming out of that darkness. Because at the end of the day, human beings are resilient. Even when we don't want to be. Even when we don't have to be. It's just in our nature and that is also magical. And I take magic, my magic, very seriously.

Kelsey   I feel like in cotton candy, you put it in your mouth and it dissolves. But Wonderpuff is so magical and it's so resilient. It's so tough and it's so hopeful. And so it's very cool to see cotton candy, we usually think of being very soft and fluffy — but here it's also tough and strong here. And it shows how magic isn't always whimsy. It's not always like Disney.

JAC   Right.

Kelsey   But it's like more... like I don't know. It's really symbolically and magically strong.

JAC   Right. Right. And it's also messy. Cotton candy is messy.

Kelsey   [laughs]

JAC   And it takes magical superpowers to make cotton candy and not cover your whole body with it. And I you know, I love — Honestly, people always ask like how did I create — How did I thought up the concept. But yeah, you know, we all know that all of our concepts are not original. They came from some other source. And I was just inspired by other people around the world spinning cotton candy. And also I just... I have a very hard time with — I'm really anti-white supremacy and white anti-capitalism, even though we have to pay bills and I like to buy, I like to buy snacks and gummy bears and gifts for my friends. Like: *Wow, don't I love money but also I want to burn everything down.* And I don't know. I am that way for a reason and it's because I have a hard time learning. And when I learned cotton candy, I'm like: *Oh, this is something easy.* I want to take the easy way out when it comes to existing in capitalism. I want to use very little resources, very little energy. What can I do that — And that's also the Taurus in me.

Kelsey   [laughs]

JAC   I want to give very little and I want to get so much back. And in society under capitalism, it doesn't work like that. In order to get a lot, you have to work a lot. And oftentimes you have to kill something and that is either your soul, your knees, your back, time with your family, time with yourself. And I'm a firm believer like: *Okay if I have to exist in this hellhole and this democracy that people are suffering in, what can I do to make my life easy, not overwork myself, and bring joy to the community?* But as a small business owner you end up overworking yourself and doing all the things that you said that you aren't gonna do. You end up doing it all. You end up over-exerting yourself. You end up working, over-working, and overextending yourself and pouring from an empty cup. Especially after the pandemic, so many small businesses, like myself, we're all in the struggle bus together. You know?

Kelsey   And it's sad because so many small businesses, like your own, give so much

	back to the community. I see you do that all the time and it's such valuable work that capitalism doesn't recognize or reward.
JAC	Right, right.
Kelsey	But that's life — Everything kind of runs on capitalism, but the stuff that really matters too, that runs off of care.
JAC	Right.
Kelsey	And that's not recognized or commodified or paid.
JAC	Right. And it's not —
Kelsey	It's a whole other form of labor.
JAC	Yes it is. Giving is a whole other form of labor, especially when it is free labor. I, you know, I'm always so taken aback when people see our business and they see Wonderpuff and they're just like: *Wow, you're part of the community. You do so much.* And I'm like: *I feel like I'm not doing enough.* You know, I want to do more. You know. And also I feel like this is not work. It's just like, I don't know, being a good person. It doesn't feel like I'm contributing to the community. It doesn't feel like I'm doing something special or sacred even though actually it is sacred. But I just feel like, I don't know, giving back to the community is just you know — [JAC says hello to Chef Octavia] I just love, I love giving. I also think that could also be sometimes a very bad thing, right? Because as a small business owner you need to make money to

stay afloat. And I tend to give a lot of our products out for free. For example, a Wonderpuff is probably the least expensive. So like out of everybody here at Boxyard, my product is the least expensive and for me being the cheapest, I give a lot away. You know, I give a lot away. For example, if you are a regular customer and you come like once a week and you support everybody, you're most likely gonna get free products from me and end up spending 30, 40, 50 dollars at other neighbors. And you know, I shouldn't be giving our products away for free, but it just, it just something… You don't think about it when you're doing something like that, you know what I'm saying? And I don't feel some type of way — I feel like I can't do it enough. So yeah, I, I — we love that about ourselves.

Kelsey   Yeah. So my work is like focusing on the role of care in community with food. Also how it's really gendered too. So like there's a lot more responsibility, historically, on women to do a lot of that care and a lot of that giving and especially like women of color that their care work is all the more under recognized.

JAC   Yes.

Kelsey   All of those things then carry on into food.

JAC   Right. Right. [singing] That is very very very true. Which is so funny because living in our patriarchal society, society tells, oh tells women — I mean not only do they care, they hate uteruses, people with uteruses, but they tell people who are femmes and people who identify as women that, like, we got to be in the kitchen. However, in the food industry, it's all run by men. And it's just very weird how that dynamic is kind of like that everywhere too, right? A lot of things are run by man and oftentimes men who don't care about anyone but themselves. And for Wonderpuff and for me, and Reem, and our team members, we just pride ourselves in dismantling all of that. You know what I'm saying? Anything that is slightly close to white supremacy, we like to go the opposite. Even if, even if that means walking by ourselves. Even if that means looking crazy, because it's weird every time you speak up for what is right, people are just like: *Shut up*. You know. Unless — Unlike your phone, because when you're on the internet, when you're on social media, you meet so many like-minded individuals like a —

Kelsey   A solidarity.

JAC   Right.

Kelsey   All over community online.

JAC   That's right.

Kelsey   It doesn't feel like — I was just telling someone, sometimes I feel like Raleigh is a bubble. Like whenever I drive and go farther away from like my home where I feel comfortable and I have found a community of people that whose voices and a perspectives all feel very similar and kind of a build together — And then whenever I see lots beyond that I'm like: Am I just living in a tiny little bubble? And I might just be that naive, but that is the beauty of social media online.

JAC   And it's also the downside of social media. Like when you put your phone down, you're just like: *Alright, where are those people that think just like me?* And you're often left by yourself. But we're all doing the work. We're just far away from each other. We're all doing the work every day. And I'm grateful that

Wonderpuff was a part of that. And people take that seriously.

It's one of the reasons why I started a business, was to create my own platform, you know.

Kelsey   In being a small business owner and doing this work, what have you most learned about yourself?

JAC   Um...

Kelsey   And others.

JAC   That — That's a loaded question. I don't think I can answer that. I'm gonna be very honest with you. It's a very loaded question and I'm still learning. Every day is a learning lesson. Every day I'm meeting a new version of myself, you know. Every day I'm learning a different level of forgiveness, a different level of anger, loneliness, heartache, grief — Like all the emotions that we feel as human beings. I discover, like oh, a new way to love. A new way to be sad. And all these things and I'm — I don't know. I don't know. What I have, the biggest thing that I have learned about myself though as an entrepreneur and somebody who makes sugar for a living is like I'm still alive, you know? So, you know, I'm still alive and if I'm still alive I can try. I can try

One important thing that I stopped doing, thanks to the pandemic, is comparing myself though.

Kelsey   Yeah. How, how did you learn to stop doing that? It's hard.

JAC   I think when something bad happens to you, the world doesn't stop. The world doesn't stop because your world has stopped. And so for me, you know, surviving so, you know, so much grief and trauma and heartache and just being fully raw with myself and giving myself permission and reminding myself: *I am not a robot.*

And I stopped comparing myself when we saw millions of people die in 2020 and people were in their kitchen making sourdough bread and watching *Tiger King* and we saw all of our nurses all over the world just get a round of applause. [scoffs] You know?

Kelsey	Yeah, my sister-in-law was a COVID nurse and —
JAC	I'm sorry.
Kelsey	She just left. Well, not just — A year ago. She left nursing. She was like: *It's too much.*
JAC	Right, right. And nurses just like teachers — it's just so funny, all the important professions —
Kelsey	Are connected to care!
JAC	That's right. That's all connected to care and our well-being and keeping us alive. You know what I'm saying? They're all underpaid.
Kelsey	They are soul nourishing, like how your business nourishes souls and community.
JAC	I've never heard that before.

Kelsey	Yeah.
JAC	Is that a real thing? Soul nourishing?
Kelsey	I don't know. I feel it should be!
JAC	Did you just make that up?
Kelsey	I did!
JAC	I love that for you.
Kelsey	You do nourish souls, like how food nourishes, like of course our bodies and appetites, but also Wonderpuff also nourishes the soul. I feel like teachers do that too and nurses. And so it's all those things that are connected to care. Those are all the most undervalued, but the most needed!
JAC	Yeah, right, right. You ever notice that? The things that are most needed in our community are those that are being undervalued, underpaid? So many teachers and nurses and doctors all over the world they're quitting every day and you're like: *Oh my God!* So what does this mean? Does this mean more prison, you know, school to prison pipelines? Does it mean more homeless people in their cars? Like what, what is going on? And that is the, it's just... I think maybe I'm also learning that I may not be, maybe I'm more than an entrepreneur when it comes to Wonderpuff. Maybe I'm supposed to be doing something else. Hyping people up. Waking people up. Letting people realize that they are powerful. And we are powerful by numbers, and that's what our democracy doesn't want. That's what our politicians don't

want. If we erase the color lines, if we erase the gender lines, if you erase the class lines, if we just literally — And I'm not talking about some kumbaya bullshit like: *Oh, I don't see color.* I see color, you know. And even if I was a non-able person who wasn't even able to see, I would still be able to understand.

[we become quickly distracted by a dog left by a table near us]

I don't know what we were saying, but we were saying all the right things.

Kelsey   It was good.

JAC   You should do a podcast.

Kelsey   You should do a podcast! We should do a podcast together.

JAC   I would love that. Yeah, I'm going to do that when I close my shop. I'm doing all the things. I'm doing all the things.

Kelsey   What brought y'all to Florida?

JAC   It's just like the East Coast situation. Yeah immigrants, they come from the island and then they moved to New York and they're just like: *Oh all of our people here, but you know, the island life is in the South.* So you go to New York and then you like — Everyone from New York is either living in North Carolina or South Florida. I don't know if you ever noticed this, but there's so many New Yorkers around here. It's crazy. It's crazy. But my family, they've been in — They've been in Florida since the 80s, since I was born so Florida girl. Florida girl, through and through. And I don't say that out loud. [laughs]

Kelsey	[laughs]
JAC	You know, it's a very, it's a very Trump state.
Kelsey	It is. North Carolina feels special at times and I feel like this area feels really special because there's people like you and —
JAC	And people like you!
Kelsey	Aw. Well I aspire to be doing all the amazing things that you do.
JAC	It's very important for, for — We need white women. It's very very important for white women to do the work alongside Black and Brown women because Black and Brown women have been doing the work. Like you said, it goes unjust. It goes unseen. It goes unrecognized. And when we have people of privilege who can use their privilege to dismantle their, you know, dismantle violence — It's very important to have white women as allies and I take it very seriously. I take it very seriously. Unless you're one of those, those women, you know, how there's a lot of like during 2020, during like the BLM movement, there are a lot of white liberals who were really showing their asses and you're just like: *You are also a part of the problem and that's also a problem and it's not my problem to fix that.* You know, we're all doing the work as individuals and that means, for some people, you have to understand: *Okay, my ancestors were terrible, but that doesn't mean I have to be.* You know what I'm saying? That whole — I never knew anything about white guilt until 2020, until the Black Lives Matter movement. And I'm just like: *This is dangerous. Not only for*

the community, but for within yourself. You are poisoning yourself instead of releasing and letting go, making room for change, love, and light that you can continue to spread to your community. And I don't have time or patience for white guilt or white tears. Because there's blood on the ground. You know what I'm saying?

So many people are suffering, and suffering is not a Black or white issue. It's a planetarium issue. It's an Earthling issue. We are all suffering. And the moment we can recognize that, the moment that we understand like: *Oh damn. Like we really do need each other.*

Kelsey	Yeah, desperately. We desperately need each other.
JAC	Oh boy.
Kelsey	There's so much hurt.
JAC	So much. And I pride myself as an entrepreneur who actually lives by those words. Obviously, I'm an imperfect human being and —
Kelsey	Because we aren't robots, like you're saying.
JAC	Right.
Kelsey	There's like a show and they say as long as you try to be a better person than you were the day before, even if you make mistakes, as long as you're trying and putting in the effort to do good and better and produce betterment, that's all we can ever ask — It's all we can ever do.

JAC Right! And it's just — That also starts within though. That also starts within. It really comes within. And the moment you surrender to that and you accept it and — I don't know life is short, you know?

Personal photographs of Wonderpuff's storefront at Research Triangle Park.

Personal photograph of Wonderpuff's storefront at Research Triangle Park.

Videri Chocolate Factory

"I always understood that you have to tell the story of like: *Why is this important*? And the easiest way for us to do it is to show people why it's important. You know, show people that we literally hand sort every bag of beans. If we didn't show that to somebody, would they believe it?"

Sam Ratto
Head Chocolate Maker and Co-Founder of Videri Chocolate Factory

Videri Chocolate Factory is the place my family recommends folks to visit when they come to Raleigh for the first time. It feels fancy to say we have a local chocolate factory — and a factory that feels, looks, and operates much differently than the UTZ Quality Foods tour I went on when I was 5.

And the chocolate, by all accounts, is fancy. It is not Halloween trick-or-treat candy (unless you are very, very wealthy). It is special occasion chocolate. It is housewarming present/moving away gift/Valentine's or birthday or retirement celebration or I love you or I love chocolate chocolate. It is savor this one bite because we are going to split this quarter-sized bonbon and it was expensive chocolate.

It is certainly not the chocolate I grew up with.

By the end of our talk, Sam and I are swapping phones to share pictures of our children.

Personal photograph of Videri Chocolate Factory.

Personal photograph of Videri Chocolate Factory.

an interview with Sam Ratto

Kelsey So, a dissertation is usually very scientific. It's usually very traditional academic writing and again, I'd argue that there's a lot of knowledge that exists that isn't coded as traditionally academic — but it's still knowledge. So same as when Downtown Raleigh had all those beautiful street murals, like that is art even though we see it every day, so people don't read it as such. So, same thing. I want the dissertation to be more utility oriented, not academic-y at all. So I'm making a cookbook for my dissertation.

Sam Oh, no way, that is wonderful.

Kelsey Yeah. And so with that I think that cookbooks are a lot more interesting to engage with than like an instruction manual.

Sam Yep.

Kelsey Like I can't read an instruction manual. Every time I get one, I just throw it away. Like I don't know how to read it.

Sam I do this weird thing where I just skim it.

Kelsey At least you skim it.

Sam I'm like: *Why am I skimming this? There's no point. Like, just throw it away, if you aren't going to use it.* [laughs]

Kelsey Yeah, and it's very boring. Like the drawings are boring. Everything about it is very boring. And so a cookbook is like the same thing, but it's way better in every regard. It's still an instruction manual.

Sam	Yeah.

Kelsey	Yep, but it's also more feminized. It's more every day, like we were saying, so we don't pay attention to it.

Sam	Yeah. I'm here for this. Okay. Well, what do you want to do with Videri? How do you want to like use us?

Kelsey	Well, I'd love to talk to you about how you all work with food and also like you — Videri is so part of the state motto and you're so saturated in the community. So I'd love to hear how that community facilitation happens, how you all kind of build in care — Because chocolate feels very... I remember growing up where Hershey's chocolate was the chocolate we ate in my household. Now it's really exciting to eat Videri, but it feels really accessible if that makes sense. So I'd love to hear how you've achieved that.

Sam	So two of our core values are friendly and welcoming. It started — so my ex-wife and I started the business with a business partner in 2011. I started in the chocolate business in 2009 working at Escazu. This is being recorded, but you can see the comparison if you walked into that business versus walking into Videri. Both my ex-wife and I's backgrounds — Both of our grandparents and parents were small business owners on some level. My grandfather on my dad's side ran a family farm, like leafy greens produce, with his nine brothers in Oakland, Alameda, California, and they still operate a large plot of land out in Modesto. But me growing up, I would always interact with my grandfather in a way where like, you know, we would do something where it's like: *Oh, I got to go pick this up for my buddy.* And we're like: *Oh, what's your buddy doing?* And he went: *Oh, he makes pasta.* And as a kid, you're just like: *Oh, this is really neat.* [train horn blasts] We are by a train station.

Kelsey [laughs]

Sam And, you know, that's a very small sampling of just like the community. So part of my upbringing was just being friendly, business partner, interacting with people —

[train horn blasts, over and over]

I'm one of 26 or 28 grandkids on my dad's side.

Kelsey Wow!

Sam I'm one of, I think, 12 or 13 grandkids on my mom's side.

Kelsey It's a very big family.

Sam And both families are very family-oriented, but community-oriented. So it wasn't like you go to a family event and there would just be like your family. It's like a family event, but plus like you and other people that were like friends with other people. So we were always kind of like in a community group setting. And then when — my career before this was, I worked in the skateboarding industry, which is all about community. It's all about, you know, who do you know — like this person that person and you connect the dots or you're in a room where you're doing something and then like somebody that owns a distillery is like you're working on a partnership or a beverage company or, you know, a sound company or whatever it is. There's always this thing of connecting with people. It's not a straight line, but that's the way that I always looked at. It is that I was always making friends or partners or business relationships with people in that way.

And then when we got into the chocolate business in 2009, I was like: *This is crazy.* Like it grows on a tree. It's fruit. And the difference between what a Hershey bar tastes like and what a chocolate bar made from high quality or they call it "fine chocolate" — Which I think is so insane, they don't call it "gourmet" for some reason, they call it "fine." Point of the story was: It blew my mind. I was like: *What is this? How does this thing that smells like vinegar once you roast it and winnow it and grind it, it tastes like this? How does this kind of work?*

And because I'm not a chemist and I didn't go to college, I don't know the technical way that it works. I just understand that it works.

You know, I take copious amounts of notes on aroma profiles and things like that, but it is — [laughs] It works. And so when I learned about it in 2009 and then when I worked through it in 2010, what sort of fascinated me was at that time, in 2009 and 10, they were, I think, like seven or eight known bean to bar chocolate factories in America. I forget the name of their first like craft guild that they were in, but it was like — I don't think the Mast Brothers were in it, but Tazza, Askinosie… what's the name of that guy — Amano Rogue. I think Escazu was in it. Maybe let's call it two other people, two other known companies. Tazza. Askinosie. Patric Chocolate was another one in that group. Those ones are still going and growing. Like they're still big companies. Rogue I don't think is in there anymore. I'm not sure if Amano does it.

But the point of it was I got into this thing and I was like: *This is amazing. I will do this forever. Like you get to sort these beans you roast them and it turns into this chocolate this is absolutely out of this world.*

And so I was just jacked up. *This is amazing.* And I actually moved to Raleigh to go to college, to get into NC State, to go into the PGM program to be a superintendent of golf courses or Land Management or something like that because I'm a golfer. And I was like: *I can't buy land to be a farmer like my relatives, but I gotta do something outside.* I'd spend so much time doing other things that I was, I gotta do something associated with that.

And I got lucky and I got a job at a chocolate factory.

And then fast forward: What I like to eat and how my brain processes cocoa beans into chocolate other people like to eat. That's one part of it, right? The next part is my ex-wife and I, when we were working at Escazu, I'd always watch her interact with customers in this really wonderful way and I thought: *Well, maybe we can build a counter for you and I'll make the chocolate and you sell it to people.* It's like: *That's great.*

Life has weird way of turning and twisting and stuff like that. We got divorced in, technically, 2019, but 2018.

But from the first day of opening our doors, our whole goal was to be friendly and welcoming. So that was like what our whole thing was. I think at the time we made like four chocolate bars. We didn't have bonbons until the end of 2012-ish. So it was literally, there was no coffee counter and it was just an open space essentially. So from that point forward we had to say, like: *What's our goal?* And our goal was to create a community around this really neat thing that is chocolate. And then the space that we're in, because when we moved here in 2011 and this building — The Pit was here and there was nightclubs essentially everywhere else. Boxcar was I think a place called The Sky Bar, or something like that, and they were a Thursday-Friday-Saturday night kind of club. Crank Arm wasn't here yet. Trolley Pub wasn't here. The Single Store wasn't really there yet. Baldwin& the marketing company moved in a couple years. But like Tasty Beverage was here. Jose and Sons which was called Jibara. And then I think Tuscan Blu Italian restaurant was here. And then at the end, I think it's always a Junction Salon. The warehouse districts foot traffic was a concern in 2011 and 12 — There wasn't a whole bunch of foot traffic.

And so we were like: *How do we get people here? What are we, how are we engaging them in our factory?* And then in a dollars and sense way, we were triple the cost, quadruple the cost of most chocolate. Every single day somebody goes: *Why is it so expensive?*

And we have to, in a friendly and welcoming way, say: *This is why it's so expensive.* Or: *This is why it's so high quality.* And that part of it is the engagement and the educational piece, for us it's why we want to talk to people.

When you come to the counter you go: *Hey, what does this taste like?* That's when someone goes: *Oh, it tastes like "this" because of "that."* Or: *Would you like to try a sample of this chocolate bar?* That's friendly and welcoming, it starts our whole process.

So as a comparison point, you may have gone into other chocolate factories or chocolate spaces where they kind of look at you like: *You don't know?* And you're like: *I actually don't. That's why I walked in here. I would like you to tell me.*

For us, we're more interested in having a conversation and chatting with people. And a lot of times our conversation will lean into — *So you walked in here, are you from out of town? Did you just move here? Where are you going for dinner or lunch?* Or: *Have you tried this place? Have you tried that place?*

And that's why we have all of the different places that use our chocolate over there and why we think of it as partnerships because, to me, when we first moved in to Raleigh in 2009, we got plugged into a community through a record store called Schoolkids Records that I think is over in Mission Valley now, but it was on Hillsborough Street and my ex-wife worked there when she lived here. I forget what year it was in early 2000, but we started meeting people and it was like: *Oh, this area is full of amazing people!* And then I started meeting people that I knew from my skateboard career. It was a light bulb moment: *Oh, this is community and here's how we're gonna you know, go.* And then we met some really neat people that were restaurant owners that were into the idea of all, you know, all tides rise all boats kind of a thought process. And that momentum was just really fun. And then you know, we just kept on doing it and thinking about it.

And then I always go back to both sides of my family, but, specifically my grandfather, my dad's dad. At his funeral he had 700 people. And about 300 were his family members and the other, the literal majority of the people, were people he worked with, connected with, and touched his life. And at one point my Uncle Don, who's a really neat man, he gave, one of the eulogy speeches... I forget exactly... I'll butcher it, but essentially said: *If Ray Ratto ever bought you a meal, raise your hand.* And literally the whole church raised their hands. He asked: *If Ray Ratto ever asked you a question about your family, raise your hand.* Everybody did it. And so I think going all the way through it and thinking about that is we want to interact with as many customers that want to interact with us. And we want people that come in here to understand and feel as special as they should when they come into a chocolate factory — Because how many people walk into an actual bean to bar chocolate factory on a regular basis, you know what I mean?

Physically when we get the POS report from Square, 80% of our customers are new every day.

Kelsey   That's incredible. Wow.

Sam   So if you think about it, not 80% are regulars. 80% of people that walk through that door have never been here before.

Kelsey   Every day?

Sam   Every single day.

And, in a larger sense, if you think about that in a very abstract way, every single time a new person walks in the factory, they probably have never been into a bean to bar chocolate factory before. So if we aren't friendly and welcoming, they would be like: *Why would I come back here?*

Now you can kind of pull that out a little bit further and — I don't know when the first time you came in here, but if you can remember, did you walk out of here and tell somebody about it?

Kelsey   Yeah, absolutely. I think I told my entire family.

Sam   So I think that's what our connection is. In that way, we're connecting in that way where somebody and especially the people that work at The Pit always go: *If you don't want this kind of dessert, go across the street to Videri.* That to me is that part of that community and how we become a part of the community is because we *want* to be a part of the community and we really enjoy this community.

I say this dumb dad joke all the time. I moved here in 2009 and I'm never gonna leave unless they kick me out. I hope they never kick me out.

So that's the most concise way I can tell that story of how we became a fabric of this community. Because we really enjoy talking to people, number one. Number two, we enjoy talking to people about chocolate.

With the exception of myself and Mordecai, nobody in here had ever worked in a chocolate factory before they came to work here. So we hope to impart that joy and that sense of wonder with everybody that works here.

And we don't really give a shit if you went to culinary school, it's great if you did, or if you have a literary degree like Carrie does. We're like: Great. You want to learn how to make chocolate? And if people do, then they do.

Kelsey	That's awesome. It's so accessible too. And the first time I came here was probably back in. I don't know it was I think 2015 or 2016 — And with your space and when I was growing up, Willy Wonka Chocolate Factory was my only understanding of a chocolate factory.
Sam	Same. I thought it was candy. I thought chocolate was candy. Yeah, I had no idea it was a fruit or that it could be good for you.
Kelsey	Yeah! The first time I came here I went for a tour and it's like everything is open. So you get to see all the machines and it's very accessible. So I wonder: How do you all here and how do you conceive of that accessibility with a factory versus like the really problematic factory systems in the world? And this is so different from that, and instead based on fun and joy and learning. So how do you conceive of all that?
Sam	The part of my *why* is that the first thing I want to be able to do is I want to be

able to making enough chocolate, sell enough chocolate that I can buy tonnes and whole lots of beans from farmer communities, farms, or co-ops or groups in cacao growing countries that can affect and change their lives in a positive way. As opposed to mass market chocolate, their whole goal is to keep those people in poverty so that they can keep buying their cocoa beans for a very low price. That's my first one.

How do we do that in here is that we educate people that a chocolate bar should cost 9, 10, 12, 15, 20 dollars. Not a dollar, right? So, how do you do that without beating somebody over the head with it?

The the word "videri" comes from the North Carolina state motto, which is "esse quam videri," which means "To be rather than to seem." But in Latin it loosely translates to "to be viewed upon." It's where the word "video" comes from. So if you think about it, it was a really nice tie-in — The word "videri" sounds delicious. The V is iconic in that sense. But really if you think about it, we're to be viewed upon. *What are you looking at? What are you seeing?* And how am I supposed to charge somebody— I mean, shit, when we first started it was six dollars for 40 grams of chocolate... I don't think it was two ounces of chocolate. And when you went to Whole Foods and they do like the price comparison of like per ounce cost or whatever, I mean we were at like $3.50 an ounce or something. Like it was some ludicrous amount of money compared to, you know, even a Green and Black or Endangered Species or something like that. People are like: *What's the difference?* And we respond: *Well, here's a difference. Here's the flavor. Here's the profile. Here's this. We're nut free. We're peanut free. We're legume free. We're gluten-free. We're soy free.*

And people would ask: *Why is that important to you?* And we, you know, would tell a story about it, but the important part about it was — Honestly for me, what I saw in the chocolate industry coming into it, coming out of skateboarding, because skateboarding is all about marketing — You are marketing a product where there were five shoe companies that weren't Vans or Nike or Adidas or whatever. They were made in the same little work factory district in South Korea. Same materials. Same whatever. Technically the same — I'm sorry, *functionally* the same kind of shoe. How did you differentiate yourself? It was with marketing. How did you tell your story or these personalities? When I was working there, Rob Dyrdek was huge for DC and I worked for another company where one of our main athletes was Daewon Song. Well, how do you market those two different types of people to different types of skateboarders or lifestyle or whatever?

So I was like, going back to this, I always understood that you have to tell the story of like: *Why is this important*? And the easiest way for us to do it is to show people why it's important. You know, show people that we literally hand sort every bag of beans. If we didn't show that to somebody, would they believe it? They'd be like: *Oh, that's BS*. But if you're like: *Look. Here it is.*

And now, we're in the pandemic, we're able to have the time and space to make videos. With the little QR codes that we have you can walk up to the Sorting Room and if there's nobody there sorting like on a Saturday night, you can scan the QR code and watch like a minute and a half long video of like what sorting looks like and why are we sorting.

Roasting. Winnowing. Grinding. We're finding all those things. So we had to show people that it was fun. And then you get a lot of good, fun conversations about people saying: *I had no idea that when you say you're tempering bars or chocolate, like you literally put a plastic mold and three bars are made and you're shaking it —*

Kelsey	It's so cool.

Sam	*Put it in the fridge. You bring it back out.* So that was, for us, it was the whole impetus of it. And then you go back to it. As you can probably tell, I'm a talker.
Kelsey	[chuckles]
Sam	It gave something for you to talk to somebody about. It gave something for you to engage with somebody. And then, you know, people always ask us why we're nut free because nuts and chocolate go perfectly together. Amazing. But we're nut free because when I first started, one of my best friends has a severe tree nut allergy. So I thought: *Well, I gotta have everybody I know eat this. So let's just start out this way.* And then you kind of zoom out, there wasn't really any chocolate factories in America that were tree nut free specifically, peanut guaranteed or soy or legume or gluten-free. It was another selling point: *Oh, that's another differentiating factor.* Thinking about business and all this stuff. You are constantly asking yourself: *What would differentiate us from other brands?* And so you have this first part, and there's always this tug of being like: *Oh, man. I really want an almond dark chocolate sea salt bar.* And you know, I'm about to pull the trigger on the idea to not be nut free anymore: *We're not nut-free anymore. Like we just want to make delicious things with nuts.* And you'll have a mother and a teenage, like, 13, 14 year old boy and we're like: *Oh, do you want samples?* They respond politely: *No. Sorry. We can't eat chocolate. It has nuts in it.* Then we respond: *Oh my God, we're nut free.* And they go: *Really?* And we go through the thing and we say: *We've been nut free since the beginning.* And literally both of them start crying. So if you think about it, that's connecting a community, right? Unintentionally, we connected a community of people who are nut free. And then people talk, you know. Nut free. They say: *You're the only chocolate we have in our house and we tell*

people about it. And we've gotten bulk customers, like restaurants or things like that or bakeries, that are also nut free that buy chocolate from us because we're the only ones that are actually nut free. And like we do like surface swab testing. We get our chocolate tested at NC State yearly to see like: *Are there any of these things in there?*

So, we have the trust of our community because the backbone of it is I had a really great friend of mine, but then you move forward and you go: *This is a safe place for people.*

And we've had some situations where you know — We've had people that, you know, bring in a bag of nuts and eat them on the tabletop. Or I made a mistake once where we had a party and we had like some charcuterie trays and actually put them in the wrong place. Not the production area, but, you know, then we go and sanitize everything in there and go: *We made a mistake.* And then we swab and see if there's any remnants of it. But that's kind of that level of, like, transparency, but you're connecting communities.

Kelsey	And it's just like this kind of radical inclusivity.
Sam	Sure.
Kelsey	Which is wonderful and it'd be a lot easier not to do that. So I think that's great.
Sam	Yeah.
Kelsey	[laughs] No, that's amazing. And so my work is focusing on how we learn by making things. So like how have what have you learned? Probably a lot about the food itself, but what have you learned by making chocolate? About

yourself. About the food. And maybe about other people.

Sam   So what I've learned about making chocolate is that there is no straight line. From an agriculture product, if you're trying to do it with less inputs. So like the single origins that we have, like the 75, 90, now we have 100% bar.

Kelsey   Oh gosh, I didn't know that. [laughs]

Sam   Yeah, it's really delicious actually. It's quite astounding how good it is. But you're looking at cocoa nibs and sugar. So what we've learned is that there is not a straight line to a bar of chocolate that's delicious. And then we've also learned that if I like a 75 Guatemala, you may not like a 75 Guatemala. So in the beginning, I think we had like three or four single origins, and it was more of a stance: *This is what we're making. And you should try this because this is different or new or it's fascinating us or tasted really good.* Now we have I think six or seven single origins and they all have different flavors in them. You know, one of them has — The 75 Ecuador has this like hazelnut somewhat blueberry flavor. The Dominican Republic has like a dry Cherry kind of cocoa flavor. The Uganda has like a sweet, almost like pomegranate kind of flavor to it. And this is all chocolate, not putting anything in it.

There's that learning experience of what we've done and how we've done it over the course of — It'll be 12 years in December [of 2023].

What do we learn about chocolate making? I learned that your best laid plans are only plans. And the whole goal is to make something that people will enjoy, right? So if there is something that I, as a person, and us, as a company — We don't ever force you to want something. So we're not gonna just make this thing and never change or never adjust it based upon customer feedback or our own feedback. So a question we get a lot is like: *What's your favorite thing?* I'll be like: *Well right now my favorite thing is this X.* But everything we make we eat. There isn't anything in this building that we don't eat.

You may go into, and I'm not saying this in a negative way to other people, but some businesses cater to their customers more than they cater to their spirit and their, like: *This is what we love.* You know, the first seven years I worked here, we would get this question all the time: *Do you make turtles?* Which are caramel pecans covered in chocolate. They are delicious. There's no debating that they're delicious. I mean we got it 20 times a week: *Do you make turtles? Do you make turtles? Do you make turtles? Do you make fudge? Do you make turtles? Do you make fudge?* And it was like we'd have these meetings with our team: *Should we start doing this?* And it was like: *I don't. I don't want to make that. Like it is delicious. There are other people who do it really well. But is that what we want to make?*

And so we kind of balance that learning of chocolate making — We're learning how to roast a certain variety of beans. Grind it. Refine it. And turn it into something that tastes delicious. And we're trying to get it to taste delicious so that customers will buy it on a regular basis, but that we also can stand behind it and say: *When we smell this bag of beans, this is what we thought it could make in a bar of chocolate.*

And then the constant learning, that just physical constant learning of everything. I mean there are countries that we get beans from that go through political instability or even natural disasters and you can't get those beans anymore. And or you have to raise money for that community just to get them back to being a regular community before you can even farm anything again.

And then you just get beans that from one season to the next, they taste and smell completely different. And you have to go: *All right. This has a little bit of whatever new flavor in it now. It used to just have cinnamon and this in it. Now it has this new flavor and aroma. How do we do — Do we bring this into our flavor profile, or do we figure out a way to, like, reduce that so that it isn't a shock to somebody who's been buying like a 70% sea salt bar for years?*

Kelsey   Ugh. That's my fav.

Sam   Right? So I think that's the other part for us. It's a constant learning process because it's an agricultural product. And we're also trying to communicate to people that it *is* an agricultural product. A Hershey bar has 12 ingredients in it and I think the fifth one is the word "chocolate." And the word "chocolate" can be three ingredients. And they do not have to tell you what those three ingredients are.

Kelsey   [sarcastically] Cool.

Sam   So, that other part of it is the reason they're doing it. And I say this with all due respect, it is a Scientific and an Industrial Revolution magic product — That they could figure out how to go and take a very wide variety and vastly different cocoa beans from wherever they're getting them for their mass production to taste the same.

I think they say that customers' or consumers' pallets change every five to seven years. So they adjust their flavor every five to seven years based upon, like, what is in vogue, essentially.

Kelsey   I didn't know that. That's interesting.

Sam   Yeah, NC State Food Science Department, actually. They are flavor and sensory masters, they always update us on what is going on in the world of flavor:

Yeah, this is what we're doing now. Like X customer has been doing this thing for this many years and they're trying to get it to be more, a little bit less sour, or trying to get it to be a little bit more this. Like you think about it just kind of tweaking a dial of being like: *How do you do this?*

And so that's like another part of it for us. It's: *What do we get and how do we make it into something?* So with the exception of the 70% classic dark which coats all of our bonbons and makes 70% sea salt and the milk chocolate — Everything else is like: *What is this? How did this come into that? And how can we turn into something people eat?*

Kelsey — I like that because I growing up, my mom told me that Libby's Pumpkin, the canned pumpkin that you can get like at Food Lion that comes from Texas, I remember her telling me one time that depending on the weather, the pumpkins will taste differently, but that company has to modify how it gets canned. That way when people make the pumpkin pie recipe on the back of the can, it tastes the same every single year. I like that you all kind respect the flavor of the beans a little bit more. And with your bonbons too — I remember we had family friends that were moving out of Raleigh and we gave them a going away gift of your bonbons and it's like — It's just nice because you really appreciate them a lot more. Like you think: *Oh, these are really small, but they're so good and they're so beautiful.* You really savor that a lot more. And there's far more intentionality with eating this chocolate than like a Hershey's bar.

Sam — Yeah, like if you're gonna buy a $25 box of eight bonbons, right, versus buying — What are those, the like the bite size? You know, any of the bite size things from Hershey or Mars? That's six bucks and you're just, you're not just gonna scarf $25 worth of chocolate. Now if you do, good for you. And there's a lot of people who do it and I'm like: *That's amazing*. But we tell people: *This, you know, sea salted caramel, which is one of my favorite things, take two bites of it. If you think of it as a square, bite it and make two triangles. Eat one and then savor it.* We're not trying to make candy. We're making bean to bar chocolate. And, you know, a lot of people don't like that our bonbons are $3.25. And I mean we get reviews all the time and, please if you have time, read the Google Reviews, because I'm the one that responds to them and I respond to them in dad joke verse. Somebody wrote one recently that said: *$3.95 for one piece of chocolate? No, thanks.* And I responded [laughs], my response was: *So good you upped the price.*

That's my version, again, still friendly and welcome. I didn't rage respond to them. But intentionality and savoring are a larger part of what we do. And again how once you buy something from us, however you treat it or enjoy it or whatever — It's on you. We have guidelines and parameters. We say: *Don't put it in the refrigerator, freezer. It doesn't make it taste any better. You know, you know if it melts and it turns kind of brown, light brown, put it in a microwave for 10 to 15 seconds, add whatever you want to or pour over ice cream or just eat it like that — Also delicious.* So it's even that level of detail we have a parameter. We have a, I wouldn't call a boundary. We just say: *Once it's yours, it's yours, right? It's yours.* Like we get the opportunity to get a raw product that are fermented cocoa beans, smell them, roast them, and go: *This is what we want to do*. And every once in a while, going back to what we learned in chocolate, there are times in the roaster, because that's where we really put our creative flavor profile on it — every once in a while in that roaster, we'll forget to flip a switch or see something or maybe the burner goes up a little bit higher and when it comes out, we're think: *Well this tastes better. We're gonna start doing it this way.*

So even to that point, that's how we're kind of constantly learning. There are people that have worked here before that do not like that way of producing. They want you to have a step 1 to step 100 and we're gonna follow these steps all the time. And I have to kind of look at them and say: *I hate to break it to you, but I can't tell a farmer that. If it's raining when the perfect harvest is coming and they don't want to go out in the rain or they can't and they have to wait three days and it's a little bit past a little bit past —* Am I gonna complain to them that they should have went out in the rain and put themself in danger or did it show up three days late? Showed up three days late. What does it taste like now?

So, I think that the learning aspect of it is constantly like at the forefront of what we do.

Kelsey
Yeah, and also seems like care is too. Like it feels like the whole infrastructure is very caring, which is really —

Sam
We try and do it. I mean, we are a commercial enterprise that is a part of, as they call it, now late stage capitalism. We all have bills to pay. I have investors. We have Roundup Charities that we like round up for. There's things that we have to pay for. So there's part of it where we still have to make money on some level. We're in America. I am not independently wealthy so I can't just keep being like: *Yeah, whatever. Here's another hundred grand, two hundred grand. Whatever.*

We still have to run a business and we have to run a business so that we can buy raw goods from the people, right? There's sort of that part of it.

I was raised in a very Catholic household and my family background is very interesting in that, like, my dad's side of the family — I think every one of his, with the exception of one or two people, everybody has married somebody in a like multicultural or different race. Most of my cousins are not — It's not like I grew up in a family, and no offense to anyone that has done this, but it's not like everybody married like an Italian Catholic. What's interesting about that is most of my aunts and uncles have a very interesting perspective about immigration. They have a very interesting perspective about race and politics. And of the 28 cousins that I have on my dad's side, we'll kind of look at our parents like: *How did we turn out like this? How are we just like:* "Oh, you're a person? Great. Oh, you want your name to be Elaine now, not Tom? Great." Whatever I'm more interested in the idea: *Do you want to talk to people about chocolate and do you want to have a good time with it?*

And you can see in our Roundup causes and things that we donate for charities, we try as much as we possibly can to find things that are about involving more people than narrowing their focus on people. And I think we're on our fourth Black Lives Matter sign. The people take it out of the ground. I'm like: *Is it really that intense? Like, do you really have to take this out and throw it in the street?*

Kelsey People steal the signs?

Sam Yeah, all the time. But I got a little off track there. But the learning part of it is the central part. When we hire somebody here, we tell them, openly: *We're learning.*

You may know this as a company that has been around for 11 years and you, you've been in 2015 — *Oh, my God. This is a great company.* Well, I am a founder of a company that I did not go to school for specifically, or have a degree in business management, or I've not run a company before this. I am learning how to run this company. In that learning, the same way you're gonna learn how to make chocolate, I'm learning how to run a business. I'm also learning how to make chocolate. You know, I can't blindfold make a 70% blend right now. I still have to follow an SOP and make sure the numbers are right and see if the flavors are going this way. And again, some people are interested and some people are not interested in that word. Some people that aren't interested don't work here anymore.

Kelsey And that's okay because it seems like you're really pruning and making something really beautiful and also it seems like everyone's just everyone here is learning how to be a kinder human too. That's all we can ever hope for.

Sam That's our goal.

Videri's classic dark chocolate pudding

A rich, creamy treat that's perfect for any occasion. Top with Videri's Cocoa Nib Streusel to take it up a notch! Makes 6 cups of pudding.

Ingredients

4 tablespoons sugar
3 tablespoons cornstarch
½ teaspoon salt
1 ¼ cup heavy cream
1 ¼ cup whole milk

1 teaspoon vanilla extract
8 ounces 70% Classic Dark Chocolate, chopped
1 tablespoon unsalted butter, room temp

Directions

1. Place the sugar, cornstarch, and salt in a medium saucepan and whisk to combine.
2. Combine cream, milk, and vanilla in a separate bowl.
3. Whisk 1 cup of the cream mixture into the dry ingredients mixture until the cornstarch is dissolved.
4. Whisk in remaining cream mixture until smooth.
5. Place saucepan over medium heat; whisk constantly until the mixture comes to a boil and thickens. The mixture is thick enough when it can coat the back of a spoon.
6. Add chocolate and whisk until melted.
7. Remove from heat and whisk in butter until melted.
8. Use a 3-oz ladle to pour pudding into 6 dessert cups. Cover and refrigerate until set, approximately 1 hour.

Serve as is, or top with whipped cream or cocoa nib streusel.

Videri's classic dark brownies

Ingredients

1 ¼ cups (5 ounces) cake flour*
12 tablespoons (6 ounces) unsalted butter, cut into tablespoons
¾ teaspoon baking powder
1 ½ cups (10 ½ ounces) sugar

1 teaspoon salt
4 large eggs
About 1 ½ cups (8 ounces) Videri 70% baking chocolate

*If you don't have cake flour: measure 1 ½ cups all-purpose flour minus 3 tablespoons. Add 3 tablespoons of cornstarch to the flour and sift the mixture twice. Use this in place of the cake flour.

Directions

1. Grease a 9"x13" pan.
2. In a medium bowl, whisk flour, baking powder, and salt until combined.
3. Place chocolate and butter in a separate heatproof bowl. Set bowl over a saucepan of just simmering water to melt, stirring occasionally, just until smooth.
4. Remove chocolate from heat and gradually whisk in sugar.
5. Add eggs to the chocolate mixture one at a time. Whisk after each addition to thoroughly combine.
6. In three additions, fold the flour mixture into the chocolate mixture just until the batter is smooth and no flour is visible.
7. Spread batter into prepared pan and smooth the top.
8. Bake for 30-33 minutes at 325° F on the middle rack of oven. Rotate the pan halfway through baking. Brownies are down when a toothpick inserted in the center comes out with a few moist crumbs.
9. Cool brownies in pan on a wire rack to room temperature. Once cool, cut into 2-inch squares to serve.

Underwood & Underwood. Sorting cacao for shipment to American and European chocolate factories, Guayaquil, Ecuador. New York: Underwood & Underwood. Photograph. Retrieved from the Library of Congress.

Two Roosters

"I think it goes down to our core values which are: be responsible, be a good neighbor, and be generous. And so we do all of those things in just the way that we present ourselves in the community, in the way that we connect."

Sarah Romeo
Director of Kitchen and Logistics at Two Roosters

Two Roosters proudly boasts: "Love people. Love ice cream. In that order." And their ice cream shops, the way they run and are sustained, are wholly based on this relationship and care between people and the love for ice cream. We can see this in how Two Roosters offers 6 guest flavors, designed by community participants, local authors and musicians, school children, and local businesses. In doing so, they commit to a mutual exchange of collaboration and support — demonstrating a more ethical form of capitalism that runs on the philosophy of Be Generous, Be a Good Neighbor.

Two Roosters in Durham, NC. Photograph provided by Two Roosters.

Gabi holding Two Roosters ice cream and Larry's Coffee's Gabi's Grounds. Photograph provided by Two Roosters.

a chat with Sarah Romeo

Kelsey — Well, thank you so much for being able to meet with me. Something that I know about Two Roosters is that — I go to the one, it's in the Mordecai area. I always get really excited when there's the month where the kids get to design the flavors. It's just so cute and it's also just sweet. And I remember my favorite flavor I have ever had at Two Roosters was one of the kid flavors. It was like lemon with rainbow sprinkles and lemon zest. And it's really amazing to see kids getting to take part. So it's just wondering if you can talk to like how that all happens and how Two Roosters is kind of dependent on these guests' flavors.

Sarah — Yeah. So, as you know, our guest flavors — We change six rotating flavors every month. It's been kind of a work in progress over the years to try to get to the point where we are now where it's not as difficult to switch over. Specifically with the kid chefs. So what the process for that is usually about a month before the month we're gonna have them on the menu, we put out an application. And we send it to local schools and the teachers help the kids put in applications as well as parents at home. But actually most of ours come from schools now. But they'll put an application with their flavor idea. And then what we do is we take them all, there's usually hundreds, and we sort it through. And some of them are just really silly ideas. Vanilla with rainbow sprinkles. And it's like: *Well, you can get that if you come to the store right now.* So we're not gonna make that into this specialty flavor.

But then sometimes they have these really great ideas. So then what happens is we take it to the recipe testing level. So we narrow down the list. We usually get it to about 10 to 12. And then we take it to the next group — Like our team the production team goes through and like: *Okay, what do we think will make sense all together?* Because we also have to factor in like: These are all chocolate based. So we're not gonna do these six. We're gonna try to make it a little bit more... I guess creative.

So we do that and then I take it to recipe testing. So I'll pick out what I think will work best and then we make them all and see kind of how they work. And so then once we do that, then when we go to the picture stage, we bring the kids in and they get to taste their ice cream and learn a little bit about the process. And then we take pictures of them and we put it on our menu. And it's usually one of our more popular months.

Kelsey	And you've worked with local authors and musicians. So, how do you do it? Is it the same process of you sending out applications to musicians?
Sarah	It's a little bit different because what our owner does is he actually creates a list and contacts them. So that he comes to them for those flavors. We don't ask them to come to us. We do have tons of authors and musicians and different — Whatever like collaborations we've done, those people like people send names in. So that's how we got ideas for like the second round of authors was because we did the kids lit authors the first time, and then like everybody and their mom was commenting on Instagram and emailing us and saying: *You got to do this author! They live here!* That's really how we're doing it now. It's just all about the connections we have with people around here.

Yeah those months, we usually — It's a similar process in that we send out a kind of like an interview almost, like a bunch of questions. We just have them answer them. And then I take those answers and kind of figure out: *Okay, this person says they like to drink coffee and eat something while they work.* So then we pull that out and make that into a flavor. If it works, we'll go for it. And then we bring them in here, and take pictures, and all that. The last time, the first time we did it last May we did some book signings type things at Quail Ridge. We had, I think, an event at a school — A teacher had requested that we bring this one flavor for this book.

So we did that. We didn't do as much of that this time around just because there wasn't a lot of like interest. We couldn't get any kind of anything moving quick enough. So.

Kelsey — That's amazing. It's just so cool to see how it's like fully saturated in the community to me. It's really exciting. And so with y'all at Two Roosters — like ice creams are happy. So what have you found to be a great lesson about working with folks in the community to make ice cream — Because it'd be so easy not to do that, but you all do that every month.

Sarah — Yeah, I mean I think it goes down to our core values which are: be responsible, be a good neighbor, and be generous. And so we do all of those things in just the way that we present ourselves in the community, in the way that we connect.

Jared got his start and kind of found this space because of Sola Coffee.[23] So it started there. And I'm not sure if you're familiar with what they have going on, but it's just like they are so community driven. And Jared, because of his own personal values, but as well as it's just how he wanted to operate a business. Like he just took that from them. Like they helped him kind of get started. Like they were storing some things in their fridge for him in the early days when he was still like at home testing with an ice cream maker on his counter like before he ever got into like opening a shop.

---

[23] Sola Coffee is a local coffee shop in Raleigh, NC. And it is situated in the same shopping complex as at the Two Roosters I met Sarah at.

They were helping him and I think that's really where like — It's just his personal values. And then when he hires people, he wants to find people that fit into those values, from all the way to the top to the bottom. Like that's always the goal. Like if we have people that share those same values, like that's how we give back in the community. That's how we make these connections.

Kelsey

And do you find that when you work with people — You mentioned the kids get to learn about ice cream, but I'm hoping that they also get to learn about some of these values as well.

Sarah

Yeah. Jared talks about them all the time. It's like that's how we want to present ourselves. So I think it's just making it a practice, even in our own personal life. That helps us to be able to do that here too. Being able to give back and help.

Like we have the Girl Scouts. We had a whole Girl Scout troop in here in February making ice cream with us. [laughs] That one was interesting. We used to have Girl Scout Mint on the menu. It was a whole situation. But because they only make Girl Scout cookies in the winter and you can only get them in the month. Like we couldn't buy them. They wouldn't let us buy them from the bakery directly. We had to go through the troops. And we bought, this was in 2021, we bought them and we ran out by August. And we were supposed to make it all the way till February with what we bought but we just grew and got so much bigger so quickly that we did not realize we were gonna go through that much ice cream. And so we just — We ended up opening an additional store that was not originally on the plan.

Kelsey

Yeah. So that's an exciting problem to have.

Sarah	For sure. So that's why we decided to go full force into an all Girl Scout month. So all of our flavors are Girl Scout cookies. The community loves that. It's fun to have the girls here — to have them come in.
Kelsey	Something with you working here and being part of all of this — You've mentioned the values and how that translates to the flavors, the hiring, and the involvement the community. But like what role does care play with all of that?
Sarah	When I started working here, almost two years ago now, it's like Jared was always very big on like: *Take ownership of your role, but take ownership of the way that you operate.* And so I think that I am heavily involved now in this business because I care about people. But even even bigger than that, it's like this is where my skill set was and it just fits perfectly with like my personal values, my like level of involvement and investment into the company. Like I would say that's really where my care comes in.
Kelsey	Mmm. And what are some of your favorite things and working here?
Sarah	[laughs] Eating as much ice cream as I want. Really my favorite part is flavor development. Like I want to take an idea and make it into an ice cream. And then like I get really excited when the people love it — Like when the community is just so excited.
Kelsey	In my family, it's like actually a ritual to have ice cream. And it's so *fun* to have ice cream. It's just really really joyful and fun. And so whenever we go to Two Roosters, it's fun to like sit outside and see so many people at picnic tables and so many kids like covered in melted ice cream. But is there anything else you think about in relationship to like Two Roosters, the ice cream work that

you all do, and like community, care, or making?

Sarah | I would say, like, I just appreciate working somewhere that, like, allow, like, encourages this type of community idea and like giving back and local collaborations. Because we're getting bigger in the community and like we're having a fifth store and we're gonna add like Wake Forest opens and three-ish weeks. Sometimes this month.

Kelsey | Congratulations!

Sarah | It's crazy. But like because we're able to do that and work in like multiple communities — Like Wake Forest. We're in Durham. We have a presence here. We're in Raleigh in three different places. Very different areas of Raleigh with very different demographics. But it's just cool to be able to make these connections for people. Like we make an ice cream with cinnamon donuts from Sola. So then somebody in Wake Forest is like: *What's Sola?* But then they get to go and they get to find out what that place is. Or we worked with Morning Rolls, a cinnamon roll place — They're very small and they were fairly new when we were able to work with them. And it almost, like it gives us the ability to help somebody, but just to provide a really good product. Like they make really good cinnamon rolls that made a delicious ice cream. But at the same time, we were able to work with a brand new business owner and like help them do some marketing from our end. Like: *Oh, have you been to Morning Rolls? You should go check this place out because these cinnamon rolls are phenomenal.* Because you don't know about it. Or like places like Slingshot Coffee. who are much bigger than us. We're working with them. So then somebody's like: *I've never heard of Slingshot.* And then they look it up and they're able to find it. Or Mystic Bourbon with our coffee bourbon — they're in Durham. These places all are like right here. Like Tin Roof Teas — we are working with them. It's just a way to like make those connections for even the people that don't live in North Raleigh where some of these places are. It's like: *Oh, I've never heard of that. But now I'm gonna go there because I learned about it at Two Roosters.*

Kelsey   It's cool. It'd be amazing if other businesses did the same thing where there was all this kind of mutual help and support happening all the time.

Sarah   I'd love to see more of that in the community.

Two Roosters: Flavor Creation Contest. Image provided by Two Roosters.

Ice cream by Two Roosters. Photograph provided by Two Roosters.

Fleischhauer, C. (1980). "Kitchen." Paradise Valley Folklife Project collection, 1978-1982 (AFC 1991/021), American Folklife Center, Library of Congress. Retrieved from the Library of Congress.

Chapter 6.
Sharing the table

(Between 1780 and 1830). "Architecture vivante [*Living Architecture*] - La Cuisiniere / chez Martinet." No known restrictions on publication. Retrieved from the Library of Congress.

Below I illustrate patterns of care across the various folks I spoke with, including Michael Evans, Sophie, and Rene from 321 Coffee, Leigh-Kathryn Bonner from Bee Downtown, Maggie Kane and Andrew Gravens from A Place at the Table, Chef Sera Cuni from The Root Cellar Cafe & Catering, Lilias Pettit-Scott at Well Fed Community Garden, Dr. Erin McKinney, JAC M from Wonderpuff, Sam Ratto from Videri Chocolate Factory, and Sarah Romeo from Two Roosters.

As emphasized in Chapter 3. Conversion charts: the methods, these findings were elicited through the prioritization of data feminism and design justice principles, as well as the use of intersectional feminism and critical pedagogy theory as frameworks of analysis. As such, the results are shared with the cognizance of power differences and systems, an embracement of my role as a facilitator of knowledge sharing among those who have participated (rather than a director or producer of knowledge development) to bring attention to knowledge and caring processes already in existence and practice, the emphasis on feeling, and to center the lived experience of the various communities and care-givers here in this work — as well as those who receive and are affected by their care.

Walker, E. (1935). "Women selling ice cream and cake, Scotts Run, West Virginia." United States Resettlement Administration. No known restrictions. Retrieved from the Library of Congress.

Makerspaces are, intended to be, democratized labs — focusing on easy access of making. Making 3D prints and creations. Making felt and cloth designs. Making Shrinky Dinks. Making pet rocks. Making everything. But the kitchen was the first Makerspace, the first lab (Livio and Emerson, 2019). Drawing our focus to making alongside and with food, while simultaneously prioritizing and reclaiming the communal, shared, and collaborative nature of cookbooks (via recipe sharing, co-constructing, mediating, and remixing) is drawing attention to role of "feminized" making that has occurred throughout history through "feminized" means of analysis and consideration.

In "The Feminist Makerspace: Smashing the Patriarchy with Crafting, Mentorship, and Connection" (2019), Meaghan Moody and Chava Spivak-Birndorf explore the "erasure" of women in makerspaces. They argue that this has occurred due to the narrow focus on male-centric technologies (including 3D printers) without an emphasis on crafting, which has historically been aligned with women: "Despite the fact that these activities are generally understood and accepted as forms of making, a culture of privileging high-technology over low-tech, crafting, and art projects prevails in makerspaces" (p. 184) and "This sends a message not only about the kinds of activities valued in the Maker Movement, but also about the kinds of people; while crafting, low-tech, and art are often coded as feminine, more complicated forms of technology are typically coded as masculine" (p. 185). And while these authors address the gendered projections unto making products, they also identify that "For women, making is often grounded in advocacy or resistance to oppression: the tools remain a means to an end" (p. 186). If we apply this to the making found within cookbooks, where the making is rooted in historically gendered and sexist spaces and roles, how might we continue considering the role of making with food? Cooking, baking, and food preparation are also grounded in such advocacy and resistance to oppression — as clearly demonstrated by the food and care work of Chef Sera and JAC at Wonderpuff, where Chef Sera speaks and works against food scarcity and JAC focuses on the happiness and community-building in Durham found within sharing cotton candy. Much like other forms of making that have often been discredited, devalued, and under considered, the making of food can serve as a rather radical means to an end rooted in resistance.[24]

Importantly, across the various conversations that this investigation followed, community was firmly rooted in *place*. For JAC, this was Durham. For those at Videri Chocolate Factory, this was Raleigh and the customers that visit their storefront — aligning with the areas and people that Two Roosters reaches with their various locations. Chef Sera identifies her restaurant as a community center, serving those in Chapel Hill (and the Pittsboro location serving those there in that area). Through this, she also focuses on procuring food from local farmers: "And it's just nice to know that here's this guy in my community. So my money is staying in the community, his money is staying in the community. So it's also helping our community, you know." Michael identities how a community has formed at their 321 Coffee's Pendo location when their staff and customers meet and have lunch together. Likewise, Sophie and Rene both speak to the powerful atmosphere they have found and engage with at 321 Coffee. The Well Fed Community Garden relies on folks physically coming to their garden facility, situated within a neighborhood, to tend to the plants. This community-rooted-in-locality signifies the importance of face-to-face interactions, connection, and exchanges of care. Much as the kitchen (historically and often now) was seen as the heart of the home, a space of domesticity, but also a place of making and sharing, we see how these businesses and people have found and created similar values within their cities, neighborhoods, blocks, and physical establishments.

the work of care

Across the various folks I spoke to, care and community are both enacted and engaged in vastly different ways.

At A Place at the Table, community centers around food; its preparation, its consumption, its clean up, its sharing, etc. And while their mission is "Community and good food for all,

---

[24] I want to draw attention to the phrasing of "can serve" here. As the role and process of making with food is not always liberatory, is not always radical, and is not always rooted in care. Because of the history of food preparation, we know that it can be, and often is, oppressive.

regardless of means" — they really are focused on facilitating community within their restaurant space and through food, as a vehicle for unification and commonality. Likewise, at the Well Fed Community Garden, food, and its care before it ever becomes part of a meal, is that which unifies the folks that visit and volunteer there.

For 321 Coffee, care is rooted in the necessity of constructing and maintaining a safe place for employees to help show all that the community (their employees) are capable of, but also in their prioritization on teaching the skill of hospitality — ensuring that anyone that goes to their shops "feels cared for and taken care of" (Michael). Here, treating others with care in this manner is an employable skill that their business relies upon, but also helps facilitate a work environment that acts as a "family" (Sophie).

Importantly, many of these folks may not immediately identify the work that they do as care work. For Leigh-Kathryn at Bee Downtown, she more readily leaned on the word "cultivate":

> Because the root of the word "cult," which, you know, positive negative whatever people want to say, but it means a deep sense of adoration. So the fact that cultivate is the word we use when we are raising bees and we are farming and we are growing crops and we are maintaining our farms and our livestock and we cultivate our land... It means to deeply adore something to the point where you will nourish it and care for it and take it from seed to harvest and make sure that it's fed and it's watered and it has the right sun and it's got shade when it needs it and that, you know, it's not too cold in the winter. And I think that that word cultivate is very much care at the end of the day.

For Bee Downtown, they are helping to channel care within and across Fortune 500 companies (that I, admittedly have, and perhaps still do, view as rather care-less and out of touch when we see how much far smaller companies care, and struggle, such as Wonderpuff, while they continue to be profitable) — namely environmental stewardship and care for others, in the form of bees. Yet, this interesting and valuable business of care only came to be because of the care that Leigh-Kathryn herself received:

> I was like the hometown, you know, NC State entrepreneur. Just the state poured into me. This community poured into Bee Downtown in a way where it probably shouldn't have worked, but because I was from here people were willing to take a chance to just try to support what I was trying to do.

At Two Roosters, we see community rooted in locality and the physical neighborhoods in which the different ice cream shops are located. As Sarah says: "We're able to do that and work in like multiple communities — Like Wake Forest. We're in Durham. We have a presence here. We're in Raleigh in three different places. Very different areas of Raleigh with very different demographics. But it's just cool to be able to make these connections for people." And then by existing and working and housing a business in these different physical locations, Two Roosters has seemingly construct a web of supporting infrastructure — A web that draws customers, a large force of their community, from their business, another force in their community, to others in the area. As Bee Downtown looks to the word "cultivate," Two Roosters seems to adopt the word "connection": " I think it goes down to our core values which are: be responsible, be a good neighbor, and be generous. And so we do all of those things in just the way that we present ourselves in the community, in the way that we connect" (Sarah). And these connections are perhaps the largest force of their community, the kids, the Girl Scouts, the authors, the musicians, and the folks that help develop their Guest Flavors each and every month.

Such as Two Roosters looks to their customers as part of their community, we see this also with Videri Chocolate Factory. At Videri, we see how the core values of being friendly and welcoming help to draw in customers, of which they see 80% new ones everyday, and these values most often take the form of interacting with customers. As such, their community is rooted and largely composed of people that are their customers, changing everyday. Because of this, Videri has to re-validate the work that they do each time a new person walks through the door.

> And so we were like: *How do we get people here? What are we, you know, like engaging them with?* And then in a dollars and sense way, we were triple the cost, quadruple the cost of chocolate. Like almost every single day somebody goes: *Why is it so expensive?* And we have to, in a friendly and welcoming way,

> say: *This is why it's so expensive.* Or: *This is why it's so high quality.* And that part of it is the engagement and the educational piece, for us it's like why we want to, like, talk to people. (Sam)

At The Root Cellar, Chef Sera focuses on community in terms of locality, much like Two Roosters. As such, The Root Cellar has, and continues to be, a champion of support and equity development for the folks that may (or already do) come into their restaurants, including farmers, girls, the LGBTQ+ community, local sports teams, those who may be hungry and in need, and more. With a location in Pittsboro and one in Chapel Hill, Chef Sera and her wife have really focused on *how* to help and then *doing* that help, as seen in their leadership in developing Pittsboro's first Pride event and Chatham County's Community Fridge program. In doing so, the Root Cellar has done work beyond their restaurants' intended capacity and labor to solve problems, including providing representation for LGBTQ+ youth and their families in a rural location in North Carolina and creating opportunities to combat food insecurity. Through this, the Root Cellar, and the hard care work of Chef Sera and her family, becomes about more than food within their restaurants' walls. It is about helping those around them.

Likewise, JAC at Wonderpuff holds a deep love and passion for their locality, Durham and the community found there:

> I just love good people. I just love good people. And I grew up in South Florida where it was very hard to find like-minded radical thinkers, like myself. And it's nobody's fault. It's just, unfortunately, we as a society — we've been conditioned and programmed, thanks to white supremacy and capitalism. And when I moved here seven years ago with my family, I found people who thought just like me and I'm like: *Okay, there are Freedom Fighters everywhere and North Carolina has so many.* I mean this entire land of ours has so many Freedom Fighters, but something about Durham, North Carolina.

And while the above businesses and folks cater to communities in their local areas or of the customers that they engage with daily, Dr. Erin McKinney offers a unique stance of working within the community of NC State University and the broader fields of their study and research, but also microbial communities that most people never think about.

> Well, I'm a universal empath. Like I love people but if it's alive, there's a chance I can relate to it. Like it just makes sense to me. So, like what does that community want? What do each of the microbial players in that community want? They just want to live. And if we provide enough nutrients or, you know, complexity then there's space, niche space for everybody. But like if there are limitations, that's when we start to get more toward opportunistic competitive microbes and that's a lot of what's in a sourdough. Yeah, it's really really fun to me to think through those dynamics.

Through this, Dr. McKinney speaks to the non-human and more-than-human community members of our world — aligning with the care research of Donna Haraway (2016) and María Puig de la Bellacasa (2017), both of which draw acute attention to the capacities, roles, and needs of those that are more-than-human.

Above, each participant and collaborator illustrates how their work intersects with their aims and goals of care, namely for community and giving. Yet importantly, JAC offered one of the only instances of acknowledgement of care work as labor and its corresponding effects, stating "Giving is a whole other form of labor, especially when it is free labor." This aligns with much scholarship and research pertaining to the often unseen, unpaid, undervalued, and absolutely vital care labor that exists within capitalism that most often falls on the shoulders of women (DeVault, 1994; Perez, 2019). In framing giving as labor, JAC poignantly distinguishes this form of care-based work, that which is rooted in care and is most often supplemental for business owners, from that which is needed to be done to maintain and sustain a small business. Moreover, in this acknowledgement, JAC demonstrates how giving and care are indeed labor and *work*, regardless of the fact that that it is something that one may enjoy doing or performing.

Jewish Historical Society of the Upper Midwest. (circa 1940). "A spontaneous family snapshot capturing the delight of being a woman in the kitchen cooking the family meal." No restrictions, via Wikimedia Commons.

Importantly, across the many interviews and discussions, there were few (if any) discussions or mentionings of challenges, of hardships, or of difficulties. Overall, the conversations were quite well-spirited, uplifting, and overwhelmingly positive and optimistic. The Well Fed Community Garden didn't mention if there may be fiscal pressures from occupying land in a location that is in prime real estate. 321 Coffee did not address any challenges of working with and for the disabled community, and how they, the owners, manage and navigate this as individuals that do not have the same disabilities as their employees. Two Roosters didn't share if there have been times when their philosophy of being a good neighbor was not reciprocated — and what the consequences of their mission may be.

These are all hypothetical challenges that may have never afflicted these establishments, yet we know that nothing exists without challenge — especially small businesses in this global economy.

However, the absence of the negative in these conversations is not consistent with reality, as we know, and the realities of care work — as evidenced by the lived experiences of caregivers, care providers, those who are dependent upon care, and the research that has been mentioned thus far.[25] Moreover, the absence of the negative here is not consistent with reality and the realities of care work — as seen in images, in literature, and in pre-existing research.

Through an intersectional feminist lens, we see that perhaps here we see the various folks that I interviewed as performing an image of care as that which aligns with and upholds their business values and protects the care of their establishments. Yet, in doing so, they are also upholding a performance of care that is rooted in optimism and joy, and the historically and stereotypically feminized dispositions associated with performing such labor. As such, these overtly joyful and positive associations and performances of care obscure the layered complexities, difficulties, and labor associated with such work.

---

[25] See: Care as labor, Care as radical intersectional feminist action, Care as survival, Care as nourishment, Care as making, and Care as cute.

In interviewing emerging businesses, which many of these participants were, I was engaging with young businesses and owners that are tending to their growth as the survival of this business. Through the pervasiveness of positive legacies and reputations, they were practicing and performing care for their business, company, and work. Our corresponding discourses on care were shaped by and with the organizational values and missions of these folks, but also acute self-awareness and consciousness about representing their businesses.

And yet, as JAC illustrates so poignantly, there can be a tension between the care of our business and the care of our communities and our selves:

> I just love, I love giving. I also think that could also be sometimes a very bad thing, right? Because as a small business owner you need to make money to stay afloat. And I tend to give a lot of our products out for free. For example, a Wonderpuff is probably the least expensive. So like out of everybody here at Boxyard, my product is the least expensive and for me being the cheapest, I give a lot away. You know, I give a lot away. For example, if you are a regular customer and you come like once a week and you support everybody, you're most likely gonna get free products from me and end up spending 30, 40, 50 dollars at other neighbors. And you know, I shouldn't be giving our products away for free, but it just, it just something... You don't think about it when you're doing something like that, you know what I'm saying? And I don't feel some type of way — I feel like I can't do it enough. So yeah, I, I — we love that about ourselves.

And while optimism is pervasive across all these conversations, there is also great pride in doing work that prioritizes care and community.

New York Public Library. (1890s). "Kitchen (preparing dinner)."Repository: The New York Public Library. Photography Collection, Miriam and Ira D. Wallach Division of Art, Prints and Photographs. No restrictions, via Wikimedia Commons.

the careful stories

We see theory and praxis aligned for feminist efforts through the method of storytelling and storysharing (Johnson, 2022; Christle, 2019). As Bellacasa writes: "Even more than before, knowledge as relating— while thinking, researching, storytelling, wording, accounting— matters in the mattering of worlds" (2017, p. 28). Additionally, as Morales emphasizes, stories and their power are not limited to that which is conveyed orally or written down: "Actions are also a form of storytelling. Sitting in the front of a bus, lying down in front of a train, stopping work, leaving a school building, blocking the loading of a ship—these are all new stories about reality that contradict official versions meant to uphold the horrible status quo" (2019, p. 45) and "Listening to, analyzing, creating, and disseminating stories, and doing so with courage, keenness, skill, and cunning, with the clear purpose of changing human consciousness in the direction of choosing justice—this is what organizing is all about" (2019, p. 46). This concentration on the capacity and power of storytelling is exemplified in the conversations I experienced with those who participated in this work.

Unlike many of the businesses mentioned that focus on locality, Videri's community is rooted in their love of chocolate: "And our goal was to create a community around this really neat thing that is chocolate" (Sam). But Sam's lived experience of working in the skateboarding industry also revealed the importance of marketing — and how a story is a valuable tool for that. Their chocolate is currently free of many common allergens, and Sam now turns to storytelling to emphasize the significance of this within the chocolate industry, and how this has, in turn, resulted in trust and vulnerability across the community: "So, we have the trust of our community because the backbone of it is I had a really great friend of mine, but then you move forward and you go: *This is a safe place for people* " (Sam).

Likewise, Chef Sera at the Root Cellar shared how her own lived experiences surrounding food shaped the stories of her childhood and the stories she seeks to preserve and share now:

> Sera: You know, I have books like my grandmother would write recipes. You know, one side of my family is Italian so they're always very good about, you know,

> making sure everybody knows how to do everything. And my grandfather was a president of an Italian American Club, so they would put out a cookbook. So this cookbook I found moving. I found it all dirty and stuff. So I scan into my phone. I scanned every page. And then I printed it so that my aunt could have it and everything like that. But it has, it'll say things like: *Don't use this, don't use it.* Like my grandmother would write: *Don't use this. This was Eleanor's recipe and it doesn't work.* But it's so great.
>
> Kelsey: And it's so much better than a manual!
>
> Sera: Yes!
>
> Kelsey: And I love seeing like olive oil —
>
> Sera: Oh my god, it's so dirty! Even like my scans have like the coffee stain on the cover and everything like that. But eventually that paper is going to deteriorate. And I have it now. And my grandmother, my mom's mother, wrote everything on those little index cards. So I've been scanning all those in because, like, eventually I want to write a cookbook.

And while Chef Sera's stories are rooted in food and family, and the deep desire for the preservation of memory and its nostalgia, Dr. Erin McKinney's use of storytelling is more so found in their role as an educator and her search to better reflect her work, who she is, and how she came to be a "celebrity scientist."

Similarly, Leigh-Kathryn sees how storytelling aids in communicating to others the need and value of work, but she also draws upon the role of the familial — much like Chef Sera:

> But in the world of startups, like we're young in the world of corporations. We're a super young company. But whereas, you know, some startups are trying to sell something that nobody knows anything about — everyone has a memory in agriculture. Everyone's grandfather or grandmother was a farmer or gardener. Everyone grew up with a farm or, you know, wanted a horse when they were little.

> And people today, they want land and they can't afford it yet, but they have this dream of living on the land in a way that the bees make it nostalgic. And so it's like safe to them in this way, because it evokes memories in a really beautiful way. And then everything we do is storytelling. It's just the core of who we are and what we do. We find ways to tell beautiful stories and help corporations tell their stories in relation to the bees as well. And that makes me happy — like finding how the stories fit each company because every company is a little different and the story we want to tell is a little bit different, but once we find it — like it's so exciting to help them tell it…
>
> …And I deeply believe that food brings people together. The stories of food brings people together. Bees do that in a great way. You just have the ability to have that story. But all food does that. And care goes into cultivating it and growing it, but it also goes into how you prepare it and how you cook it and how you wash it and how you, you know, dry different things and can things and preserve things.

Here, Leigh-Kathryn illustrates the power of storytelling and nostalgia in relation to food and agriculture. In doing so, she posits these avenues, and their use in stories, as a powerful tool and avenue for equalizing experience. While not everyone has grown up on a farm or near a farm, many can relate to playing pretend with a toy horse or watching plants grow as the seasons change. Like Sam, Leigh-Kathryn identifies the capacity of storytelling and story sharing as a business maneuver; one in which stakeholders are reminded of their own youth, their own relationships to food and nature, to create a unifying force to tie them to Bee Downtown. It is effective because nostalgia and storytelling are powerful devices that strive to equate and draw parallels between the human experience through similarities, emotion, and affect. Moreover, relying and looking to storytelling, in the ways that Sam and Leigh-Kathryn, as well as Chef Sera and Dr. MicKinney, do, illustrates the multifaceted capacities of storytelling — and how this skill and art are invaluable tools and treasures that are infused in and with care.

the capitalism of care + the care in capitalism

Importantly, each of these folks are connected to businesses[26] — whether that be their own business or one that they are employed for or with.

This context is important because it is easy and simple, yet reductive and misleading, to look whole-heartedly at each of these's folks efforts towards care and community as just that: efforts towards care and community for the sake of care and community. However, taken with the significance of their business standings, we must reckon and reconcile with the fact that, as businesses, care and community effort are also effective strategies in the scheme of capitalism, which contributes and ensures the oppression of some, namely those who are already most vulnerable, including people of color, children, people of the global south, those who are disabled, women, and more (Morales, 2019).

And, on one hand, the mission and strategizing of inclusion makes business sense: when more folks are included, more will spend their money there. This is seen in how Videri Chocolate Factory strives to make their food more accessible through their exclusion of many ingredients that are common allergens. Or how Bee Downtown works with many huge companies that contain a high saturation of wealth. But, the sustained effort to make something (cotton candy, honey and bee education, chocolate, meals, coffee, recipes, opportunities, memories) alongside and for a diverse, inclusive, and pointedly welcoming force is something to be noted.

For Two Roosters, we see a form of capitalism that is rooted in and dependent upon collaboration and the mutual exchange of services, ideas, goods, and customers. JAC at Wonderpuff resists capitalism boldly, while recognizing that the United States exists within and through a capitalist system that we can only fight against so much. As JAC states:

> I'm really anti-white supremacy and white anti-capitalism, even though we have to pay bills and I like to buy, I like to buy snacks and gummy bears and gifts for my friends. Like: *Wow, don't I love money but also I want to burn everything down.* And I don't know. I am that way for a reason and it's because I have a hard

---

[26] One could argue that NC State, where Erin McKinney teaches, *is* a business. I argue that.

> time learning. And when I learned cotton candy, I'm like: *Oh, this is something easy.* I want to take the easy way out when it comes to existing in capitalism. I want to use very little resources, very little energy. What can I do that — And that's also the Taurus in me. I want to give very little and I want to get so much back. And in society under capitalism, it doesn't work like that. In order to get a lot, you have to work a lot. And oftentimes you have to kill something and that is either your soul, your knees, your back, time with your family, time with yourself. And I'm a firm believer like: *Okay if I have to exist in this hellhole and this democracy that people are suffering in, what can I do to make my life easy, not overwork myself, and bring joy to the community?*

As JAC emphasizes, to work, let alone to care or live or survive, under capitalism requires participation within it. Similarly, as Sam states:

> I mean, we are a commercial enterprise that is a part of, as they call it, now late stage capitalism. We all have bills to pay. I have investors. We have Roundup Charities that we like round up for. Like there's things that we have to pay for. So there's part of it where we still have to make money on some level. We're in America. I am not independently wealthy so I can't just keep being like: *Yeah, whatever. Here's another hundred grand, two hundred grand. Whatever.* We still have to run a business and we have to run a business so that we can buy raw goods from the people, right? There's sort of that part of it.

While A Place at the Table and 321 Coffee are non-profits, we see how other businesses use their profits to help benefit the communities that they serve and the localities that they are home to — see most notably with The Root Cellar Cafe & Catering and Two Roosters. At The Root Cellar, Sera has devoted great time and energy to not only relying upon local farmers and food producers, but also strategizing how to solve hunger issues in her county — in addition to leading the development of Pride events in places where these have never been before. With Two Roosters, we see how the prioritization of *being* a good neighbor comes to fruition: by looking to other locals (artists, businesses, restaurants, Girl Scouts) to help develop and drive their own production and consumable goods. Moreover, they hope to see their own way of doing business emulated by others — something that also aligns with 321 Coffee:

> 321 was founded first and foremost on this mission and there are a lot of companies where it may be more like a secondary thought, but there's also nothing wrong with that, you know. Like that is how change is going to come about is that we need more people to get to that almost, like, second step. (Michael)

Similarly, the Well Fed Community Garden practices sustainability with their profits by sharing the harvest (literally) with those who have a hand in the garden, and using commercial profits from Farmers Markets to support operating the garden and urban farm.

While these businesses and individuals all expressed their goals of a more just, ethical, and fair business model operating within a capitalistic system, these conversations and findings demonstrate a gap in and potential need for more research surrounding the intersection of care and capitalism. Most research identifies and acknowledges the complicity of capitalism in upholding and reinforcing oppressive systems, yet where do capitalistic endeavors that try to do good within this framework fit? How do they add a layer of complexity?

equity + justice + making

How are equity and justice supported in the community through the process of making? What role do critical making, critical pedagogy and experiential inquiry play in supporting equity and justice?

Throughout the various conversations explored here, we see several instances in which equity and justice are worked towards through the focus on making alongside and with food. This is perhaps most immediately seen with Chef Sera's work through the Root Cellar in Pittsboro and Chapel Hill, where Chef Sera is currently employing and supporting two young women and even paying for one to attend culinary classes. Employing the young women at all is a step towards equity in the professional kitchen where, as Chef Sera reminds us, many women are unable to find work due to pervasive sexism in the food industry. Moreover, Chef Sera's work in the development of community fridges throughout Chatham County to combat food insecurity is a clear demonstration of working towards equity through food access, and using the privilege of owning and operating a restaurant to help others that need food. Chef Sera says:

> We are supposedly in the greatest country in the world. In Chatham County one in eight are hungry. It's one in eight. They don't know where their next meal is coming from. That hits so hard for me that I am like: *That can't happen...* I mean, I understand that it's food and it counts and they need nourishment. Whatever. It's so part of a human right to be able to sit down and eat dinner with somebody that they shouldn't have to worry. Kids should never have to worry about that.

Likewise, 321 Coffee and their various shops and locations demonstrate how leading with a mission rooted in equity works towards justice. The building of 321 Coffee itself is a poignant testament to the celebration of its mission: while a small building that is easily physically/literally overshadowed by its neighbors, its pseudo-stained glass windows and bright atmosphere offer a sharp contrast to the cold, gray, metal aesthetic that is claiming (aka: gentrifying) the street. As Michael stated:

> [Other opportunities for the disabled community weren't] challenging or it wasn't right. It was — It wasn't about them. It was: *Oh, you can wash the dishes, but you're not allowed to be out front.* And so we wanted to create a business that was, like, centered around: *Hey, look at everything that this community is capable of.* So I'd say the mission came first, coffee came second.

And yet, Michael recognizes that while they at 321 Coffee led with their mission to work with and for folks with disabilities, there is still great value in businesses that approach similar work secondarily — because they are getting and working towards equity and justice, which is the point.

Conversely, Bee Downtown seems to be offering opportunities to work towards equity and justice through their focus on environmental stewardship — namely for Fortune 500 companies.

By fostering environmental stewardship, responsibility, and care among these companies and employees who possess great corporate (and otherwise) privilege and wealth, there is a placement of responsibility and onus among those who, perhaps, should and have the capacity to bear it. This is not to say that not everyone should care about nor care for the environment, but that there is something subversive occurring when responsibility, care, and accountability are placed on the hands of massive corporations with massive power. In learning to care for the bees, Leigh-Kathryn identifies that they will care more and do more. But perhaps this extends beyond the environment. In learning to care for the bees and the environment, they will also learn how to care for those in the world who need it. As she explains:

> And it's our goal, in essence, to help cultivate great places to work — but rooted in agricultural education which leads, typically, to increased environmental stewardship: when you know a little bit more, you care a little bit more. But we do it in a way that we try to make it fun and very inviting to people where if you do a little bit, it'll make a big change in the world.

By making care fun, and focusing it on bees, these companies and their employees will learn how to care. And I would argue that this care must trickle down and we must hope that the bees, who already do so much for our planet, will help us to take better care of each other.

Collectively, each of the individuals that participated in this work engage in experiential inquiry through the "factory" or business model that necessitates them working with their hands to develop and make a product for others. At Bee Downtown, the team teaches folks how to take care of bees themselves and how to analyze and think through the food we eat through their Honey Camp. Dr. McKenney encourages students to work with microbial matters to better understand the subject at hand. JAC spins and shares cotton candy to facilitate the spreading of magic in sugar form. In this sense, there is an exchange of experience. For example, at Videri Chocolate factory we see great attention focused on the experience of making chocolate to then teach others about the beauty and importance of ethical chocolate production. Through this, customers then experience it for themselves upon speaking with employees and then eating and consuming the chocolate.

With this in mind, each of these businesses and individuals all engage in critical making alongside food — from cotton candy and ice cream to sourdough and honey; however, not all participants engage in critical pedagogy as explicitly as experiential inquiry and critical making. While critical pedagogy is perhaps elicited to support and lead to critical making, many of the participants included here have not, or did not in their conversations with me, address their goals or methods to "empower the powerless" (McLaren, 2015, p. 122).

Nor did they ask questions such as: Who is not present or included within our customer base? Who have we unintentionally left out? What are the effects of this? Who is harmed by our work? How can we invite more people to the table? How can we center those who are most underserved and oppressed? Recognizing the complicity within capitalism, how can our business help those most affected by the negative effects of capitalism? How might a culture and attitude of benevolence patronize those who wish to come to our establishment?

While these participants did not engage in instances of critical pedagogy with me, that is not to say that they do not. Moreover, many of them do exchange in striving towards the outcomes of critical pedagogy, including justice and equity — as addressed above.

As such, we may need new terminology in the future to investigate how critical pedagogy occurs out in the world beyond traditional pedagogical frames or to further consider the processes of such work.

the responsibility + burden of care

In considering the role of care in reimaging power, who is responsible for the care, labor, and power of ancestral and community stories, histories, and affect? Moreover, how does gender intersect with care? What is the relationship between gender and care? Who is responsible for care (and all that is cared for/is made through care)?

As I hypothesize above of how the responsibility of caring for bees is placed on major corporations through the business of Bee Downtown, we also know that care is regularly placed on those who understand the need and importance of care as they themselves are often individuals that need it or practice giving it — and they simultaneously are often among the undervalued and underappreciated. As JAC at Wonderpuff addressed:

> You ever notice that? The things that are most needed in our community are those that are being undervalued, underpaid? So many teachers and nurses and doctors all over the world they're quitting every day and you're like: *Oh my God!* So what does this mean? Does this mean more prison, you know, school to prison pipelines? Does it mean more homeless people in their cars? Like what, what is going on? And that is the, it's just... I think maybe I'm also learning that I may not be, maybe I'm more than an entrepreneur when it comes to Wonderpuff. Maybe I'm supposed to be doing something else. Hyping people up. Waking people up. Letting people realize that they are powerful. And we are powerful by numbers, and that's what our democracy doesn't want. That's what our politicians don't want. If we erase the color lines, if we erase the gender lines, if you erase the class lines, if we just literally — And I'm not talking about some kumbaya bullshit like: *Oh, I don't see color.* I see color, you know. And even if I was a non-able person who wasn't even able to see, I would still be able to understand.

While JAC focuses on the professionalization of care, and its subsequent undervaluing over-dependence, she also emphasizes the consequences of lack of care, including increased homelessness and a widening of the school to prison pipeline, which already impact different people of different positionalities in uneven ways. And while JAC emphasizes the importance of unity in the face of oppression, discussions of care cannot and should not be divorced from discussions of race, gender, class, ability, and the historical contexts and lineages of all of these.

And in focusing on gender specifically, both JAC and Chef Sera address the role of gender in making with and alongside food. Aligning with Perez's *Invisible Women: Exposing Data Bias in a World Designed for Men* (2019), JAC states:

> Right. Right. [singing] That is very very very true. Which is so funny because living in our patriarchal society, society tells, oh tells women — I mean not only do they care, they hate uteruses, people with uteruses, but they tell people who are femmes and people who identify as women that, like, we got to be in the kitchen. However, in the food industry, it's all run by men. And it's just very weird how that dynamic is kind of like that everywhere too, right? A lot of things are run by man and oftentimes men who don't care about anyone but themselves. And for Wonderpuff and for me, and Reem, and our team members, we just pride ourselves in dismantling all of that. You know what I'm saying? Anything that is slightly close to white supremacy, we like to go the opposite. Even if, even if that means walking by ourselves. Even if that means looking crazy, because it's weird every time you speak up for what is right, people are just like: *Shut up*. You know.

In identifying the pervasive and oppressive sexism in patriarchal systems and the deep seeded racism of white supremacy, JAC expresses great intentionality in working against and in opposition to these oppressive systems and ideologies and the pattern of professional and commercialized food-making dominated by men, and, thus, devoid of care.

Likewise, Chef Sera and I discussed the role of gender in her kitchen and others:

> Sera: But also, It's so, you know women traditionally cooked in the house for, you know, like families. But there's no women in the profession. Like we don't get that, we don't get gratitude and all that for being in the restaurant.
>
> Kelsey: Why do you think that is?
>
> Sera: I think it's just that you know, it's everything is male-based, you know. Like everything. Like there's, you know, your mother might have cooked for the family down the street and then you know this and this and this. And then like so, you know, my grandmother might have done this and I'm like: *Well, I'm gonna be a chef*. And they're like: *Why?* You know, like I went — One of my first jobs I went and I interviewed, I was out of college, hadn't even gone to culinary school. And I

> said: *I want to do this*. I had worked in a pizza restaurant making pizza so it wasn't like I didn't know anything. And he's like: *Well, I would hire you, but you're never working in the kitchen. You could be a waitress*. And I was like: *I don't want to be a waitress*. He's like: *Well, no woman's ever gonna work in my kitchen*. I was like: *Well, this woman is not working for you*. And I left. But like that was 30 years ago, and I'm still telling the story.

And now, Chef Sera employs young women — working against the precedent that was established in her own life, against working towards equity and justice. Yet, this demonstrates, as JAC illustrates, that the burden of responsibility for care, for change, and for betterment does not fall upon those who are upholding the oppressive and discriminatory systems and establishments, and often falls on the shoulders of those who care. All the more, JAC illustrates how this work of care is unevenly experienced and carried:

> We need white women. It's very very important for white women to do the work alongside Black and Brown women because Black and Brown women have been doing the work. Like you said, it goes unjust. It goes unseen. It goes unrecognized. And when we have people of privilege who can use their privilege to dismantle their, you know, dismantle violence — It's very important to have white women as allies and I take it very seriously. I take it very seriously.
>
> Unless... during like the BLM movement, there are a lot of white liberals who were really showing their asses and you're just like: *You are also a part of the problem and that's also a problem and it's not my problem to fix that*.

Here, JAC illustrates the significance of positionality and the matrix of domination in relation to care labor, work, and burdens (Crenshaw, 1989; Collins, 2015) and how women of color have been engaging in work, especially that pertaining to justice and equity, long before white women joined the conversation. In performing this labor, they have also experienced the duality of this vital labor being unseen and unrecognized. Moreover, JAC addresses how white women are complicit in oppressive systems, and that the burden of teaching white women to recognize and remedy this does not fall on the already laden shoulders of people of color (hooks,

2000/2015; Eltahawy, 2000; Kendall, 2021).

In furthering analysis from an intersectional feminist lens, and differing from Jezer-Morton's identification of care within the "tradwife" model (2023), there seems to be a fetishization of care as fixated on the performance of a grandmotherly-like figure: an older woman in the kitchen with an apron covered in flour making biscuits for family.[27] To evoke this grandmotherly performance is to evoke a sense of nostalgia, as demonstrated with A Place at the Table where the folks that operate the business want the restaurant to *feel* like a mother's kitchen with grandmother's food. In doing so, they strive towards a culture, climate, and atmosphere that is rooted in the performance, feeling, and memory of care (as these archetypal characters of Mom and Grandma are dripping in historically-associated performances and responsibilities of care). While this upholds a fetishized performance, it aids in facilitating a space that feels safe, familiar, and welcoming to all. It also showcases how a restaurant/business can embrace a historically feminized atmosphere to great success, operating in contrast to the man that refused to hire Chef Sera 30 years ago.

---

[27] A Pumpkin Pie Porter beer in my fridge from Clayton, North Carolina's Deep River Brewing Co. reads: "Our Pumpkin Pie Porter won't stick to your ribs like Grandma's cooking but it sure packs a fistful of flavor. We pack over 7 pounds of pumpkin per barrel into this beer along with our perfect blend of pumpkin pie spices. We know Grandma always said 'Don't spoil your supper with too many drinkypoos' but we say indulge because Grandma is in the kitchen drinking dandelion wine anyways!" It also has an illustration of a pie with "#NotYourMemas" written on the pie tin.

Muray, Nickolas. (1939). "McCall's magazine cover, family arriving in the kitchen for the holidays." No restrictions, via Wikimedia Commons.

This feeling and essence of the grandmother was also evoked by Leigh-Kathryn: "there's the ability to have care in all of our food. And I think, you know, women especially in the South like that is, for so many of them, that's their legacy. *How do you bring your grandchildren to the table?*" Notably, Leigh-Kathryn also speaks of her multigenerational beekeeping legacy that includes her grandfather and uncle, but not her grandmother or other female family members. The legacy that Leigh-Kathryn speaks to, and that which is elicited by the performance of a grandmother in spaces or in dishes, is firmly connected to the kitchen and the food preparation that occurs within — not the fields, meadows, or seas where food may be found, harvested, and sourced. Similarly, A Place at the Table aims to make their space feel like a home, specifically a grandmother's, Leigh-Kathryn looks to story sharing and memory making to demonstrate the legacy power, and perhaps the burden, of care work in relationship to food. And perhaps because of the effect of speaking and looking to maternal family in this way, I myself unintentionally referenced and spoke about my mother in relationship to food, making, and care in nearly every conversation.

Moreover, Chef Sera also demonstrates how she is, happily and proudly, documenting the recipes, and their corresponding stories, from her family, her wife's family, and encouraging that same practice among friends. For Chef Sera, this is a practice of pride, of love, and of familial remembrance — yet it also exists as another avenue of labor. Importantly, as these conversations help to illustrate, we can find great joy and happiness in a form of labor that is focused on care, while also experiencing fatigue and pressure from it. Labor and care are not mutually exclusive. This is best demonstrated by JAC, who stated:

> But as a small business owner you end up overworking yourself and doing all the things that you said that you aren't gonna do. You end up doing it all. You end up over-exerting yourself. You end up working, over-working, and overextending yourself and pouring from an empty cup.

This speaks to the work of care, but also the burden of care. More importantly, throughout the conversations I engaged in, those that addressed fatigue (in relation to their paid labor or childcare) occurred with women or femme-identifying individuals, seen in JAC's comments above or how I spent a great deal of my time with Dr. Erin McKenney discussing childcare and balancing being a working mother before and after our official discussion about this project. This aligns with past scholarship, as addressed in Tools + frames + theory and Care materials, while also highlighting that care work that engages in critical making and experiential inquiry also necessitates labor that is experienced or acknowledged unevenly.

the capacity of cookbooks for change

As seen with the capacities of cookbooks, how can systems and manners of knowing more equitably and critically enable exploration, learning, and care to reimagine power (of care, literacy, and justice) and knowledge (production, recognition, and legitimacy)? How can cookbooks serve as a template for more equitable and better knowledge sharing?

Importantly, many of the folks that participated in this investigation spoke to working against traditional academic knowledge models or expectations. When talking about his journey to become a chocolate maker, he said: "I'm not a chemist and I didn't go to college, I don't know the technical way that it works. I just understand that it works." Similarly, when teaching me about the various levels of beekeepers and their retrospective testing and legitimatization processes, Leigh-Kathryn stated: "Those tests are hard and they're not necessarily… it's the, like, academic knowledge versus the applied to knowledge." While Leigh-Kathryn herself is a Journeyman Beekeeper, she identifies how this testing accreditation has affected beekeepers: "it's like you start to lose some beekeepers where, you know, fantastic beekeepers that aren't Master Beekeepers. And you'll have not great beekeepers that are actually Master Beekeepers because they know how to test." Leigh-Kathryn herself, a fourth-generation beekeeper that learned much from her family, shared that neither her grandfather nor uncle have gone through all the testing. This demonstrates how familial knowledge and that which is firmly rooted in experience and praxis is not weighed with as much value as that which is assessed with a test, with credits, and with an academic framework. Furthermore, this very framework to measure and award legitimacy has turned away and excluded many expert beekeepers for whom such testing processes are not accessible, useful, or realistic.

Likewise, Dr. Erin McKenney spoke to the issue of accessibility in learning and teaching as a gut microbial-ecologist: "And [sourdough is] the perfect conduit and framework for citizen science and outreach because it's countertop science, right? Flour and water and a spoon are generally much more accessible than like sequencing materials or any guts and poop" and "making this sourdough accessible, like, you don't have to be an expert baker." Through this, she focuses on how this hands-on, accessible, and experiential learning that occurs through making and maintaining sourdough starters enables a form of citizen science, or science that exists beyond a classroom. Moreover, Dr. Erin McKenney identifies that in research, "publications are the currency of academia" and lack a relevance or air of necessity among those who aren't in the academy — echoing Leigh-Kathryn's concerns about beekeeper accreditation, and perhaps Sam's own acknowledgment and example that academic knowledge is not always needed.

Collectively, these all (ironically) corroborate much pre-existing research that illustrate that academic, traditional, and/or credited, legitimized knowledge is not always needed, that it can indeed be limited and exclusionary, and that there is great value to other sources of knowledge (Apple, 1999/2014; hooks, 2000/2015).

And in looking to cookbooks specifically as sources and objects of knowledge, Chef Sera addresses her goals of constructing a cookbook herself and I look to a story that Leigh-Kathryn shared about her grandmother to emphasize the value and capacity of cookbooks, as I hope to have done throughout this work:

> It was she you know, like she always cooked... She always cooked. We always cooked. Yeah, she made a cake. Granny's chocolate cake. But when she got sick, she told me, she said: *I'm gonna teach you how to make my husband catchers*. And that was, like, what she wanted to teach me how to make. She wasn't gonna be here and so she's like: *Well, I need you to figure out how to catch a husband.* So I was like: *Okay, Granny*. Like: *Let's make husband catchers*. And she's like: *Great!* So we start cooking and all this stuff and I'm kind of looking around like:

> *Oh, Granny, what are we making?* She said: *Sug, I told you husband catchers!* And she said: *Cuz then you gon catch yourself a husband.* I was like: *Okay.* I said: *Granny, are these Hush Puppies?* She's like: *Mmm and if you can make 'em like I can make 'em, you're gonna catch a husband.* And she wanted me to learn how to make husband catchers and she wanted to pass on that, you know, knowledge.

This story demonstrates the care that is infused into making food, as something that is nourishing and, as Granny would perhaps argue, something that can ensure one finds (a husband and) security. Food, and its making, is about more than just food. In this instance, it is about the craft and process of making in community and collaboration, and the communal experience of doing something together — memory making.

And while Leigh-Kathryn shared this story as a reflection on the importance of the link between food and care, it is also a testament to the knowledge exchange that can, and often does, occur alongside the preparation and making of food. Here, Leigh-Kathryn's Granny performs the actions and instructions of a cookbook, sharing why one should try to learn/make a recipe and then teaching and instructing how to make a dish. But Leigh-Kathryn performs the beauty and value of cookbooks by infusing her storytelling, positionality, and memories into this mentioning of hush puppies.

Moreover, her story represents a great power of cookbooks to elicit, document, and transfer feeling and emotion — which serves as a valuable tool of intersectional feminism (Ahmed, 2017; D'Ignazio & Klein, 2020; hooks, 2000/2015). These texts become a vehicle through which these feelings are permitted and enabled to be shared alongside the exchange of information, namely recipes, escaping beyond the limiting wall of academic knowledge (Moraga, 2015; Eltahawy, 2020; hooks, 2000/2015; Kendall, 2021). And, as such, they rely, intentionally or not, on their unofficial knowledge recognition (Apple, 1999/2014) and identification of "simply a cookbook" to reach more and more people, and to "include the historical experiences and cultural expressions of labor, women, people of color, and other who have been less powerful" (Apple, 1999/2014, p. 52).

As such, cookbooks offer the capacity to transfer the care of making (and its responsibility, its burden, its pride, its joy) into a text that is then able to be read, used, cared for and by anyone. In doing so, they serve as democratized and accessible works of teaching and learning that are reliant upon construction and making led by the reader (rather than a teacher, an expert, or a professional). Through this, power and autonomy are shifted to the reader to lead their own efforts.

In addition to offering strategies for cooking and baking, they also offer advice, informal positionality statements and local contextuality. Small vignettes will often accompany each recipe — notating how the author, baker, developer came to this food and how they found this version that they want to share with you.

Additionally, cookbooks operate with a primary medium that we all engage with: food. As I learned throughout the various conversations, the value and unity surrounding food cannot be understated. As Dr. Erin McKinney stated:

> Because it is a basic need, right? Like we all have to eat. We don't, we can't all eat gluten, but we all have to eat. And so for people who can engage without a visceral reaction, food provides such a fabulous opportunity to bond. And it reminds me of different peace efforts like Community Gardens in Israeli and Palestinian communities, right? But like: *You can grow a garden together.* And you realize slowly: *Oh, right. They have to eat too. Oh, because we are all humans.*

In acknowledging that we all eat, Dr. Erin McKinney identifies a strong commonality across all people. We may eat different things, in different ways, at different times, in different settings, but we *all* eat.

And while Dr. McKenney does much research on sourdough, JAC pointed out a great issue with the fad of sourdough baking that proliferated during COVID-19: "And I stopped comparing myself when we saw millions of people die in 2020 and people were in their kitchen making sourdough bread and watching *Tiger King* and we saw all of our nurses all over the world just get a round of applause. [scoffs] You know?" Through this, JAC is addressing how a great portion of people were fixating on TV shows and baking, rather than the humanitarian crisis of the pandemic. She further states: "So many people are suffering, and suffering is not a Black or white issue. It's a planetarium issue. It's an Earthling issue. We are all suffering. And the moment we can recognize that, the moment that we understand like: *Oh damn. Like we really do need each other.*" As such, both JAC and Dr. Erin McKenney illustrate a powerful sense of unity and connection in efforts to reach betterment. For Dr. Erin McKenney, an avenue to connection and togetherness is achieved through the power of food. For JAC, unity is in closer proximity when we realize and acknowledge that we are all experiencing pain and we can help each other.

And while discussions of food elicit opportunities to consider and evaluate unity across and within communities, cookbooks themselves offer a bit more complexities. There are, as Dr. Erin McKinney emphasized to me, limitations and disadvantages to the form of cookbooks in of themselves:

> Erin: Cookbook. Follow this, you expect to get this. And if you don't get that, then it's wrong. You messed up. But they don't even tell you how to troubleshoot it, right?
>
> Kelsey: That's true. Right.
>
> Erin: It's just: *Well you did that wrong. Here's what it's supposed to look like.*

Whereas I have illustrated the wonders of cookbooks, here Dr. McKinney draws attention to the isolating solitude that one experiences when working through and alongside a cookbook. There is no one to explain the recipe to you if you do not understand, if the recipe is poorly written or documented, or if you need to make adjustments or modifications. Worse still, you are alone (without the author, developer, cook) in your making. As such, there is perhaps a latent sense of abandonment that exists within cookbooks, due to the lack of assistance, reassurance, and help. And while there are ways to supplement this (like making with family or friends, Google-ing how to adjust a recipe to be egg free, accounting for differences in oven types) — one could argue that the default of cookbooks is the banking model of education that Freire argues so strongly against (1985). *Take these things, make this thing this way. This is what it looks like.*

All the more, cookbooks can be identified as objects and texts that uphold patriarchal oppression by situating knowledge production, dissemination, and experimentation within the most historically feminized of spaces: the kitchen. In doing so, one could identify the subversive nature of cookbooks, yet we must also acknowledge their complicity in and going with-ness of the patriarchy (Eltahawy, 2020). How could a cookbook become even more radical and revolutionary? What would this look or read like?

While I have demonstrated, however, that there are also many facets of cookbooks that work against the banking model and do align with critical pedagogy, it is worthwhile and necessary to recognize these significant limitations in the nature of cookbooks as they exist at a rudimentary level.

Summary

Importantly, care isn't soft. Care isn't idealistic, but makes room for contradictions and complexities when the system doesn't have ethics baked in. And while enacting care, even when community oriented, cannot be divorced from capitalism and economic systems, with many of the folks here, care provides an opportunity for a more viable, more ethical (if there could ever be such a thing) flavor of capitalism.

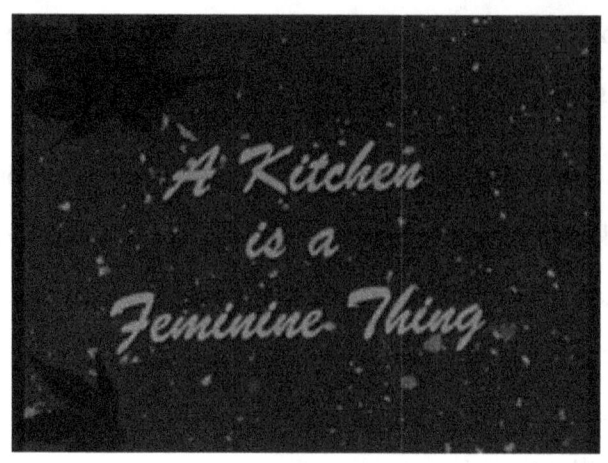

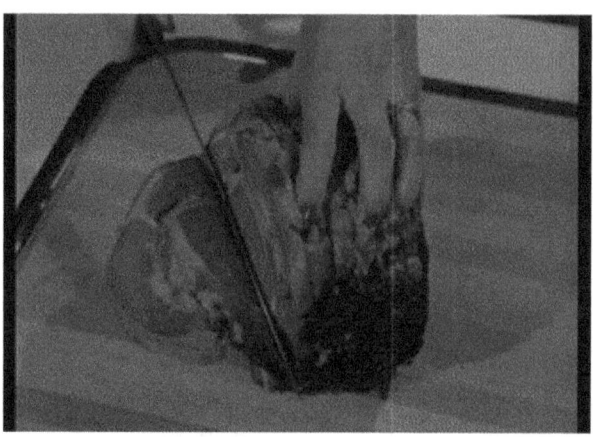

Robert Fisher Productions & General Motors Corporation. (1960). Frigidaire Division. Stills from: "A Kitchen Is a Feminine Thing." Library of Congress, Motion Picture, Broadcasting, and Recorded Sound Division. Retrieved from the Library of Congress.

"A Kitchen is a Feminine Thing" we are reminded as the bright cursive stands out against a splattered background with dark leaves. Yet, these stills visually illustrate a more beastly and eerie kitchen scene than the associations of femininity that plagued the American 1960s.

While black and white, I imagine the fingernails digging into the meat as a knife serrates clean slivers are just as red as the meat filling into the nail beds. The knife is just as bright, cold, and silver as the wedding ring. The same hand then dotingly holds a plastic-wrapped wedding cake. Here, the bright white frosting draws parallels to the marbleization of the meat just cut, but the light reflecting off the plastic encompassing the slab of dessert is all the more eye-catching. The woman, the owner of the hand and the fingernails and the ring, looks down upon the miniscule groom figurine, trapped atop white frosting and underneath suffocating plastic, as she goes to set the cake in the dark fridge with a knowing smile. The real life groom may be the owner of the knife, the fridge, the home, and even the woman, but here, in the kitchen, she shuts his miniature away.

Chapter 7.
A recipe for necessary disaster + disruption: A manifesto

Here I have practiced interrogating the genre conventions of an academic mode of knowledge production and how academic arguments are and can be made in a way that is just as credible, but far more accessible — and emulates the way knowledge has been communicated and transmitted via gendered routes of community resources, namely cookbooks. In doing so, they illustrate a disarray of traditional models and expectations of how knowledge performs. However, cookbooks are not alone as potential models of more equitable, inclusive, and creative forms and avenues of knowledge sharing and preserving. Indigenous knowledge practices remind us to look to nature to see how the world around us has been preserving knowledge that we often do not even draw our own awareness to (Kimmerer, 2013). Familial legacies and histories, told through stories, journals, and diaries, also demonstrate the power of preservation and lineage — as well as how we are all capable of such documentation (Cuni, 2023; Bonner, 2023).

Yet in looking to cookbooks, as I have done here, we can see how these texts serve as a powerful model of how knowledge can be, and has been, made public-facing and accessible through its multimodality, its intended engagement, its simplicity and humanness, and more.

The recipe (or manifesto) below outlines how we can continue striving towards that which cookbooks achieve and what they can teach us, beyond food, and towards the needed disruption of the pervasive knowledge systems:

1. **Collaboration + community-centered**

   When knowledge is focused on that which is produced in collaboration, people and learners are able to gain access to a more dynamic, more enriched form of knowledge than that which may have been produced in isolation. As such, knowledge and information that is produced and disseminated communally should become a norm, rather than the exception or novelty.

2. **Accessibility + differentiation**

   By prioritizing accessibility and differentiation in knowledge production, dissemination, and sharing, we are also prioritizing inclusion and equity in reaching a variety of people and learners with different needs, experiences, and expectations. As such, this knowledge sharing and dissemination must also rely on transparency, including clarity in how data and ideas were obtained, in how that information is conveyed, and how it is to be found and shared.

3. **Multimodality**

   One of the most exciting parts of a cookbook is the different ways in which something is represented, communicated, and shared. Readers are provided with stories, recipes, and photos of one meal — all to best aid in the reader's own understanding and development of their own personal making and application. By including multiple representations and multiple modes of information, cookbooks are better equipped to reach their readers — once more increasing accessibility through differentiation.

4. **Making-centered**

   There is great benefit to our learning when we get to *make* something and see a process of creation from start to finish.

   > Sera: They don't comprehend and they have that goldfish, 30 second thing. They sit there and they write and write, they don't — They might just memorize it, but they don't understand it. But when you sit there and you show them something like: *This is how you make a muffin.* Like: *It's egg and it's milk. And then you take*

> *it and froth. And then they're like: Wow, that's really cool. We're just like, I mean — Even science things. Like, you know, like we grew up making volcanoes and all those kinds of things and these kids they don't. They learn how to do, I don't even know what, from YouTube.*

Likewise, the benefits of critical making enable implementers of such making to apply knowledge through an exploratory project-based process. As such, knowledge forms and representations that encourage folks to *apply* and *put to action* evoke similar advantages of critical making.

5. **Heart-led**

    The current knowledge economy is rooted in institutional ownership and prowess — where knowledge must adhere to a performance established by an elite, racist, sexist system, or it is not recognized as such by the masses. However, what might a knowledge system rooted in care look like? How may it be better equipped to serve a broad, expansive, and diverse public?

6. **Critical care**

    Most importantly, we need critical care as a framework through which we conduct knowledge production. I define critical care as:

    a. Enabled through the prioritization of critical theory — or the radical questioning, exploratory interrogation, centering of lived experience — in efforts to work against, fight, and overturn oppressive systems and strive towards equity for all.
    b. Alongside the methods of critical theory, critical care is enacted when care is at focus. Care for self, others, our communities, and particularly those who are most vulnerable and needing of care. As such, care is a strategy of attention, of work, and of equity.

c. Critical care is a reminder that: Care is not soft, care is not liberally given or entitled, care is not expected, care is not without cost, care is not an expected duty, care is not without fault, imperfection, and mistakes. And: Care is liberatory, care is hard, care is labor, care is historically complex and messy, care is effort towards betterment.

Wong, Nancy. "Poet Cyn Zarco in kitchen of her apartment on 8th Avenue in San Francisco, California, 1975." CC BY-SA 4.0, via Wikimedia Commons.

Chapter 8.
Cleaning the table

As someone who is not an expert cook, making a meal and then enjoying that edible meal can feel like a magical moment. When olive oil pools on top of a soup in shallow rivers of gold, that feels magical too. Or when you scoop ice cream on top of the boxed brownie you just pulled out of the oven at the end of a long day to eat as you watch a movie. Magic.

For Leigh-Kathryn, magic is found in the bee boxes and the way she is able to blend that which is entrepreneurial with honoring "legacy and history in a way that is really special." For JAC, magic is connected to their childhood, through their relationship with their father and their roots in Haiti, but also hope. Sam sees mass marketed chocolate as a "Scientific and an Industrial Revolution magic product."

Making food and engaging with care have strong ties to magic — no matter how you define care, making, or even magic. And while this framing reinforces the complexities and problems I addressed in Rose-colored care, there is something to be said about how food does carry the capacity to tie us together and to help spread something good.

overview + overarching findings

This research found that food is a valuable vehicle through which care and memory can be fostered, shared, and experienced, yet its corresponding labor falls on the shoulders of those who are already most facing hardship and oppression. The businesses and individuals that participated and contributed to this work root care and its labor in community-making and sustaining, focused predominantly on place, space, and locality. As demonstrated and explored in Sharing the table, this work found that care and community investment is intertwined. The various participants here rooted their care into those that may most immediately engage with and receive it through proximity and locality.

For all collaborators involved in this work, their care work is important to them and their businesses (as well as those who receive the corresponding care), yet is unavoidably complicit within capitalism and its corresponding oppression due to the business component of their work. This does not mean that there is not value to their work, nor that their care work is inherently bad or wrong, but rather that we cannot divorce discussions of care from the systems in which it exists within. Moreover, the participants here recognize that they conduct and operate businesses under capitalism while simultaneously trying to prioritize care in their values, processes, outreach, and more.

Furthermore, the role of storytelling alongside care became a common experience and method across the various participants — demonstrating the utility and value of cookbooks as knowledge sharing texts that draw upon storytelling and multimodality to share information to a broad audience.

Lastly, these discussions and work found and affirmed the importance and value of cookbooks as knowledge sharing devices and artifacts. By combining care, multimodality, storytelling, access, and emotion, cookbooks provide a template and avenue through which we can produce better, more caring knowledge.

Rawleigh, EJ of Buffalo or Buffalo Express. (circa 1915-1925). "Two First Nations women hold pots at an outdoor kitchen arrive in an unknown village in Ontario, Canada." Bibliothèque et Archives nationales du Québec, Public domain, via Wikimedia Commons.

contributions

This work, research, and "cookbook" makes significant contributions to the well established fields of study surrounding critical pedagogy, experiential inquiry, and critical making. Moreover, this contributes to intersectional feminism (both in research and praxis), cookbook studies, multimodal learning, and knowledge ethics through its subject matter focus and output. While drawing connections and identifying commonalities in research across these disciplines, my contributions are rooted in the unification of these avenues of analysis. Moreover, through its interdisciplinary analysis and innovative methodology, this research expands the boundaries of existing knowledge in these domains.

This more valuably serves as a case-study and tangible manifestation and display of that which is possible when the confining and exclusionary metrics and expectations inherent in academic knowledge are interrogated, critiqued, and pushed against. In illuminating the significant and well-known limitations within the realm of academic knowledge sharing, this work prompts critical engagement, reflection, and revaluation of these existing and established practices. Additionally, by further intentionally and outwardly working against these boundaries, this work exemplifies that which is possible beyond, within, and across scholarly pursuits — as well as knowledge creation that is not contained by or awarded the "scholarly" identification.

A worthwhile feature of this book is found in its commitment to embody the principles it advocates for and draws upon. Rather than performing traditional academic norms and precedents, the research takes the very form it scrutinizes and actively performs the work it investigates. This purposeful meta-awareness not only provides a unique perspective, but also features the importance of reflexivity and self-awareness in academic endeavors. In doing so, this work further illuminates significant and known limitations of academic knowledge sharing, while also highlighting alternative avenues for sharing and disseminating knowledge as rooted in multimodality, stories, feelings, and experiences. In striving toward a holistic and inclusive approach, this research serves as an example for future practitioners and academics, encouraging them to explore new, underrepresented, and discredited pathways in their pursuit of knowledge creation and sharing.

limitations

A significant limitation of this work, naturally, is the interviews themselves. In wanting to focus on face-to-face conversations, extended dialogues, and stories, I focused on a small pool of folks to speak with — thus excluding many that would have further enriched this work and the investigation. How might these conversations have compared if I spoke with the big-chain restaurants and establishments that many referred to as a point of contrast? How might the conversations, and subsequent themes of care and making, have been different if I had focused on speaking with folks from all over North Carolina, the south, the country, the world?

By prioritizing connection, conversation, and collaboration throughout this investigation, I was reliant upon the work and labor of other individuals to help bring this work to fruition. As such, I was assigning more labor (labor on care even) to those who already perform great amounts of labor. This research benefited greatly from this participation, yet it was also complicit in re-allocating care and labor work to those who already carry that load.

Additionally, the conversational focus of communication with the various participants elicited wonderful, insightful moments. But it also enabled various instances where I was not necessarily prepared. For example, I did not know I was going to be able to speak with Sophie and Rene at 321 Coffee until Michael asked if they wanted to talk to me and I them. Had I known in advance, I would have prepared questions specific for employees of the businesses participating.

Moreover, as this work currently stands, I obtained no information about how care is received, engaged with, or perceived. What if I had been able to speak with and learn from the recipients of care, including the customers, the community members, the folks connected to these businesses — rather than or in addition to the owners?

And while I was able to identify that conversations that addressed fatigue and excessive labor occurred with participants that were women or femme-identifying, my participants were self-selected and represent a very small, very biased pool. As such, it would be worthwhile to evaluate the relationship between care and fatigue alongside gender identity among those who work with food across a far broader pool of participants and collaborators.

Importantly, intersectional feminism leads me to remember my own influence on this work — how my positionality, biases, and power affected those who participated and the subsequent findings. Here, I met with individuals and collaborators in sharing that I was a PhD student at NC State University and that I wanted to include them within my dissertation. While this is completely true and open about my intentions and goals, it does establish an air of academia (specifically through language like "PhD," "dissertation," and "NC State University") that could have influenced if folks decided to work with me, and how they then did. Moreover, my own lack of food expertise and practical knowledge aided in my broad analysis and appreciation of cookbooks, making with food, and their role with care, yet it very likely limited my own participation in the conversations I was engaging in with those who are experts in their work.

Lastly, when revisiting the various conversations that took place, I was reminded of my personal experience in engaging in these dialogues with these people at this specific moment in time. I could recall how much we laughed or how I ate a biscuit during the chat. But reading back and seeing "[laughs]" does not carry the same emotional weight as it did to experience it. I cannot read how my inherited New York accent accidentally pops up every now and then when I get excited talking to someone, or how someone starts tearing up when sharing a memory with me. There is a limitation in reading something secondhand that was so wonderfully experienced firsthand, despite the efforts to maintain the spirit of the conversation throughout the transcriptions. What does this reveal about the mediation of experience — even one that is investigating experiential inquiry?

opportunities for further consideration

Furthermore, due to the very nature of research as a flawed, limited, and contained entity — this work is limited due to its scope and that which was yet to be explored. In the future, it would be worthwhile to continue considering the exploring the capacities of cookbooks as more equitable knowledge sharing artifacts, but to also investigate:

The humanness of cookbooks: As culturally significant objects and artifacts, cookbooks are beloved texts that are also beautifully and dutifully used. With markings and indications of past cookings, they are also scrapbooks of living moments. How might this innately human and messy component of these works influence their knowledge sharing? How do cookbooks invite these instances of co-collaboration? What other forms and objects similarly invite readers in?

The relationship between author and cook: My analysis of care, as catalyzed within cookbooks, did not offer consideration of the author in relation to the cook, or the creator/recipient of care. In exploring the knowledge exchange found in these texts, what is the relationship between the author and the cook?

The modality of cookbooks: How does this relationship between author and cook change depending on the type of cookbook, or even the form of recipe? Here I wonder especially of the proliferation of online recipe hubs and databases. I myself have a tin box full of recipe cards, magazine clippings, index cards, notebook paper, printed recipes. My mother has a binder full of clippings from magazines, the paper wrapping on a can that contained a recipe for tomato soup, or the back of a bag of chocolate chips for a cookie recipe. Many folks compile these self-made cookbooks. Pinterest presents a whole new array of types of recipes online. Some may print these recipes out to make their own compilation of recipes, an ad hoc and patchwork cookbook often found in a box or binder, but others save these recipes on Pinterest or an app. How are these different? And what are the effects?

Cookbooks as literature: In literature, we do not consider the intent of the author, so much as the impact of their work, their stories, their characters. But in cookbooks, might this be different? How might we study and read cookbooks as literature? All the more, how may cookbooks align with literary genres such as memoir, diaries, and commonplaces? What may be the advantages of such analysis, and what may be the limitations?

Cooking as critical failure: I am not particularly good at cooking. More than half of the things I try to make end up as kitchen failures (too much vinegar, mixing baking soda for baking powder, using dark brown sugar instead of light brown, substituting too many things, cutting the edges off of a cake and then trying to cover it all in icing just to learn that this is a big mess). How can we consider the role of failure in making, in cooking, in conversation with critical making? How are the stakes higher when we fail in making with food? And how can we understand such failure within an intersectional feminist framework?

Hollem, Howard R. (1942). "This image shows the life of a typical housewife during the Great Depression. Women were taking care of their children and working around the house to make sure things were taken care of, such as washing the dishes." Public domain, via Wikimedia Commons.

Forever Equal Pie

3 c. long lasting equality
2 c. love (liquid)
1 heaping cup education
1 c. joy
1/4 (liquid) peace
1 c. nonviolence (liquid)
1 c. (powdered) truth
1 c. faith
3/4 peace (powdered)

    Gently stir liquid peace nonviolence and love in a large bowl. Slowly add in long lasting equality and powdered peace and truth. Calmly mix in faith and education as you do this the mixture should firm and rise above the wrong doing in the world. After it rises pour it into a pie pan and refrigerate for two days. Serve on square plates so you can experience the thrill of being treated equally.
    This recipe serves the United States, or those who believe in equality.

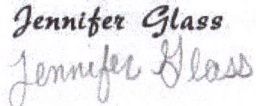

Glass, J. (2000). "Forever equal pie / Jennifer Glass." Retrieved from the Library of Congress.

references

a

A Place at the Table, personal communication, June 29, 2023.

Ahmed, S. (2017). *Living a feminist life.* Duke University Press.

And Also Too: Community accountable design. Accessed from https://www.andalsotoo.net/.

Apple, M. (1999/2014). Chapter 1: Introduction: The politics of official knowledge. In *Official Knowledge: Democratic Education in a Conservative Age. 3rd Edition.* Routledge. pp. 1-15.

Apple, M. (1999/2014). Chapter 3: Cultural politics and the text. In *Official Knowledge: Democratic Education in a Conservative Age. 3rd Edition.* Routledge. pp. 45-66.

Ashton, J. (2017). The feminists are cackling in the archive. *Feminist Review, 115*(1), pp. 155–164. https://doi.org/10.1057/s41305-017-0024-

B

Bee Downtown, personal communication, May 22, 2023.

Bellacasa, M. P. de la (2017). *Matters of care: Speculative ethics in more than human worlds.* University of Minnesota Press.

Bjerede, M. (2012). Critical making: Make: A place for genders to intersect? Edited by G. Hertz. (Zine). Telharmonium Press.

Bledsoe, J. T. (1959). "African American woman at refrigerator holding a pitcher as she pours out drinks for children, probably Little Rock, Arkansas / JTB." No known restrictions on publication. Retrieved from the Library of Congress.

Board of Education. "Lessons in domestic science for seventh and eighth grade students. Includes lessons in preparing food, baking, and clean up. Created by the Toledo Public Schools Board of Education 1919." Public domain, via Wikimedia Commons.

Booker, M. (2020, April 23). *Why do people care for sourdough?.* Fermentology. https://fermentology.pubpub.org/pub/tw9kpb4x/release/1.

Bower, A. L. (1997). *Recipes for reading: community cookbooks, stories, histories.* University of Massachusetts Press.

Bower, A. L. (1997) Our sisters' recipes: Exploring "community" in a community cookbook. *Journal of Popular Culture, 31*(3), pp. 137-151. ProQuest, https://proxying.lib.ncsu.edu/index.php/login?url=https://www.proquest.com/scholarly-journals/our-sisters-recipes-exploring-community/docview/195362557/se-2?accountid=12725.

Bradbury, H. and Associates. (2017). Cooking with action research: Stories and resources for self and community transformation. *AR+*.

C

Cameron, K., & Fitzpatrick, J. (2021). Restoring the 'Lived space of the body': Attunement in critical making. *Electronic Book Review*. https://doi.org/10.7273/j480-c578.

cárdenas, m. (2022). The stitch. In *Poetic operations: Trans of color art in digital media.* Duke University Press. pp. 129-166.

Cerpina, Z. & Stenslie, S. (2022). Introduction. In *The anthropocene cookbook: Recipes and opportunities for future catastrophes.* MIT Press. pp. 1-17.

Charny, D. (2012). Critical making: Power of making. Edited by G. Hertz. (Zine). Telharmonium Press.

Christle, H. (2019). *The crying book.* Catapult.

Colford, A. L. "Front title page of *A friend in the kitchen: Or, what to cook and how to cook it,* published in 1899." Public domain, via Wikimedia Commons.

Collins, P. H. (2000). *Black feminist thought: Knowledge, consciousness, and the politics of empowerment.* New York: Routledge.

Costanza-Chock, S. (2020). *Design justice: Community-led practices to build the worlds we need.* MIT Press.

Cramp, H. (1913). "The institute cook book." Public domain, via Wikimedia Commons.

Crenshaw, K. (1989). "Demarginalizing the intersection of race and sex: A Black feminist critique of antidiscrimination doctrine, feminist theory and antiracist politics." *University of Chicago Legal Forum, 1989*(1). Available at: http://chicagounbound.uchicago.edu/uclf/vol1989/iss1/8

Cuni, Sera from The Root Cellar Cafe & Catering, personal communication, July 11, 2023.

Curtis, E. S. (1927). "Drying meat - Cheyenne." Museum of Photographic Arts Collections, No restrictions, via Wikimedia Commons.

D

Data 4 Black Lives. Accessed from https://d4bl.org/.

Design Justice Network. Accessed from https://designjustice.org/.

DeVault, M. L. (1994). Introduction. In *Feeding the family: The social organization of caring as gendered work*. University of Chicago Press. pp. 1-35.

Dewey, J. (1934). *Art as experience.* New York: Perigee Books, 1980. Print.

D'Ignazio, C. & Klein, L. (2020). *Data feminism.* MIT Press.

DiSalvo, C. (2014). Critical making as materializing the politics of design. *The Information Society, 30*(2), pp. 96-105.

Doran, W. (2023, April 27). *NC Republicans take aim at diversity initiatives in universities, State Government.* WRAL.com. https://www.wral.com/story/nc-republicans-take-aim-at-diversity-initiatives-in-universities-state-government/20832587/

Douglas, T. R., & Nganga, C. (2013). What's radical love got to do with it: Navigating Identity, Pedagogy, and Positionality in Pre-Service Education. *International Journal of Critical Pedagogy, 5*(1), pp. 58-82.

Dwight, H. L. "The Golden Age Cook-Book, published in 1898. This is an early American vegetarian cookbook." Public domain, via Wikimedia Commons.

E

Earthseed Land Collective. Accessed from https://earthseedlandcoop.org/.

Eltahawy, M. (2020). Introduction: Defying, disobeying, and disrupting the patriarchy. In *The Seven Necessary Sins for Women and Girls*. Penguin Random House. pp. 1-14.

Equity-Centered Community Design: Our Approach, by Creative Reaction Lab. Accessed from https://crxlab.org/our-approach.

Escobar, A. (2018). Introduction. In *Designs for the pluriverse: Radical interdependence, autonomy, and the making of worlds*. Duke University Press. pp. 1-22.

Evans, M., Sophie, & Rene. 321 Coffee, personal communication, May 29, 2023.

Ferguson, K. (2012). Intensifying taste, intensifying identity: Collectivity through community cookbooks. *Signs: Journal Of Women In Culture And Society, 37*(3), pp. 695-717.

Ferguson, K. (2020). *Cookbook politics.* University of Pennsylvania Press.

Fleischhauer, C. (1980). "Kitchen." Paradise Valley Folklife Project collection, 1978-1982 (AFC 1991/021), American Folklife Center, Library of Congress. Retrieved from the Library of Congress.

Fleitz, E. J. (2009). The multimodal kitchen: Cookbooks as women's rhetorical practice, Bowling Green State University, Ann Arbor, *ProQuest*, https://etd.ohiolink.edu/apexprod/rws_etd/send_file/send?accession=bgsu1240934967&disposition=inline.

Fleitz, E. J. (2010). Cooking codes: Cookbook discourses as women's rhetorical practice." *Present Tense: A Journal of Rhetoric in Society 1*(1), pp. 1-9. https://www.presenttensejournal.org/vol1/cooking-codes-cookbook-discourses-as-womens-rhetorical-practices/

Freire, P. (1985). Reading the word and reading the world: An interview with Paulo Freire. *Language Arts, 62*(1), pp. 15-21.

Fleischhauer, C. (1980). "Making Lunches for School." [Thomas, Jean (Depicted) & Thomas, Cheryl (Depicted)]. Paradise Valley Folklife Project collection, 1978-1982 (AFC 1991/021), American Folklife Center. No known restrictions on publication. Retrieved from the Library of Congress.

Food Youth Initiative. Accessed from https://cefs.ncsu.edu/youth/food-youth-initiative/.

Freire, P. (2018). *Pedagogy of the oppressed : 50th anniversary edition.* Bloomsbury Academic.

Gharabaghi, K., & Anderson-Nathe, B. (2017). The need for critical scholarship. *Child & Youth Services, 38*(2), pp. 95–97. doi.org/10.1080/0145935X.2017.1327692.

Gilbert, Lynn. (1978). "Julia Child in her kitchen as photographed ©Lynn Gilbert." Cambridge, Massachusetts. CC BY-SA 4.0, via Wikimedia Commons.

Glass, J. (2000). "Forever equal pie / Jennifer Glass." Retrieved from the Library of Congress.

Gollihue, K., & Browning. A. (2019). Towards an intersectional feminist critical making. In L. Bogers & L. Chiappini (Eds.), *The critical makers reader: (Un)learning technology* (pp. 227-236). Institute of Network Cultures.

Greene, M. (2009). Teaching as possibility: A light in dark times. In *Critical pedagogy in uncertain times* (pp. 137-149). Palgrave Macmillan, New York.

Haraway, D. (1988). Situated knowledges: The science question in feminism and the privilege of partial perspective. *Feminist Studies, 14*(3), pp. 575-599. doi:10.2307/3178066

Haraway, D. J. (2016). *Staying with the trouble: Making kin in the chthulucene.* Duke University Press. *Project MUSE*, muse.jhu.edu/book/69253.

Hastie, A. (2007). Introduction: The collaborator: At the cupboards of film history. In *Cupboards of curiosity: Women, recollection, and film history*. Duke University Press. pp. 1-18.

Hertz, G. (2012). "Critical making: Interview with Natalie Jeremijenko." Telharmonium Press.

Hertz, G. (2016). What is critical making? *Current*. https://current.ecuad.ca/what-is-critical-making.

Herst, D. (2019). Destandardizing design? Learning from critical users. In L. Bogers & L. Chiappini (Eds.), *The critical makers reader: (Un)learning technology* (pp. 206-217). Institute of Network Cultures.

Highsmith, C. M. [Between 1980 and 2006] "1950s kitchen at Strawbery Banke Colonial Village, a restored city neighborhood in Portsmouth, New Hampshire." No known restrictions on publication. Retrieved from the Library of Congress, https://www.loc.gov/item/2011631583/.

Hill, J. M. "The Boston Cooking School magazine of culinary science and domestic economics (1908)." No restrictions, via Wikimedia Commons.

Hill, J. M. (1922). "Table laid for Sunday-night Tea. 'Sunday clears away the rust of whole week.'—Addison." Public domain, via Wikimedia Commons.

Hobart, H. J. K., & Kneese, T. (2020). Radical care: Survival strategies for uncertain times. *Social Text, 38*(1), pp. 1–16. doi: https://doi.org/10.1215/01642472-7971067

Hollem, H. R. (1942). "This image shows the life of a typical housewife during the Great Depression. Women were taking care of their children and working around the house to make sure things were taken care of, such as washing the dishes." Public domain, via Wikimedia Commons.

Holmes, K. (2018). *Mismatch: How inclusion shapes design.* MIT Press.

hooks, B. (1994) *Teaching to transgress: Education as the practice of freedom.* Routledge.

hooks, b. (1999). *All about love: New visions.* Morrow.

hooks, b. (2000/2015). *Feminism is for everybody: Passionate politics.* Routledge.

hooks, b. (2010). Touching the Earth. In Moore, Kathleen D, and Michael P. Nelson (eds.). *Moral ground: Ethical action for a planet in peril.* Trinity University Press.

Imagining America. (2018). Artists and scholars in public life: Refreshed vision, mission, values. Accessed from https://d2zhgehghqjuwb.cloudfront.net/accounts/11780/original/VISION_MISSION_VALUES_FINAL.pdf?1545238498.

Inness, S. A. (2001). Introduction. In *Dinner roles: American women and culinary culture.* University of Iowa Press. pp. 1-16.

Ireland, L. (1981). The compiled cookbook as foodways autobiography. *Western Folklore, 40*(1), pp. 107–114. https://doi.org/10.2307/1499855

Janks, H. (2013). The importance of critical literacy. In J. Pandya & J. Ávila (eds.) *Moving Critical Literacies Forward.* (pp. 32-44). Routledge.

Jansen, S. L. (1993). 'Family Liked, 1956': My mother's recipes. *Frontiers: A Journal of Women Studies 13*(2), pp. 65-74.

Jewish Historical Society of the Upper Midwest. (circa 1940). "A spontaneous family snapshot capturing the delight of being a woman in the kitchen cooking the family meal." No restrictions, via Wikimedia Commons.

Jezer-Morton, K. (2023). Is tradwife content dangerous, or just stupid? *The Cut.* https://www.thecut.com/2023/09/tradwife-content-influencers-conservative-ideology.html

Johnson, G. (2022). February 1 and 8. *Designing Ecologies of Care.*

Johnson, G. (2020). *The slow grind: Finding our way back to creative balance.* Independently published. https://www.theslowgrind.world/product/the-slow-grind-book.

Johnson, G. N., & Eiler, T. (1978). "Carrie Severt milking cow, Alleghany County, North Carolina." Blue Ridge Parkway Folklife Project collection (AFC 1982/009), American Folklife Center, Library of Congress. No known restrictions on publication. Retrieved from the Library of Congress.

Johnson, G. N., & Eiler, T. (1978). "Carrie Severt in kitchen, Allegheny County, North Carolina." Blue Ridge Parkway Folklife Project collection (AFC 1982/009), American Folklife Center, Library of Congress. No known restrictions on publication. Retrieved from the Library of Congress.

Kazmi, A. (2014). Burqa girls. (art exhibition).

Kendall, M. (2021). *Hood feminism: Notes from the women that a movement forgot.* Penguin Random House.

Kimmerer, R. W. (2013). *Braiding sweetgrass: Indigenous wisdom, scientific knowledge, and the teachings of plants.* Milkweed Editions.

Lanser, S. S. (1993). Burning dinners: Feminist subversions of domesticity. In Rader, J. N (ed.) *Feminist Messages: Coding in Women's Folk Culture*. University of Illinois Press. pp. 36-53.

Lee, R. (1939). "Kitchen scene in Spanish-American home near Taos, New Mexico, Taos County. Making tortillas." No known restrictions. Retrieved from the Library of Congress.

Lee, R. (1947). "Mrs. Elige Hicks and her daughter in the kitchen of the four room house which rents for $10.50 monthly. Mrs. Hicks' husband and son are now working in a coal mine in Virginia and are looking for a home to buy. Southern Coal Corporation, Bradshaw Mine, Bradshaw, McDowell County, West Virginia." Public domain, via Wikimedia Commons.

Livio, M., & Emerson, L. (2019). Towards feminist labs: Provocations for collective knowledge-making. In L. Bogers & L. Chiappini (eds.) *The Critical Makers Reader: (Un)learning Technology* (pp. 286-297). Institute of Network Cultures.

Lomen Bros. (1916). "An Eskimo kitchen outdoors." Retrieved from the Library of Congress.

Lorde, A. (2015). The master's tools will never dismantle the master's house. In Moraga, Cherríe and Anzaldúa, Gloria (eds.) *This Bridge Called My Back, Fourth Edition: Writings by Radical Women of Color*. State University of New York Press. pp. 94-97.

Luke, A. (2014). Defining critical literacy. In J. Pandya & J. Ávila (eds.) *Moving Critical Literacies Forward*. (pp. 19-31). Routledge.

Lupi, G., & Posavec, S. (2016). *Dear Data*. Princeton Architectural Press.

M

McKenney, E., personal communication, June 9, 2023.

McLaren, P. (2015). The emergence of critical pedagogy. In *Life in Schools: An Introduction to Critical Pedagogy in the Foundations of Education*. Routledge.

McLaren, P. (2015). Critical pedagogy: A look at the major concepts. In *Life in Schools: An Introduction to Critical Pedagogy in the Foundations of Education*. Routledge.

Merkner, S. (1996). "A sense of community - Plain or fancy, group cookbooks reflect spirit of sharing." *San Antonio Express-News*, Sep 11, 1996, p. 1. ProQuest, https://proxying.lib.ncsu.edu/index.php/login?url=https://www.proquest.com/newspapers/sense-community-plain-fancy-group-cookbooks/docview/261757162/se-2?accountid=12725.

Miller, C. R. (1984). Genre as social action. *Quarterly Journal of Speech, 70*, pp. 151–176.

Milner, J. O. B., & Milner, L. F. M. (1999). *Bridging English*. Merrill.

Moody, M. & Spivak-Birndorf, C. (2019). The feminist makerspace: Smashing the patriarchy with crafting, mentorship, and connection. In Melo, M. & Nichols, J. (eds). *Re-Making the Library Makerspace : Critical Theories, Reflections, and Practices*. Litwin Books. pp. 183-202. ProQuest Ebook Central, https://ebookcentral.proquest.com/lib/ncsu/detail.action?docID=6624797.

Moraga, C. (2015). La güera. In C. Moraga & G. Anzaldúa (eds.) *This Bridge Called My Back, Fourth Edition: Writings by Radical Women of Color*. State University of New York Press. pp. 22-29.

Morales, A. L. (2019). Part 1: The ground on which I stand. In *Medicine Stories: Essays for Radicals*. Duke University Press. pp. 1-52.

Morin, J. from Wonderpuff, personal communication, June 13, 2023.

Muray, N. (1939). "McCall's magazine cover, family arriving in the kitchen for the holidays." No restrictions, via Wikimedia Commons.

𝒩

Nelson, M. (2015). *The argonauts.* Graywolf Press.

Neuhaus, J. (1999). The way to a man's heart: Gender roles, domestic ideology, and cookbooks in the 1950s." *Journal of Social History, 32*(3), Oxford University Press, pp. 529–555, http://www.jstor.org/stable/3789341.

New York Public Library. (1890s). "Kitchen (preparing dinner)." Repository: The New York Public Library. Photography Collection, Miriam and Ira D. Wallach Division of Art, Prints and Photographs. No restrictions, via Wikimedia Commons.

Nijenhuis, W. (2019). Making (things) as ethical practice. In L. Bogers & L. Chiappini (Eds.), *The Critical Makers Reader: (Un)learning Technology* (pp. 127-139). Institute of Network Cultures.

Noddings, N. (1984). Why care about caring? In *Caring: A Feminine Approach to Ethics and Moral Education.* University of California Press. pp. 7-29.

Nosrat, S. (2017). *Salt, fat, acid, heat.* Simon and Schuster.

Nxumalo, F., & Villanueva, M. T. (2020). Listening to water: Situated dialogues between Black, Indigenous and Black-Indigenous feminisms. In Taylor, C.A., Hughes, C., & Ulmer, J.B. (Eds.) *Transdisciplinary Feminist Research: Innovations in Theory, Method and Practice* (1st ed.). Routledge. https://doi.org/10.4324/9780429199776. pp. 59-75.

𝒫

Papert, S. (1980). *Mindstorms: Children, computers, and powerful ideas.* New York: Basic Books.

People's Kitchen Collective. Accessed from https://peopleskitchencollective.com/.

Pettit-Scott, L. from Well Fed Community Garden, personal communication, July 12, 2023.

Perez, C. C. (2019). The long Friday. In *Invisible Women: Exposing Data Bias in a World Designed for Men.* Abrams Press. pp. 69-91.

Piepzna-Samarasinha, L. L. (2018). Preface-Care webs: Experiments in creating collective access. In *Care Work: Dreaming Disability Justice.* Arsenal Pulp Press.

Porter, M. E. (circa 1907). "Baking Bread; Photograph showing two Pueblo Indian women baking bread in an oven." No known restrictions on publication. Retrieved from the Library of Congress.

Pupusas for Education. Accessed from https://www.pupusas4education.com/.

R

Radner, J. N. & Lanser, S. S. (1987). The feminist voice: Strategies of coding in women's cultures. *The Journal of American Folklore, 100*(398), Folklore and Feminism, pp. 412-425.

Raley, R. (2009). Introduction: Tactical media as virtuosic performance in *Tactical Media*. (pp. 1-30). Minnesota Press.

Ratto, M. (2011). "Critical making: Conceptual and material studies in technology and social life." *The Information Society 27*(4), pp. 252-260. (online)

Ratto, M., & Hertz, G. (2019). Critical making and interdisciplinary learning: Making as a bridge between art, science,,engineering and social interventions. In L. Bogers & L. Chiappini (eds.), *The Critical Makers Reader: (Un)learning Technology* (pp. 18-28). Institute of Network Cultures.

Ratto, S. from Videri Chocolate Factory, personal communication, May 26, 2023.

Rawleigh, EJ. (circa 1915-1925). "Two First Nations women hold pots at an outdoor kitchen arrive in an unknown village in Ontario, Canada." Bibliothèque et Archives nationales du Québec, Public domain, via Wikimedia Commons.

Robert Fisher Productions & General Motors Corporation. (1960). Frigidaire Division. Stills from: "A Kitchen Is a Feminine Thing." Library of Congress, Motion Picture, Broadcasting, and Recorded Sound Division. Retrieved from the Library of Congress.

Romeo, S. from Two Roosters, personal communication, July 5, 2023.

Rosener, A. (1942) "'Share The Meat' recipes. Braised stuffed heart. Fill hearts with stuffing and sew up the slit with coarse thread." United States Office Of War Information, Public Domain. Retrieved from the Library of Congress.

Rosener, A. (1942). "'Share The Meat' recipes. Braised stuffed heart. Make gravy of the pan drippings and serve the hearts piping hot, garnished with crisp greens." United States Office Of War Information, Public Domain. Retrieved from the Library of Congress.

Russell, L. (2020). *Glitch feminism*. Verso.

Santos, B. de S. (2018). Conclusion: Between fear and hope. In *The End of the Cognitive Empire: The Coming of Age of Epistemologies of the South.* Duke University Press. pp. 293-301.

Santos, B. de S. (2018). Bodies, knowledges, and corzaonar. In *The End of the Cognitive Empire: The Coming of Age of Epistemologies of the South.* Duke University Press. pp. 87-103.

S.D. Butcher & Son. (circa 1908). "Pine Ridge Indians drying meat / photo made by S.D. Butcher & Son, Kearney, Neb." No known restrictions on publication. Retrieved from the Library of Congress.

Shabatura, J. (2022, July 26). *Using Bloom's taxonomy to write effective learning outcomes.* Using Bloom's Taxonomy to Write Effective Learning Outcomes. https://tips.uark.edu/using-blooms-taxonomy/#:~:text=Bloom's%20Taxonomy%20is%20a%20classification%20of%20the%20different%20outcomes%20and,at%20the%20University%20of%20Chicago.

Simeoni, F. (2021). Acnephobic: Faces for a feminist data practice. *Nightingale: Journal of the Data Visualization Society.* Accessed from https://nightingaledvs.com/acnephobic-faces-for-a-feminist-data-practice/.

Sperrazza, W. (2019). Recipe books as digital feminist archives. *The Recipes Project.*

Springgay, S. (2022). Introduction: Feltness: On how to practice intimacy. In *Feltness: Research-creation, Socially Engaged Art, and Affective Pedagogies.* Duke University Press. Internet resource. pp. 1-30.

Theophano, J. Introduction. In *Eat My Words: Reading Women's Lives through the Cookbooks they Wrote.* New York: Palgrave Macmillan, 2002. pp.1-10.

Thomas, H. W. (artist)

Tie, Y. C., Birks, M., & Francis, K. (2019). "Grounded theory research: A design framework for novice researchers." *SAGE Open Med.* doi: 10.1177/2050312118822927. Toledo (Ohio).

Transplanting Traditions. Accessed from https://www.transplantingtraditions.org/Statements-of-Principles.

Tsing, A. L. (2021). *The mushroom at the end of the world: On the possibility of life in capitalist ruins.* Princeton Press.

Twitty, M. (2018). *The cooking gene: A journey through African American culinary history in the old south*. Amistad.

U

United States Extension Service. (between 1925 and 1930). "Women Canning Food Outdoors in a Wooded Area." No known restrictions on publication. Retrieved from the Library of Congress.

V

Vasquez, V. M., Janks, H., & Comber, B. (2019). Critical literacy as a way of being and doing. *Language Arts, 96*(5), pp. 300-311. (online)

W

Walker, E. (1935). "Women selling ice cream and cake, Scotts Run, West Virginia." United States Resettlement Administration. No known restrictions, Retrieved from the Library of Congress.

Wiley, K. (artist)

Wong, Nancy. "Poet Cyn Zarco in kitchen of her apartment on 8th Avenue in San Francisco, California, 1975." CC BY-SA 4.0, via Wikimedia Commons.

Wtewael, Peter. (1620s). "Kitchen Scene." CC0, via Wikimedia Commons.

Wyeth, N. C. (1948). " The Ladies' home journal." No restrictions, via Wikimedia Commons.

Z

Zaliwska, Z., & Boler, M. (2018). Troubling hope: Performing inventive connections in discomforting times. *Studies in Philosophy and Education, 38*(1), pp. 71–84. (online) *additional references*

(Between 1780 and 1830). "Architecture vivante [*Living Architecture*] - La Cuisiniere / chez Martinet." No known restrictions on publication. Retrieved from the Library of Congress.

(1905). "A Kitchen Nymph." No known restrictions on publication. Retrieved from the Library of Congress.

(1909). "Washington Women's Cookbook by Linda Deziah Jennings." Public domain, via Wikimedia Commons.

(1916). "Fort Street Public School - [making jam]." Photographs by the State Archives and Records Authority of New South Wales. No restrictions, via Wikimedia Commons.

(1940). "Butchering a buffalo." National Archives and Records Administration, Department of the Interior. Bureau of Indian Affairs. Pine Ridge Agency. Public domain, via Wikimedia Commons.

(between 1941 and 1943). "Madison County, Ala., --Mrs. Frank Jacobs likes to can fruits and vegetables." No known restrictions on publication. Retrieved from the Library of Congress.

thanks

I would like to express great gratitude to Crystal Chen Lee, Lesley-Ann Noel, Elizabeth Jones, Jason Miller, and Fernanda Duarte. Thank you, Crystal, for your endless mentorship and guidance throughout my journey as a pre-service highschool English teacher to doctoral candidate. I am forever thankful for Jason's unwavering support and enthusiasm for carving a path led by the power of stories. To Lesley-Ann and Elizabeth, thank you both for welcoming me with open arms into your worlds of study and learning. And to Fernanda, who also served as my dissertation advisor and chair, I am especially thankful for your insight, support, and kindness throughout this writing process.

To the wonderful folks within the Data Science and AI Academy, especially Ray Levy, who believed in and kindly championed this work as it continued to find its footing, I am forever thankful that you welcomed this English teacher-turned-data science researcher into your midst.

Thank you to David Tully, Will Cross, John McLeod, and Sophie Dickerson for your insight, advice, and work in making this book come to be. We did it!

Many thanks to Micah Vandegrift who introduced me to and taught me the foundations of open knowledge and to Scott Bailey who always talked to me about all things *Data Feminism*. These conversations inspired this work.

To each of the participants and collaborators who made this work possible: thank you thank you thank you. You did not need to participate in an abstract and exploratory academic investigation into care and food, but you did — wholeheartedly and enthusiastically.

To my family and friends who never fully understood what I was doing, thank you for your support and kindness — especially when it came to asking me about deadlines. To Alessandra: thank you for dreaming of better worlds, reading books, and sharing stories of love and care with me. Thank you, Bridget, for always reminding me how care for the self, the family, and the country is messy, tough, and gritty. Jenna, I am forever thankful for the great joy, fun, and laughter we have together in navigating care, motherhood, and un/paid labor.

I especially want to thank Kim and Mary (my mother-in-law and mother) — the care you showed me, and always show me, is what enabled this work to come to be. Thank you.

I am forever thankful for my sons, Teddy, who was present for 90% of the writing found here and slept on me while I wrote on my phone or played with his blocks and under the table as I typed away in efforts to see this project to the end, and August, who joined us just two weeks after I "finished" this work and reminded me of the brute power that is found in care and love.

Lastly, Daniel: thank you for everything. You are my favorite cook.

further reading

Black Food: Stories, Art, and Recipes from Across the African Diaspora
- a cookbook by Bryant Terry (Editor)

Cake Zine
- a print magazine (https://cakezine.com/)

Ciudad de México: Recipes and Stories from the Heart of Mexico City
- a cookbook by Edson Diaz Fuentes

Cook Korean!: A Comic Book with Recipes
- a cookbook by Robin Ha

@DreamBoatCafe on Instagram
- chef, zine creator, and journalist

Filipinx: Heritage Recipes from the Diaspora
- a cookbook by Angela Dimayuga and Ligaya Mishan

Gohan: Everyday Japanese Cooking: Memories and Stories from My Family's Kitchen
- a cookbook by Emiko Davies

In Her Kitchen: Stories and Recipes from Grandmas Around the World: A Cookbook
- a cookbook by Gabriele Galimberti

In the Kitchen: Essays on Food and Life
- a book by Juliet Annan, Yemisí Aríbisálà, Laura Freeman, Joel Golby, Daisy Johnson, Rebecca May Johnson, Rebecca Liu, Nina Mingya Powles, Ella Risbridger, Rachel Roddy, Mayukh Sen, Ruby Tandoh, Julia Turshen

Lost Bread Co
- zines and recipes (https://www.lostbreadco.com/zine)

Recipe for Disaster: 40 Superstar Stories of Sustenance and Survival

    a book by Alison Riley

Salt, Fat, Acid, Heat: Mastering the Elements of Good Cooking

    a cookbook by Samin Nosrat (Author) and Wendy MacNaughton (Illustrator)

Slow Noodles: A Cambodian Memoir of Love, Loss, and Family Recipes

    a book by Chantha Nguon with Kim Green

Summer Kitchens: Recipes and Reminiscences from Every Corner of Ukraine

    a cookbook by Olia Hercules

The Cooking Gene: A Journey Through African American Culinary History in the Old South

    a James Beard Award Winner book by Michael W. Twitty

The *Home Cooking* Podcast

    https://homecooking.show/

The *TASTE* Podcast

    https://tastecooking.com/category/the-taste-podcast/

Why We Cook: Women on Food, Identity, and Connection

    a book by Lindsay Gardner

Women on Food

    a book by Charlotte Druckman

Virginia Story, my great-grandmother, shucking corn from the family farm. Her last-born son is the namesake of my first — and his favorite food is corn. Story Farms, Catskill, New York.

www.ingramcontent.com/pod-product-compliance
Lightning Source LLC
Chambersburg PA
CBHW080437170426
43195CB00017B/2806